THE BIBLE:
What's in It for Me?

THE BIBLE: What's in It for Me?

J. Stephen Lang

Chariot VICTOR
PUBLISHING
A DIVISION OF COOK COMMUNICATIONS

The author wishes to thank Bob Hosack, who conceived this project and Baker Taylor, its first enthusiast.

Editors: Afton Rorvik, Barbara Williams
Designer: Andrea Boven

Victor Books is an imprint of ChariotVictor Publishing,
a division of Cook Communications, Colorado Springs, Colorado 80918.
Cook Communications, Paris, Ontario
Kingsway Communications, Eastbourne, England

contents

If you're looking for . . .

- brief summaries of each book of the Bible, see chapters 12 and 13.

- a clear, concise "nuts and bolts" explanation of chapter and verse divisions, how the Bible books were named, differences between Old and New Testaments, and other "square one" issues, see chapter 1.

- a list of "basics," Bible stories and teachings that everyone ought to know, see chapter 10.

- a concise glossary of key words and concepts in the Bible, see chapter 14.

- "pathways through the Bible," helping you find your way to key stories, biographies, and teachings, see chapter 11.

- tips on using the Bible to help you learn to pray (or pray better), see chapter 7.

- tips on using the Bible in making decisions in your life, see chapter 6.

- different ways to begin your study of the Bible, see chapter 5.

- tips on organizing a group study of the Bible, see chapter 9.

- an easy-to-understand explanation of what we mean when we call the Bible "inspired" and "authoritative," see chapter 3.

- good Bible verses to memorize, and tips on memorizing, see chapter 8.

- a simple introduction to interpreting the Bible as its authors intended, see chapter 4.

- a brief (and fascinating) history of the Bible, from papyrus scrolls to the printing press to the computer age, see chapter 2.

- help in choosing reference books to help you study the Bible, see chapter 15.

- a timeline showing when key Bible events took place and where you can find them in the Bible, see chapter 16.

Introduction ◄··

Making the Bible User-Friendly

At the end of the twentieth century, can an ancient book be "user-friendly"? Can the life of King David, who lived around 1000 B.C., be accessible—or interesting—or relevant—to contemporary individuals?

Granted, the Bible isn't as accessible as MTV and VH-1. It isn't supposed to be. It's the Word of God to human beings, not a multi-image promo for some throwaway pop culture. The Bible is serious. It's concerned with morality, with ethics, with values. It's concerned with where we came from, how we should live, and what our destiny is beyond this present life. In other words, it answers the basic human questions about the meaning of life.

But it is accessible. It is interesting. If sex and violence help sell books and videos, then the Bible should sell well, for sex and violence are there. (Mark Twain snickered at libraries that banned his books but kept the Bible on the shelves.) The Bible presents the human tale, warts and all—and adds the Divine element, making the picture complete. It's even more interesting than pop culture because it has everything the secular world has, plus a loving, forgiving, saving God. The Almighty God is, according to the Bible, approachable—friendly, if you will.

"User-friendly" means that an average, normal human being can approach without feeling threatened. Bible handbooks flood the market—and many seem to assume that the reader already knows the Bible fairly well and enjoys reading it. The book you are now holding assumes no such thing. It assumes you are at least *interested* in the Bible—maybe slightly familiar with it, but maybe puzzled, curious, perhaps even hostile. It doesn't assume you know the order of the Bible's books, its main characters, its key teachings, its history, or its place in the everyday life of real human beings. It does assume that knowledge of these things is important—as important as knowing how to drive a car, program a VCR, operate a microwave oven, fill out a tax return, or shop for nutritious food. In fact, this book assumes that knowing the Bible is *more* important than all these things. It does not assume that you must be a scholar or a college grad to know the Bible.

The Bible: What's in It for Me? is written for several people:

• The new Christian believer, who wants to become familiar with the Book of books because it is the foundation of Christian belief and Christian living. The new believer can profit from studying this handbook alone, but I encourage group study when possible. Classes of high school age or older should find the book eminently user-friendly.

• The person who wants to get "reacquainted"—that is, the person who realizes he has too long neglected the Bible and would like to become more familiar with it. Surveys consistently show that long-time churchgoers are often ignorant of basic Bible teachings. We hope this book will help to remedy that problem.

• The Christian who is familiar with the Bible but would like a refresher course, a kind of review of Bible 101, if you will.

Pastors and professors fall into this category.

• The non-Christian who is curious—curious as a seeker after truth, or maybe curious as one who opposes Christianity but wonders if the failings of Christianity are traceable to the Bible itself. For the seeker, I hope this book leads to further inquiry and commitment. For the hostile person, I hope at least to clarify some issues. Certainly I include nothing here that should make a non-Christian less respectful of the Bible and Christianity.

In 1988 I published *The Complete Book of Bible Trivia*. It sold extremely well, which made me realize that a lot of people are interested in the "tidbits" of the Bible, its many interesting snippets of events, people, places. Having looked at the Bible as *trivia*, I now move on to *significa*—the Bible as something that is, or can be, very significant in human life. My trivia book answered the question "Can the Bible entertain me?" The book you are now holding answers the question "The Bible—what's in it for me?

chapter 1

Beyond the Words: ◄···
What Is the Bible All About?

Bibles are sold by the thousands every year across the globe. Are they being read? Some are, some aren't. If the sales figures meant anything, we would be a very Bible-literate people. But that isn't so.

It was so—in the past, anyway. If you read the history of the United States and England, you can't help but notice that great leaders often quoted and referred to the Bible. Even when their actions were morally questionable, they were at least familiar with what the Bible taught. It was a part of education, just like learning the mythology of Greece and Rome. But it was more important than mythology because most people believed the Bible was *true*. Even Thomas Jefferson, who questioned the miraculous elements in the Bible, still believed that its moral and ethical teachings applied to human life and that God in some way produced the Bible. Thus it wasn't just a book, like *Great Expectations* by Charles Dickens or a long poem like *The Odyssey*.

It originated because God wanted to reveal His will to the human race. The Bible was God's voice speaking to everyone who could read it or hear it being read aloud.

The word *Bible* means, simply "the book." One modern version was even marketed as *The Book*, which is accurate. But it doesn't have one author in the same way a detective novel has one author. It was written over a period of hundreds of years by many different people. Each author had—as all authors do—an individual way of expressing himself in words. No two books of the Bible are exactly alike, even ones by the same author.

WHAT ARE THESE "BOOKS"?

Before looking deeply into the Bible, consider some terminology. Pastors and teachers talk about a particular "book" of the Bible. Meaning what? Each section of the Bible—there are sixty-six in all—is called a "book," even though none of them is big enough to fill an entire book by itself. Thus we talk about the "Book of Psalms" and the "Book of Jeremiah" and the "Book of Acts." The longest one, the Book of Psalms, fills up a hundred pages in some Bibles, yet the Book of Obadiah barely fills a page. So a "book" doesn't mean "thing between two covers," but "component part." Each "book" is divided into chapters and verses (more about these divisions later), and most of the "books" are attributed to a single author. The Book of Acts, for example, is supposed to have been written by Luke (who also wrote the Gospel of Luke), and the Book of Revelation was written by John. Some "books" had several authors. Psalms, for example, was written by King David and many other authors. Proverbs was written by King Solomon, Agur, Lemuel, and possibly others.

In some cases the particular "book" may have been edited. The Book of Deuteronomy in the Old Testament is supposed to have been written by Moses, but at its end it tells about Moses' death, so we have to assume that someone else edited the book, adding the material about Moses' death at the end.

For people who accept the Bible as divine, it is *the* Book, the most important book of all.

WHAT ARE THE BOOKS NAMED FOR?

The sixty-six "books" are named for a variety of different reasons. In the New Testament, the four Gospels—the stories of Jesus—are named for their different authors (Matthew, Mark, Luke, John). So are the Old Testament prophetic books, such as Isaiah, Ezekiel, and Amos. Some other parts of the New Testament are also named for their authors (the epistles—letters—of Peter, James, and John). Some books are named for their main character, who may or may not be the author. This is the case with Joshua, Ruth, Esther, Job, Ezra.

The Book of Acts is named for its content. (It tells of the "acts," deeds, of the early Christians.) So is the Book of Revelation. (It is a "revealing" of the future.) And the Book of Exodus is also named for its content. (It concerns the exodus, the "exit," of the people of Israel from Egypt.) Some "books" are named for their intended audience. This is true of most of the epistles—letters—in the New Testament, which are addressed to, for example, the Romans, the Colossians, the Ephesians, and to individuals such as Timothy and Titus.

Some books seem to be named wrong. For example, Numbers (the fourth book of the Old Testament) tells about a census—but this is only a tiny part of the book. And some names—Leviticus, Deuteronomy, and Ecclesiastes, for example—make no sense at all. If the name seems really weird, it's because the name is probably an English form of the ancient names. (See chaps. 12–13 for a summary of each book and an explanation of the name.)

Note that a few books contain numerals in the titles. In the Old Testament you'll find, for example, 1 and 2 Samuel. When you speak of these out loud, you say "First and Second Samuel," not "One and Two Samuel." The same applies to 1 and 2 Kings and to 1 and 2 Timothy, and to all other books with numerals in their names.

Now a note about "Johns." The New Testament has a large and important book, the Gospel of John. It is usually just called John for short (as in "Our Bible study group is studying John for the next few weeks"). But the New Testament also has three epistles—letters—written by the same John. These three are 1 John, 2 John, and 3 John. They are much shorter than the Gospel and not referred to nearly as often. If you see "John" without a number preceding it, the reference is to the Gospel of John.

Don't concern yourself too much with the names of the sixty-six books. Their content is more important than their titles.

WHAT ARE THESE TWO "TESTAMENTS"?

The Bible's sixty-six books are divided into two groups. The Old Testament deals with the beginnings of the world and God's dealings with the people known as Israelites or Hebrews. The New Testament, written later, deals with Jesus, His disciples, and the earliest group of Christians. *Testament* means "covenant" or "agreement," and it refers to God's "contract" with His special people—the Hebrews in the Old Testament, the Christians in the New. You could think of *testament* as meaning "instruction manual" or "terms of agreement" for people who wanted to know and do God's will.

WHAT'S IN THESE TESTAMENTS?

This instruction manual is, fortunately, more readable than most manuals. Unlike manuals, it isn't written in one businesslike style. The sixty-six books contain histories (seldom boring), moral rules, worship rules, advice for daily living, songs of praise and thanksgiving and despair, warnings against moral decay, prophecies, sermons, and more. With sixty-six books and many different authors, this kind of variety is no surprise.

Speaking of authors: they're a mixed group. Two of the writers, Moses and Paul, were well-educated by the standards of their times. Some of the other authors were fishermen (Peter and John) and kings (David and Solomon). One author was a tax collector (Matthew), one a shepherd (Amos), one a priest (Ezra), and one a servant (Nehemiah). Not one of these men was a "professional writer" in our sense of the words. Their written words were produced over a span of 1,600 years. Written over this vast time span, by dozens of different writers, these sixty-six books compose more than just "a book." The Bible is (and has often been called) the "Book of books."

Unfortunately, the diversity can be puzzling to a first-time reader of the Bible. Where do we begin? At page 1? Is it all worth reading, or are there parts that can be skipped? Which parts are really, *really* important? Read on. The book you are holding will try to answer all those questions, and others.

WHY IS IT CALLED "HOLY"?

First, consider the Bible's other name: *Scripture*. This just means "writings," and people talk about the *Holy Bible* and the *Holy Scriptures*. What they mean is, "These writings are so honored and respected and so different from other writings that we consider them *holy* or *sacred*." That is, they exist not just because human beings wrote them and passed them on through the centuries, but because people believe they really are a revealing of God to humanity. Because people consider the Bible "holy," they think of it as something more than just pleasure reading or a historical curiosity.

Consider the great epic poems *The Iliad* and *The Odyssey*. Both were written long ago, during the same period as certain books of the Bible. People still read them (in the original Greek, but more often in translation) and discuss them. They are "classics," as is the Bible. But no one *believes* in the truth of these poems. They may contain some historical material. But they are a mixture (a beautiful and well-written mixture) of

> *The Christian feels that the tooth of time gnaws all books but the Bible. It has a pertinent relevance to every age.*
> —W.E. SANGSTER

mythology, religious beliefs, and details about life in an ancient civilization—and none of it really has any bearing on how we now live our lives and find meaning. But the author knew he was just writing poetry. He never included the words "Thus says the Lord . . ."—a phrase that crops up again and again in the Bible. So there are old books like *The Iliad* that are "classics," but not "holy." The Bible, for people who accept it, is a "holy classic."

IS IT THE ONLY "HOLY" BOOK IN EXISTENCE?

Christianity is not the only religion with "scriptures" or "holy books." Most of the great world religions have some writings that they consider special. The fact is, all religions have important traditions and teachings. In what we call the primitive religions, these may not be written down. The people of these religions may pass traditions and teachings on by word of mouth from one generation to another. These may include history, rules, and poetry—like the Bible.

The Bible had its beginnings in word of mouth. The authors believed that the traditions were so important they wouldn't rely just on the human memory. They would commit the traditions to writing. Instead of traditions being passed on orally—and possibly being changed in the process—they were "set in stone." This would serve the purpose of settling disputes. For example, if two people argued about exactly what an ethical law in the Book of Exodus said, they could "look it up" instead of just comparing one person's memory to another.

The Jews have the Bible—minus the New Testament, which they don't accept. Devout Jews order their lives around their Bible, particularly the first five books, known as the Torah. Many still follow the kosher food laws in the Book of Leviticus (against eating pork, for example). Jews have written hundreds of volumes of commentary on the Old Testament, so it is definitely a holy book for them.

The Muslims have the Quran (or Koran), written (unlike the Bible) by only one author, the prophet Muhammad. Muslims call it "the Noble Quran" or sometimes just "the Book." Muslims believe that Allah—God—was the ultimate source of the Quran. It guides the lives of devout Muslims, and the society and culture of Muslim nations across North Africa, the Middle East, and elsewhere show the reverence people have for the book.

Christians, Jews, and Muslims are "people of the book." In theory, these three religions' beliefs are supposed to be based on their holy books, and on nothing else. Tradition, of course, also plays a role, but, in the final analysis, the book is the cornerstone of belief.

Other religions also have holy books, but the religions don't have the same attitude as Christians, Jews, and Muslims do. Confucianism, for example, is based on the teachings (and writings) of the Chinese teacher Confucius. But some people aren't sure whether Confucianism is a religion or just a philosophy. Confucianists respect Confucius' writings, but they don't really regard them as sacred.

The Hindu religion of India, being very, very old, has many books—the Bhagavad-Gita, the Vedas, the Upanishads, and many others. Hinduism is more like a group of religions than just one, and there is no one book that the Hindus honor in the same way that Christians approach the Bible.

The Bible's view of humans' relationship with God is unique in all the world religions. In the Bible, God is the mighty King of the universe, Master of all things, the awesome Supreme Being, the all-seeing Judge who knows our every thought and deed. Other religions have gods like this. But the Bible shows us other sides of this mighty God. He is approachable. He loves people. He wants to be loved by us, but freely, willingly. He is not just the King, but also Father to people who love Him. He wants His followers to be not only worshipers but His children. As the Holy Spirit, this very personal God actually lives within His people, guiding them, strengthening them. So the God of the Bible is—uniquely—both "Master of the Universe" and "up close and personal."

What Is the Apocrypha?

Some Bibles don't contain the Apocrypha, some do. The books in the Apocrypha are an addition to the standard sixty-six "books" of the Old and New Testaments. All of them were written during—and most are concerned with—the long gap of time between the Old and New Testaments. When the Protestant churches broke away from the Catholic church in the 1500s, they chose to drop the Apocrypha, believing the books weren't "inspired" in the same way that the other books of the Bible are. Protestant leaders noted that the Jews' sacred books did not include the Apocrypha. All Catholic Bibles still include the Apocrypha. But the books of the Apocrypha have never been studied as closely or been considered as important as the other sixty-six books. We will deal more with the Apocrypha in a later section.

WHY ARE THERE SO MANY VERSIONS?

Every bookstore in every mall sells Bibles—and more than one version. You can't buy the "real" Bible because the "real" one was written in ancient Hebrew and Greek. So we have to trust translators who know these languages to give us an accurate idea of what the original authors meant to communicate. Since languages change over time, no translation can be "permanent"—although many people still read the *King James Version*, done in 1611. Words and phrases change, so every few years people who know Greek and Hebrew decide that it's time for a "new and improved" translation of the old Book. There are literally dozens of English translations today, though a handful qualify as the most popular.

If you look inside the front of a Bible, you will usually find a preface or introduction. This will explain when and why the translation was done. Most people today find it easiest to read a translation done after 1970.

There is no "official" version that everyone agrees is the best. The one I quote in this book is the *New International Version,* completed in 1984. It has been well-received by readers (one test of its value as a translation) and by scholars (the other test of its value as a translation). Some other popular versions are the *New Revised Standard Version,* the *New Jerusalem Bible,* the *New King James Version,* and *Today's English Version* (also called the *Good News Bible*). You'll often see these versions referred to by their acronyms—NIV for *New International Version,* for example, and KJV for (you guessed it) the *King James Version.*

WHAT ARE THE NUMBERS CONTAINED IN THE BOOKS?

If you open your Bible to the first "book," Genesis, you'll see a large 1, which indicates chapter 1. The entire Bible was divided into chapters in the Middle Ages. Like the chapter divisions in any book, the chapters break up the text and make it easier for the reader to locate a specific section. The smaller numbers in the text refer to verses—generally, one or two sentences for each verse, but not always. (The word *verse* does not mean that the material is poetry, by the way.)

The verse divisions were done in the 1500s—again, to make it easier to locate a specific section. If you're looking for the Ten Commandments, it's much easier if someone tells you, "It's in Exodus, chapter 20" instead of, "It's somewhere in Exodus." Usually, to be brief, you would simply say, "Exodus 20."

Before the Bible was divided into chapters (around the year 1214) and verses (in 1551), people had to refer to parts of the Bible by the name of the book or by the author (or whoever people thought the author was). People would refer to the Book of Isaiah by saying, "As Isaiah says . . ." Or they would say, "As Solomon says in Proverbs . . ." The chapter and verse numbers have been a tremendous help because they allow anyone to find the exact location in a particular book.

The one book in the Bible that isn't divided into chapters is Psalms. It has always consisted of 150 separate poems, and these are referred to as "psalms," never as chapters. They are, like chapters, divided into verses. Instead of saying "Psalms, chapter 23, verse 2," you would say, "Psalm 23, verse 2."

You will seldom find any book or speaker that refers to page numbers in the Bible. Instead, he or she will refer to the book, its chapter, and its verse. For example: a pastor announces on Sunday, "I will be preaching this morning on John 3:16." He means that his sermon will be about John (a book of the New Testament), the third chapter, the sixteenth verse. Note that a colon (:) always separates the chapter number from the verse number. Romans 12:1 means "Romans, chapter 12, verse 1." A few books of the Bible have only one chapter, and they have no chapter numbers, only verse numbers. So Jude 14 means "Jude, verse 14."

The numbers are always the same, regardless of what Bible translation you use. In other words, no matter what Bible you use, you will always find at Exodus 20:14 words similar to "You shall not commit adultery."

WHAT ARE THE HEADINGS IN THE BOOKS?

Most Bibles have headings, in addition to chapter and verse numbers. For example, the *New International Version* has, in chapter 2 of Genesis, the heading "Adam and Eve." These headings aren't actually part of the Bible text. They are aids the translators insert to give you an idea of what the particular section is about. They serve the same purpose as chapter titles in a regular book. These are useful if you're looking for a particular subject, or if you're just browsing. For example, if you're looking for the Christmas story in Luke's Gospel, it helps when you find the heading "The Birth of Jesus" at the beginning of chapter 2 in Luke. On the other hand, if you flip through

Leviticus and see headings like "Regulations about Mildew and Discharges Causing Uncleanness," you may (wisely) choose to skip these sections.

WHAT ARE "TEXT" AND "PASSAGE"?

When people speak of a portion, or section, of the Bible, they refer to it as a "passage." Example: "My favorite passage in the Bible is the Parable of the Good Samaritan in Luke 10." A passage is always more than one verse; it may be as long as a chapter, or even longer. "Passage" could mean the same as "verses," except that "verses" might refer to verses from different places in the Bible. "Passage" refers to a continuous set of verses.

"Text" is just a way of referring to the words. You could speak of "translating the Hebrew text into English." "Text" can also mean the same as "passage." You might hear a pastor begin a sermon by saying, "The text for my sermon today is Exodus 20:1-2." Someone might say, "The author quoted a Bible text in his novel" or "The author quoted a Bible passage in his novel"—both mean the same.

WHY ARE THE SIXTY-SIX BOOKS IN THIS PARTICULAR ORDER?

First, the New Testament follows the Old (naturally). Second, there is a chronological sequence in both Testaments—sort of. The Old Testament begins—appropriately— with Genesis and its story of the world's creation. From Genesis to the Book of Esther the Old Testament books progress forward in time. But Esther is followed by Job, a book with no specific date attached to it. And Job is followed by Psalms, poems written over hundreds of years. Beginning with the Book of Isaiah, the books known (collectively) as the Prophets fall into (roughly) a chronological sequence. Malachi, the last book of the Old Testament, is generally supposed to have been the last prophetic writing before the New Testament.

Why did the Old Testament not use a strict chronological approach? Some of the books—Psalms, Proverbs, and Ecclesiastes, for example—simply don't fit into a historical sequence. Over time, they found their niche between the historical writings (from Genesis to Esther) and the Prophets (Isaiah to Malachi).

The New Testament begins with the birth of Jesus (told in the Gospel of Matthew), then continues with the other three Gospels (Mark, Luke, and John), which are other versions of Jesus' life. They are followed by the Book of Acts, which tells the story of Jesus' followers after He had departed the earth. Acts is followed by the Epistles—letters—written to churches or individuals and concerned with issues confronting the early Christians. These letters aren't arranged historically. They are generally arranged according to size—that is, the first letter, Romans, is the longest. After the letters comes the closing book, Revelation. It is the logical end to the Bible because it is concerned with the end of the world and the beginning of an entirely new world—heaven. As in a good novel, Revelation is the climax, the "ending with a real bang."

If you are new to the Bible, face this fact:

To make your study of it easier, you can memorize the sequence of the sixty-six books, or you can get in the habit of looking at your Bible's alphabetical list of the books, which will enable you to find the book by page number. (By the way, one Bible version of the 1980s, the *Alphabetical Bible,* tried to solve the problem by arranging the sixty-six books in alphabetical order. Oddly, this version didn't sell well.)

Here are the names of the books of the Bible, along with the usual abbreviations:

OLD TESTAMENT

Genesis	Gen.
Exodus	Ex.
Leviticus	Lev.
Numbers	Num.
Deuteronomy	Deut.
Joshua	Josh.
Judges	Jdg. or Jud.
Ruth	Ruth
1 Samuel	1 Sam.
2 Samuel	2 Sam.
1 Kings	1 Kgs.
2 Kings	2 Kgs.
1 Chronicles	1 Chr. or 1 Chron.
2 Chronicles	2 Chr. or 2 Chron.
Ezra	Ezra
Nehemiah	Neh.
Esther	Est. or Es.
Job	Job
Psalms	Ps. and Pss.
Proverbs	Pr. or Prov.
Ecclesiastes	Ecc.
Song of Songs	S. of S. or Song
Isaiah	Isa.
Jeremiah	Jer.
Lamentations	Lam.

Ezekiel	Ezek.
Daniel	Dan.
Hosea	Hos.
Joel	Joel
Amos	Amos
Obadiah	Obad.
Jonah	Jon.
Micah	Mic.
Nahum	Nah.
Habakkuk	Hab.
Zephaniah	Zeph.
Haggai	Hag.
Zechariah	Zech.
Malachi	Mal.

NEW TESTAMENT

Matthew	Matt.
Mark	Mark or Mk.
Luke	Luke or Lk.
John	John or Jn.
Acts	Acts
Romans	Rom.
1 Corinthians	1 Cor.
2 Corinthians	2 Cor.
Galatians	Gal.
Ephesians	Eph.
Philippians	Phil.
Colossians	Col.
1 Thessalonians	1 Thes. or 1 Th.
2 Thessalonians	2 Thes. or 2 Th.
1 Timothy	1 Tim.
2 Timothy	2 Tim.
Titus	Tit.
Philemon	Phm. or Phile.
Hebrews	Heb.
James	Jam.
1 Peter	1 Peter
2 Peter	2 Peter
1 John	1 Jn.
2 John	2 Jn.
3 John	3 Jn.
Jude	Jude
Revelation	Rev.

WHY ARE THERE MAPS?

You don't need a map to enjoy or understand the Bible. But the Old and New Testaments both refer to events that took place in actual locations—cities, countries, rivers, etc. Because much of the Bible is history, a map is helpful, just as maps are helpful in any history book. Most Bibles contain at least a few maps, showing the key places in the Old Testament and the New Testament.

WHY ARE THERE TABLES OF WEIGHTS AND MEASURES?

Since the people of the Bible lived centuries ago, they didn't use the metric system, nor did they refer to measurements in miles, yards, pounds, ounces, etc. Nor was their money the same as ours. Most Bibles have charts or tables that show the rough modern equivalents of weights, measures, and money. A good modern translation of the Bible will probably communicate these things in the text itself.

WHAT IS THIS "CONCORDANCE" AT THE END?

A concordance is a sort of index. It lists the verses in the Bible that mention a particular word or name. Most Bibles don't contain a *complete* concordance that lists every word in the Bible and every verse that has that word. A complete concordance is large enough to require a whole book by itself. The concordances found in the backs of Bibles usually just mention selected verses and selected words. For example, a concordance might list *love* and would include such familiar verses as John 3:16 and 1 Corinthians 13:2.

WHY IS THERE A DICTIONARY AT THE END?

Your Bible may not have a dictionary, but it's a nice thing to have. What you have is really a "minidictionary." Since the Bible is so big and so full of people, places, and events, a comprehensive Bible dictionary is a full book all by itself. But the "mini" version in your Bible is usually a list of the most important people, places, and things, giving a short definition of each one and telling why it is important and where you could locate it in the Bible. This is useful for new readers. For example, many parts of the New Testament refer to a man named Abraham— whose story is in the Old Testament. Your Bible's minidictionary may explain where you can find the story of Abraham (it's in Genesis, chapters 12 through 25) and why he is considered so important in both the Old and New Testaments.

Footnotes also explain the translation of a word or phrase. For example, John 1:5 in the New International Version reads this way: "The light shines in the darkness, but the darkness has not understood it." The footnote for the verse says, "Or, the darkness has not overcome it." The experts on Greek have yet to decide which is the more accurate translation. So the footnote lets you know there are two valid translations.

WHY DO BIBLES HAVE FOOTNOTES?

You will notice that most Bibles have footnotes at the bottoms of the pages. Like footnotes in any book, these contain important information. And as with any book, the important thing is the book's text, not its footnotes. But with a book as old as the Bible, footnotes help explain some information that might otherwise puzzle the reader. Let's take some examples from the Book of Psalms in the *New International Version.*

At the end of Psalm 3, the odd word *Selah* appears. The footnote at the page bottom says, "A word of uncertain meaning, occurring frequently in the Psalms; possibly a musical term." You don't have to know this to appreciate Psalm 3, but at least the footnote keeps you from puzzling over just what *Selah* means. (In effect, the footnote says, "Don't worry, the scholars aren't sure what it means either.")

Psalm 18, verse 2, describes God as "my shield and the horn of my salvation." Horn, you say? The footnote says, "*Horn* here symbolizes strength." The footnote is bridging a gap, translating a psalm many hundreds of years old, and explaining that the horn has a symbolic, not a literal meaning. (The people in

Bible times, being closer to nature, generally thought of "horn" as "thing on an animal's head," not "musical instrument.")

Several places in Psalms the phrase "Praise the LORD" occurs, always with this footnote: "Hebrew *Hallelu Yah*." In other words, our English "Praise the Lord" is a translation of the Hebrew *Hallelu Yah*.

> *The Bible was never intended to be a book for scholars and specialists only. From the very beginning it was intended to be everybody's book, and that is what it continues to be.*
> —F.F. BRUCE

The Old Testament is quoted many times in the New Testament. In fact, almost any page in the New Testament will contain some quotation from the Old because the New Testament authors believed that Jesus fulfilled many parts of the Old Testament. In many cases a footnote will point out which Old Testament verse is being quoted. For example, Luke 22:37 reads, "It is written: 'And He was numbered with the transgressors.'" The footnote says "Isaiah 53:12." If you choose, you can look up Isaiah 53:12 and read that verse in its original context. (This is similar to when a teacher or author states, "President Reagan once said

...." If the Reagan quotation is followed by a footnote, it would tell you when and where Reagan made the remark.) Footnotes like these are useful if you're curious about the Old Testament background of verses in the New Testament.

This is called cross-referencing—telling the reader about related Bible verses. Some such footnotes also refer the reader to other verses that cover the same ground. For example: Some Bibles might include a footnote for Matthew 5:3, where Jesus' Beatitudes begin. The footnote might read: "Luke 6:20." This tells the reader that Luke 6:20 covers the same material.

By the way, footnotes in Bibles are not new. Since the invention of the printing press, most Bibles have contained notes explaining the text. Some old versions of the Bible had notes with a particular slant.

MAKING CONNECTIONS: OLD TO NEW TO OLD

In some cases you'll find a footnote in the New Testament that refers you to verses in both the Old and the New. A classic example is Matthew 22:44, where Jesus is quoting Psalm 110:1. The footnote for this might say "Psalm 110:1." It might also add several other references: "Mark 12:36, Luke 20:43, Acts 2:35, Hebrews 1:13." These are other places where the New Testament quotes Psalm 110:1, and all the verses are related because they are referring to Jesus. You could trace the way that Psalm 110:1 was interpreted by different New Testament authors. In many Bibles, you would also find a footnote at Psalm 110:1, pointing you to the New Testament verses that quote it. So this kind of footnote allows you to "make connections" between various parts of the Bible.

DIGGING ARCHAEOLOGY

The Old Testament mentions an Egyptian Pharaoh named Shishak (or Sheshonk), who attacked Jerusalem in the time of King Rehoboam (1 Kings 11:40). Archaeologists have found Shishak's record of this military campaign, inscribed on a wall in a temple in Karnak in Egypt. The Bible claims that he did not capture Jerusalem but imposed a heavy tribute (2 Chron. 12). The record in Egypt says exactly the same thing.

Do altars have horns?

The Old Testament claims that certain people held onto the "horns of the altar" (1 Kings 1:50; 2:28), and readers puzzled over just what the "horns" were. Archaeologists have uncovered altars that actually do have triangular projections on the corners—just like horns. (You might notice in the Old Testament that an animal horn is often a symbol of power.)

The Bible records the Babylonian King Nebuchadnezzar's siege of Jerusalem in this way:

"Nebuchadnezzar himself came up to the city while his officers were besieging it. Jehoiachin king of Judah . . . his nobles and his officials all surrendered to him. In the eighth year of the reign of the king of Babylon, he took Jehoiachin prisoner. . . . Nebuchadnezzar removed all the treasures from the temple of the LORD and from the royal palace, and took away all the gold articles. . . . Nebuchadnezzar took Jehoiachin captive to Babylon. He made Mattaniah, Jehoiachin's uncle, king in his place and changed his name to Zedekiah." (2 Kings 24:11-17)

Archaeologists found a Babylonian clay tablet confirming these exact details.

Bathing for health?

John's Gospel mentions a healing at the Pool of Bethesda in Jerusalem. According to John, this pool had five porches. For centuries no one found evidence of any such place. Then in 1888 diggers found the remains of a public bathhouse in Jerusalem. It had five porches (colonnades).

The Book of Acts records a strange scene.

The Christian missionaries Paul and Barnabas preach and heal in the town of Lystra, and the local people believe they are the gods Zeus and Hermes. The local priest of Zeus tries to sacrifice some bulls to the visiting "gods" (Acts 14).

Archaeologists found that, indeed, Lystra had a Zeus-and-Hermes fixation. Near the town they found a statue of the god Hermes and a stone altar dedicated to both Zeus and Hermes.

The Book of Acts records a sad racist tale.

A riot broke out in Jerusalem because the Jews believed the Apostle Paul had taken a non-Jew into the Jewish temple.

"Some Jews from the province of Asia saw Paul at the temple. They stirred up the whole crowd and seized him, shouting, 'Men of Israel, help us! This is the man who teaches all men everywhere against our people and our law and this place. And besides, he has brought Greeks into the temple area and defiled this holy place.' (They had previously seen Trophimus the Ephesian in the city with Paul and assumed that Paul had brought him into the temple area.) The whole city was aroused, and the people came running from all directions" (Acts 21:27-30).

The archaeologists dug up an inscription in Jerusalem's temple area. The stone inscription reads "No non-Jew to proceed beyond the barrier and enclosure which surrounds the Sacred Place. Any man who does so is responsible for his death, which is the consequence."

For example, after Protestants split from the Catholic church in the 1500s, there were Protestant Bibles with anti-Catholic footnotes and Catholic Bibles with anti-Protestant footnotes. For example, a Protestant Bible of the 1500s had a footnote for Revelation 9:11, indicating that the "angel of the bottomless pit" was . . . the Catholic pope. A breakthrough came with the *King James Version* in 1611. Its translators ruled that no notes could be added except "for the explanation of the Hebrew or Greek." Happily, Bibles today aren't guilty of bashing other groups of Christians.

WHY IS SOME OF THE MATERIAL PRINTED IN RED LETTERS?

"Red-letter Bibles" show the words of Jesus printed in red. Since Jesus is the key figure in the Bible, His words are more important than any other character's words so some Bibles print them in red to make them stand out from the rest of the text.

WHAT ARE STUDY BIBLES?

These are Bibles with extensive notes. If your Bible is a study Bible, it will probably say so on the cover and the spine of the book (*NIV Study Bible, Life Application Bible, Oxford Study Bible* are just a few examples). With a study Bible, you get a lot of historical and theological information, usually written by well-respected Bible scholars. These notes explain such matters as dates of events and key ideas. Some notes in study Bibles also explain how the passage applies to life.

WHY IS THE BIBLE SUPPOSED TO BE "INSPIRED"?

Harriet Beecher Stowe, who wrote the famous anti-slavery novel, *Uncle Tom's Cabin,* claimed that "God wrote it." Did she mean that God actually wrote the novel, and that she merely signed her name to it? Of course not. She meant that she wrote it, but that God's guidance was behind her writing of it. This is similar to what people mean about the Bible being "inspired." The Bible did not just fall out of heaven, nor was it found written on golden plates. It was written piece by piece over a long period by many different writers.

In any Bible translation—and particularly in the original Hebrew and Greek—you can't help but notice that the authors had different personalities. Paul's Letter to the Romans has a very different style from the Book of Acts, and the historical book of 1 Samuel is very different in style from the Book of Ecclesiastes. Every author was different, just as present-day authors are different. God did not suppress or override each author's individual way of expressing himself.

The idea of inspiration is that God took a special interest in the books that compose the Bible. *Every* human author writes with "divine guidance"—in the sense that all authors owe their lives, their intelligence, and their way with words to God. But Christians believe that the Bible authors received particular guidance from God. This guidance kept the Bible free from errors—not minor errors of science and historical fact, but errors about God Himself and what He willed for the human race. When we say the Bible is *inerrant*, this is what we mean. It is "without error," at least in the ways that count. That leads us to the next topic, historical authority.

HOW DOES THE BIBLE SQUARE WITH WHAT ARCHAEOLOGISTS FIND?

Maybe a better question is: Can archaeology and other sciences prove the Bible is true? In a sense, no—because archaeology can't prove (or disprove) that God exists. Nor can it prove that God took a special interest in the Hebrews or Christians. What archaeology *can* do is confirm that the Bible's historical data is correct. In other words, archaeology can prove that the

The New Testament in the original Greek is not a work of literary art.
—C.S. LEWIS

Bible is recounting real history, not just spinning a wild tale.

Back in the 1800s it became fashionable to believe that the Bible, particularly the Old Testament, was just a folktale or legend. For example, the Old Testament refers to a tribe of people called the Hittites, and no archaeologist had ever found evidence that the Hittites existed. Skeptics assumed the Hittites were just fiction—like the Lilliputians in *Gulliver's Travels*. But—surprise!—in 1906, archaeologists working in Turkey found evidence that confirms almost everything the Bible says about the Hittites' customs and their location. Archaeologists from time to time discover clay tablets and monuments bearing the names of people in the Bible. For example, Omri, a

king of Israel (1 Kings 16) is mentioned on the Moabite Stone, cut in the ninth century B.C. Another king of Israel, Jehu (2 Kings 10), is mentioned on the Black Obelisk of the Assyrian King Shalmaneser III. An official inscription of Assyrian King Sennacherib mentions that he shut up the Judean King Hezekiah "like a bird in a cage"—exactly the words expressed in the Bible (2 Kings 18). The Babylonian Chronicle mentions that King Nebuchadnezzar conquered Jerusalem and imprisoned its king, Jehoiachin—exactly the story the Bible tells (2 Kings 24).

Genesis, the first book and the one dealing with the oldest material, covers some very ancient times. Historians used to assume that Genesis' ancient stories of Abraham, Isaac, and Jacob were just fiction, written hundreds of years later and having no basis in reality. But archaeologists have found out a lot about those ancient times—family customs, travel, etc.—and they now believe that the early stories in Genesis reflect the times accurately.

Since the New Testament is much nearer to our own time, there is even more historical evidence. No one seriously doubts anymore that Jesus existed (although this was a trendy idea in the 1800s), and the various Jewish and Roman officials mentioned in the New Testament were all real, as confirmed by Roman inscriptions and records. In 1992, archaeologists found the family tomb of Caiaphas, the high priest who presided at the trial of Jesus. Like Caiaphas, Herod, Pontius Pilate, Felix, and other figures were real men, not just inventions of the Gospel writers. These are just a few examples of archaeology supporting what the Bible says.

As you might imagine, the farther back in time you go, the less evidence there is. For instance, archaeologists leave no doubt in our minds that King David and King Solomon were real, historical characters. But, going back farther, they find less evidence for Moses, even less for Abraham, and (naturally) none for Adam and Eve. That doesn't mean that these figures were fictional. It just means that evidence is harder to come by, the farther back you go. (If you've ever worked on your family's genealogy, you run into the same problem. It's easy tracing people in the 1900s, less so in the 1800s, even less in the 1700s, etc.) Archaeology cannot convince an unbeliever to believe in God. It can provide a believer with evidence that the parts of the Bible claiming to be history really do have a foundation in fact.

When you begin to study the Bible, you'll notice that two important historical events are critical for belief: in the Old Testament, the Israelites' miraculous exodus from Egypt; in the New Testament, the resurrection of Jesus from the dead. Archaeology has yet to prove—or disprove—either of these events. If Jesus was raised from the dead, then obviously no evidence could ever be produced. It is possible that further evidence could be found to support the Israelites' exodus—but, no archaeologist could ever prove that it occurred because of God's miraculous intervention. Archaeologists can't report on miracles, obviously. They can only report

on inscriptions, official court records, and the other leftovers of civilization—coins, tombs, tools, etc.

ISN'T THE OLD TESTAMENT JUST A CONFUSING HODGEPODGE OF LAWS AND WEIRD STORIES?

The Old Testament has no "plan" or "plot" in the way that a good novel or movie has. The only "plan" binding it all together is God's own plan of revelation. It really is a hodgepodge—songs, poems, law, ritual, historical narrative, and prophecy. The theme that somehow binds it all together is that God reveals Himself to people and saves those who are faithful to Him. It does take some sifting through the Old Testament to see this theme.

Compared to the great writings of Greek and Roman literature, the Bible is not great literature. Its style is too blunt and straightforward compared with the writings of the Greek poets. The Old Testament honestly portrays all the sins of mankind—"warts and all." Israel's heroes are not idealized storybook figures (which is one good reason to believe in the Bible's historical accuracy). The heroes—people like Abraham, David, and Solomon—have both good and bad sides. They were good, God-fearing men, but they were prone to deceit, violence, sexual promiscuity, and other vices. This is appropriate, because for the Bible authors, God is the real hero of the story. Much as the Jews honored people like David, the Bible is consistent in one thing: God alone deserves the praise for everything good. (Consider the logic of this: instead of telling us to worship all-too-human heroes with clay feet, the Bible says "Worship God—even the best human beings can be failures at times.")

At the time Jesus appeared on the scene, many non-Jews—Gentiles—had become admirers of the Jewish religion. In some cases they became full converts. Most of these people were attracted to the high moral standards in the Old Testament. Note: they were not attracted by the Bible's "heroes" but by its ethics and its emphasis on a moral God. They also were not attracted to the Bible because of its literary value. Compared to the great writings of Greek and Roman literature, the Bible is *not* great literature. Its style is too blunt and straightforward compared with the writings of the Greek poets.

But many people believed that fine writing was not enough. In a time of moral breakdown, they yearned for a high morality, and they wanted to worship a God who urged them on to a better way of life. Many of them found this in the Jews' sacred book, the Old Testament. Just as in our own day, when many politicians and preachers urge a return to biblical standards of morality, so many people in the Roman Empire promoted the moral standards of the Old Testament.

AREN'T AMERICANS A RELIGIOUS PEOPLE, FAMILIAR WITH THE BIBLE?

According to most polls, yes, Americans consider themselves religious. Most say they believe in God, prayer, heaven, and hell. They even say these beliefs are "very important" to them.

But other polls show that people—even regular churchgoers—are very ignorant about what's in the Bible. Most people responding to polls cannot identify major characters and beliefs in the Bible, the Ten Commandments, the Beatitudes of Jesus, etc.

In short, polls show that Americans say they believe in God—but since they don't know the Bible (which is supposed to be our chief source of information about God), what exactly is their "God" like? The loving and forgiving Heavenly Father of the New Testament? A cosmic "Force"? A Creator who is not really involved in human life day to day? Nature? The universe itself—us included? The average person's idea of God may be so vague that believing in God may mean believing in . . . nothing. Getting acquainted with God must involve (besides prayer, naturally) getting familiar with the Book, believed to be the Word of God Himself.

APPROACHING THE BIBLE: HOW NOT TO DO IT

A. Approach it as a "church book"

Many people grew up hearing the Bible read only in church. Not hearing it read at home, they associate the Bible with the stuffiness of a worship service. They may associate the Bible with a pompous, "reverent" tone of voice. This made the Bible seem like a "Sunday thing"—something sacred, stuffy, and separate from the other six days— "real life." In fact, the original Hebrew and Greek in the Bible are very much "everyday" lan-

"THE TONIGHT SHOW" AND THE BIBLE

"The Tonight Show" once featured Jay Leno doing a "Test Your Bible Knowledge" segment. Leno did on-the-street interviews with people who claimed they owned a Bible. He introduced the segment by saying "There are certain things we all know, whether we're religious or not. But watch these clips. This is frightening."

"Can you name one of the Ten Commandments?"
"Freedom of speech."

"How many Commandments were there?"
"Ten."
"Right. Can you name any of them?"
"Um, no. Well, OK, they say . . . you know, you can't do anything."

"Can you name the four men who wrote the Gospels?"
"No."
"Can you name the four Beatles?"
"Sure. John, Paul, George, Ringo."

"Who was swallowed by a whale?"
"Pinocchio."

"What was Eve created from?"
"Adam's arm."

"What was Eve created from?"
"The apple."

"Who was taller, David or Goliath?"
"David who?"

"Where did Noah's ark land?"
"In a tree."

"Where did Noah's ark land? It was on Mount . . . ?"
"Everest?"

---

guage, not a special "holy" language. The original Bible was written in ordinary language to communicate with as many people as possible. Just as, today, everyone understands the language of TV shows and radio talk show hosts, so the Bible's words were the "common ground" of their day.

B. Approach it as a book of rules

Well, it *does* have rules. All religions do. So do all schools, employers, sports teams, any kind of human grouping. No one joins a baseball team and gripes, "I don't like this, 'three strikes and you're out' rule." That's just baseball. Well, the Bible's assumption is that life, like baseball, has rules. They're not there to stifle and repress.

They're just there. This is the way things are. And the rules are there for a good reason. (Any married person who's ever been suspicious of his spouse understands the wisdom of the "Do not commit adultery" rule. And anyone who owns any type of property understands "Do not steal." The rules aren't all bad, are they?)

But it is wrong to see the Bible as a book of "do nots." It has so much more: images of loving fellowship with God and with other people. The "do nots" are balanced with a lot of very positive "do's."

C. Approach it as a book of mysteries

Parts of the Bible puzzle people. The Book

of Revelation, for example, has been interpreted in many, many ways. The same goes for parts of the Book of Daniel. But generally the Bible is pretty straightforward. If you're reading a good modern translation, you'll find the Bible is pretty easy to understand. Books like Acts and Mark's Gospel are easy enough for most children to grasp. We say the Bible is "holy" and "sacred," but its writers didn't intend it to be mysterious or cryptic. In its original Hebrew and Greek its language is amazingly ordinary—the language of everyday thought.

D. Approach it to prove a point

People love to do this: use the Bible to prove something they already believe. (Some people have used the verse "You must be born again" to support their belief in reincarnation—definitely *not* what the verse really means.) This is an abuse of the Bible. Instead of really studying the Bible, reading it to find out its main themes, people scrounge around to find particular verses to support their own ideas. (The classic example is the "Peanuts" cartoon where Lucy goes running to her brother Linus, pointing out that she found the word "sister" in the Bible. Then she says, "That proves you have to give me a Christmas present.")

E. Approach it as if it were dull

It isn't—not by any means. The problem is, people approach it assuming that since it is "holy," it is boring. People in cultures that have no prior knowledge of the Bible or its religion often take it up, read it, and find it fascinating. It would be interesting to see what people would do if they could clear their minds of everything they'd ever heard about the Bible. If they could approach it as they would any other book, what might happen? "The Bible? Wonder what this is? Let's read this and find out …"

Oddly, some of the same people who claim the Bible is dull will gladly tell you about some "fascinating" book on Buddhism or New Age beliefs.

F. Approach it as if it were holy

Well, isn't it? Yes, in the sense that many intelligent people really do believe that it contains God's revelation to mankind. But it—the paper and ink that make up the physical Bible—isn't holy. The revelation is. There is nothing magical about the book itself—even though people have done silly things like placing a Bible on the chest of a dying person, hoping it would help him recover. It is not a lucky charm, like a rabbit's foot or lucky horseshoe.

For centuries people have believed that the Bible's words could change human lives—assuming that the reader actually puts them into practice. Having a cookbook does not make you a cook, nor does it fill your stomach. Likewise, having a Bible does not change a human life. It doesn't fill your spiritual hunger, unless you act on what's there. You could starve to death with a cookbook in your hand (even if you'd memorized every recipe in it), and you could feel spiritual emptiness (even if you had memorized every verse). The ink and paper—and even the words themselves—make no difference in human life unless the reader acts on them.

There is a classic French novel, *The Red and the Black*, which tells the story of a brilliant clergyman who has memorized the entire New Testament—in its original

Greek. This impresses everyone, and many people think he must be a very "spiritual" person. In fact, he is a totally immoral character, selfish and cruel. Another character in the novel tells him, "I fear for your salvation."

CAN YOU SAY "MINUTIAE"?

The book you are reading is a "basic" book, not a book for scholars. (Even scholars need an occasional refresher course, though, don't they?) So the book leaves out material that you probably don't need. For example, the section with summaries of the Bible's sixty-six books does not mention the date each book was written. Bible scholars like to fight over these things. Pick up any Bible commentary and you'll find long discussions of when each book was (supposedly) written, who wrote it, who the readers were, etc. Such things are *minutiae*— the "tiny things" that we normal human beings don't find particularly significant or useful in our lives. All of us (and presumably the scholars too) must get up in the morning, go to work, relate to coworkers and friends and family members, dabble in some pastimes outside work, plan our finances, plan for retirement, take care of our physical well-being, and go to bed feeling at peace. Somewhere, in the midst of all this, we must have *purpose* (Why do I bother doing all this?) and *guidance* (Am I doing the right thing?). Beyond living, we feel the need to live *for* something. When these basic needs are met, then, if there is any time and mental energy left over, we can wrangle over whether the Gospel of John was written in A.D. 65 or A.D. 100. Do you

care about that date? I have a degree in religion, and I don't.

But the scholars, bless 'em, do serve a purpose. They—and the archaeologists—can remind us that the Bible is not pure fiction but is based on historical realities. And they can (loud applause here) explain some parts of the Bible that make us scratch our heads.

An example: At the beginning of Jesus' great Sermon on the Mount, we read: "Now when He saw the crowds, He went up on a mountainside and sat down. His disciples came to Him, and He began to teach them" (Matt. 5:1-2). Is this clear enough? Of course. But the Bible scholars offer some helpful explanation too: sitting was the normal posture for a teacher in those days. A noted teacher wouldn't stand at a lectern. He would sit, delivering His teaching from the "seat of authority," so to speak. Is this information absolutely essential for you? No. But it does help your understanding of Jesus' world. The fact that He was sitting meant that He was speaking with authority and seriousness—"putting the word" on His listeners.

Let's take something a little harder to understand, from the story of Saul becoming Israel's first king: "Samuel took a flask of oil and poured it on Saul's head and kissed him, saying, 'Has not the LORD anointed you leader over His inheritance?'" (1 Sam. 10:1) You may or may not know just what *anointing* is, nor what the oil and the kiss signify. A Bible commentary—or the notes found in a study Bible—could tell you that anointing is a ceremony of marking a person for a special task. Kings were anointed, and so were some priests and prophets. Anointing involved pouring or rubbing oil on the person's head. This is still done, by the way, in countries (like Britain) that have coronation ceremonies for the ruler.

Essential information? No, but helpful. Most readers could figure out from the context that some special ceremony was taking place, that the Prophet Samuel was playing the role of "king-maker."

Take one more example. Matthew's Gospel lists the names of Jesus' twelve apostles: "Simon (who is called Peter) and his brother Andrew; James son of Zebedee, and his brother John; Philip and Bartholomew; Thomas and Matthew the tax collector; James son of Alphaeus, and Thaddaeus; Simon the Zealot and Judas Iscariot, who betrayed him" (Matt. 10:2-4). Pretty straightforward information, not hard to grasp. But your Bible commentary might point out something important here: *Matthew the tax collector* would have been a worker for the Roman government. *Simon the Zealot* belonged to a political group vigorously opposed to the Romans—and to Jews employed by the Romans. So Jesus' band of apostles included two men who would have had reason to despise each other. This isn't critical information. But it helps us to know that Jesus chose to include different types of people among His followers.

WHY READ THE BIBLE?

Reason 1
Joy

We're so busy having fun in our culture, there's no time for joy. How often do you hear someone speak seriously about feeling joy? Along with Christianity itself, the concept of joy is definitely passé in both pop and high culture today. Yet it's an attractive idea, one that people in serious moments admit is missing from their lives.

It is not missing from the Bible. The popular image of people of faith is that they are incredibly long-faced, gloomy, and repressed. There are a few of these types around—but not in the Bible. In both the Old and New Testaments, the people of faith experienced joy in life—not the same as a temporary emotional or chemical high, but something they could hold onto in the worst of times.

Can this joy still be had? Of course. The Bible is worth reading if only to find out just what the joyful people had, and why. (In case you're curious, the words joy and joyful and rejoice occur over 300 times in the Bible.)

Reason 2
Values and Morals

You hear a lot today about "family values" and returning to traditional morals and religion for the good of society. The problem with all this talk from politicians and culture analysts is that people inevitably ask "Why?" followed by the logical question, "Do you expect me to be—or act—religious just for the sake of my kids and their kids?" The real nagging question is, "I can't do it if I don't believe the religious thing is actually true." In other words, why act Christian or semi-Christian if you aren't convinced that Christianity (based on the Bible) is true? The

WHY READ THE BIBLE?

answer "It's good for you" doesn't wash. Faith is either alive or dead, absent or present.

So getting to know the Bible will resolve one question: Is this faith based on the Bible really true? Some people have studied the Bible and concluded, "No." Many others have said, "Yes, it is. So what it teaches about life and morals is important." Not many people have believed that the faith taught in the Bible was "sort of" important or "moderately" important. After studying the Bible closely, most people conclude that it is true—and thus extremely important—or false, and thus not important at all.

Reason 3
Critiquing the Church

The Bible has been called "the church's memory committed to writing." More precisely, it's the memory book of the first generation of Christians. The history of Christianity throughout the centuries is, in essence, the story of how Christians have interpreted the Bible and attempted to be Jesus' followers. Some of the failures of so-called Christians are well-known—the medieval Inquisition, the bloody Crusades, etc. Every generation of Christians—ours included—fails in some ways to measure up to the standards set forth in the Bible. These failures are no reflection on the Bible itself. High standards are not a problem. Failing to meet them—that's a problem.

Unbelievers and believers both need to be familiar with the Bible, if only to be able to understand how Christianity does and does not square with its beliefs. When people criticize certain Christian practices, it's helpful to know if those practices are "real Christianity" (as the Bible presents it) or some sad misunderstanding of it. In other words, if you reject Christianity or certain aspects of it, at least be conscious of whether you're rejecting the real thing or some perversion of it. (For example, if you're offended by door-to-door evangelists, at least be aware the practice is vouched for in the Bible. On the other hand, if you're bothered that some of these evangelists try to pass off the Book of Mormon as sacred Scripture, this is not vouched for in the Bible.)

Reason 4
The Alternatives

A lot of people sneer at the Bible, its characters, its message. Consider some popular alternatives: TV Guide, People, Vanity Fair, Penthouse, Golf Digest. These stimulate:

1. the mind—not at all
2. the morals—not at all, or for worse
3. the imagination—a lot, but in the wrong ways.

Reading these magazines won't send you to hell (though they might help on the trip). But they won't do you much good, either. Plus, they get stale very fast. A month-old issue of People is, well, boring. So at least consider the option of reading something that has been stimulating people's minds, morals, and imaginations for 2,000 years.

WHY READ THE BIBLE?

Reason 5

Understanding Culture

I love art museums, but like many museum-goers, I look at some of the modern artworks and puzzle. "I just don't get it."

I don't have this same problem with the older paintings, the "old masters." If you don't know the Bible well, you might. Many works of art created before 1700 or so were based on Bible scenes. Art museums across the world are filled with pictures of Jesus' birth, His crucifixion, the Last Supper, David killing Goliath, God creating Adam and Eve, Moses and the Ten Commandments, etc. You can admire these pictures, finding them "pretty," but if you don't know the Bible, you might be missing the point. The artists created these works for people who knew the stories. They weren't just being clever with a paintbrush. They were portraying scenes that people would immediately understand.

Consider, for example, a painting of the Last Supper. (There are hundreds of these, not just the most famous one by Leonardo da Vinci.) If you know the Gospels, you know that Jesus and His twelve disciples had one final meal together before Jesus' crucifixion. In paintings of the Supper, one of the men is usually shown holding a bag in one hand. Who is he, and what did the bag mean? If you know the story, you know that Judas Iscariot was the disciple who betrayed Jesus for thirty pieces of silver. In the picture, Judas is usually shown with his moneybag. A minor point? Maybe. But the more you know about the Bible, the more you can appreciate such works of art.

Think about the world's great literature also. The great novelists and poets frequently refer to ideas and characters from the Bible. Some writings, like John Milton's poem Paradise Lost, are hard to grasp unless you have a basic knowledge of the Bible. Even William Shakespeare's works are full of references to people and events in the Bible. In more modern times, authors (even ones who don't consider themselves believers) use biblical ideas and phrases. John Steinbeck gave two of his novels titles from the Bible: East of Eden and To a God Unknown. In both books he based modern characters on characters from the Bible. Another great author of this century, William Faulkner, gave biblical titles to his novels: Absalom, Absalom, and Go Down, Moses, for example. His novel A Fable is a modern retelling of the story of Christ.

The Bible isn't a totally "dead" book today. In 1996 the city of Richmond, Virginia dedicated a large statue of tennis star Arthur Ashe, who had been born in the city. Engraved in huge letters on the pedestal is a long quotation from the Letter to the Hebrews in the New Testament. Our culture may not be Bible-literate anymore, but it's obvious that people still have a feeling of respect—maybe even affection—for the Bible.

Can you be a well-read, knowledgeable person without knowing the Bible? You can—but you wouldn't have the same understanding and appreciation of some of the best that culture has to offer.

Reason 6
Find Out What the Media Aren't Telling You

We learn about our world by . . . what? Watching TV, listening to radio, reading newspapers and magazines, right? There's a problem, though, because the people we rely on to inform us often overlook things—sometimes deliberately. For example, did you know that some of the best-selling books in the last thirty years have been Christian books?

And did you know that the best-selling nonfiction book of both 1972 and 1973 was a contemporary Bible translation? (It was The Living Bible, by the way.) Writing in the National Review, David Scott noted that Christian authors "will never appear on the Publishers Weekly or New York Times bestseller lists. Because of the way the bookstores surveyed for these lists are chosen, Christian books are segregated in a literary ghetto, although most of them are at least equal in literary merit to Danielle Steel's novels and The Bridges of Madison County" (June 17, 1996, p. 50).

chapter 2

Papyrus, Scrolls, ◀··· and All That:
How We Got the Bible

We take fax machines, e-mail, copiers, and desktop publishing for granted. It's quite easy today to produce a letter, a brochure, or even an entire book in a small amount of time—produce it and *re*produce it. In the great timeline of the world, mass-production of written materials is a recent blip. The printing press, the first means of mass-producing books, didn't come along until the 1400s. Before that, written materials circulated through one method—the copycat method. A real flesh-and-blood human scribe had to copy a book (or scroll) word for word. Flip through the pages of your Bible (or a Stephen King novel, for that matter) and consider how long it would take you to copy every word of the book.

Why is it important to know this? Very simply, it means that in the pre-printing press era (most of human history, that is), people didn't dabble at writing. Writing was laborious, publishing was laborious, and writing materials were usually expensive. Scratch pads and Post-It notes were not an option.

So when people wrote things down, they did so with a purpose. When archaeologists find written materials buried for thousands of years, they find mainly two things: sacred writings (like the Bible) and official writings (court records, for example). The average Joe in ancient times didn't keep a diary or dash off letters to friends every day. In fact, the average Joe probably couldn't read or write. He had to rely on professionals—scribes—to fill in the literacy gap.

All this means that the writings that got passed on generation after generation were pretty serious stuff. You wouldn't spend day after day making a copy of the Book of Psalms unless you thought the Book of Psalms was worth passing on. You would not do this just to "preserve a slice of history," and you probably wouldn't do it because you thought the Psalms were "good reading." You would engage in this painful process because you honestly thought that your own generation, and the next, *needed to have the Psalms.* This is the only real explanation we can give for why the books of the Bible have been passed on for hundreds of years. Having considered the *why*, let's look at the *how*.

YOU THINK PAPER GROWS ON TREES?

The original form of paper didn't. It grew on weeds. Specifically, it was made from a water plant, papyrus, that grows in Egypt and elsewhere. Egyptians discovered that the papyrus stalks could be cut into strips and laid in crisscross fashion to form a flat, durable writing surface. (We get our word *paper* from *papyrus*, naturally.) In the dry climate of Egypt and other parts of the Middle East, pieces of papyrus have lasted for centuries—much longer than a page of modern-day wood-pulp paper would last.

Papyrus could take the form of pages, but for anything of great length—the Book of Genesis, for example—long sheets of papyrus took the form of scrolls. Throughout the Bible, if you find a reference to someone reading a *book*, mentally insert the word *scroll*. Most contemporary Bible versions are accurate enough to use the word *scroll*. The writing appeared in columns on the scroll—only on one side, not on both sides as the pages of a book are printed.

Papyrus wasn't the only writing material available (though it had the advantage of being fairly cheap). Animal skins, leather in very thin form, could be used to write on. (Recall that people used to refer to a diploma as a "sheepskin.") Leather was a valuable commodity, and if written on, it could be recycled—the old writing scraped off and new writing put on. In the form of scrolls, sheets of papyrus were glued together, while leather pieces were stitched together.

THE CHAPTER DIVISIONS IN THE BIBLE WEREN'T PART OF THE ORIGINAL HEBREW AND GREEK WRITINGS. THEY WERE ACTUALLY INTRODUCED AROUND THE YEAR 1214 BY STEPHEN LANGTON, ARCHBISHOP OF CANTERBURY (ENGLAND'S CHIEF CLERGYMAN). LANGTON'S CHAPTER DIVISIONS WERE ADOPTED NOT ONLY BY THE CHRISTIAN CHURCH BUT ALSO BY JEWS. LANGTON DIDN'T HAVE TO DIVIDE THE BOOK OF PSALMS INTO CHAPTERS, SINCE THE BOOK WAS ALREADY DIVIDED INTO 150 SEPARATE PSALMS. THE SHORTEST BOOKS (LIKE OBADIAH, PHILEMON, AND JUDE) HE DID NOT DIVIDE AT ALL.

THE VERSE DIVISIONS IN THE BIBLE DIDN'T APPEAR UNTIL 1551. ROBERT ESTIENNE, A FRENCH SCHOLAR AND PRINTER, WAS RESPONSIBLE FOR THE WORK. ACCORDING TO HIS SON, HE DID THE WORK WHILE RIDING ON HORSEBACK ACROSS FRANCE. (SOME PEOPLE BELIEVE THAT THIS JERKY FORM OF TRANSPORTATION EXPLAINS WHY SOME OF THE VERSE DIVISIONS APPEAR IN ODD PLACES.)

THE HEBREW OBSESSION WITH DETAIL

The Hebrews/Israelites were a "people of the Book," not worshiping idols as neighbor nations did, but having great reverence for the books that we now call the Old Testament. Using their Hebrew alphabet (written right to left, by the way), they took great pains to copy and recopy the sacred books onto scrolls. Many stories have been told about how fanatical the copyists were about adding and deleting nothing in the copying process. Believing that the books really were the word of God, a copyist was denied the option of "editing" or "polishing" the words. Copyists were humble souls. No copies contain the name, or date, of the copyists. But they were good at what they did. Scholars are amazed that Hebrew scrolls made hundreds of years apart are almost exactly alike. The Jews have been very good at passing on the Old Testament as they received it.

So what became of the original scrolls—the ones actually written by Moses, Isaiah, Solomon? Who knows? There is, in fact, no way of proving that a scroll could be an original. But we do have some old, old copies. The oldest ones found were the famous Dead Sea Scrolls, discovered in 1947 in some caves. Scholars believe these scrolls are the oldest copies we have of Old Testament materials. They date from roughly 250 B.C. to A.D. 65.

The Dead Sea Scrolls are written in Hebrew, the language of the Old Testament. Curiously, at the time these scrolls were copied, most Jews in the world did not speak or read Hebrew—not in everyday situations, anyway. Jews were scattered across the Roman Empire, and though Hebrew was their "official" language, many of them spoke and read the common Greek that was the Roman Empire's unofficial international language. This Greek was not the same elegant, "literary" Greek of classics like *The Iliad* and *The Odyssey*. It was a sort of basic Greek, easily understandable to ordinary people, including tradespeople and travelers.

The New Testament was written in this common (*koine*) Greek. And, years earlier, so was that amazing Old Testament translation called the Septuagint. Completed in Egypt (which had a large Jewish community) the Septuagint became *the* Old Testament for the many Jews who no longer understood the original Hebrew. The Septuagint is important for us because of its effect on the New Testament. When the New Testament authors quote the Old Testament (and they do this quite often), they seem to be quoting the Septuagint, not the original Hebrew. So the Septuagint, the Old Testament in Greek, was the version that Paul, John, Luke, and the other New Testament writers knew well. Most important of all, the Septuagint was the Bible of the early Christians. Before they had decided once and for all which books would be included in the New Testament, they were already certain that the Old Testament—in the Septuagint version—was sacred writing.

The Septuagint is significant for several reasons. One is, being in Greek, it made the religion of the Hebrews "exportable." Greek was spoken and read in Rome, Egypt, North Africa, even as far away as Spain. Now people across the Roman Empire could read the Old Testament.

Many non-Jews became admirers of the Jews' religion. They read the Old Testament and came to expect a Messiah, or Christ. They were well-prepared to hear the message of Christianity.

Greek continued for many years as the international language, so the Septuagint was copied and recopied. The Gospels, letters, and other writings of the New Testament were also recorded in common Greek.

Bible scholars and archaeologists like to comb through ancient digs to find scrolls—or even tiny scraps of scrolls—to see just how ancient a Bible passage they can find. The oldest they've found—so far—is a tiny piece of John's Gospel, chapter 18. This scrap of papyrus dates from around the year 135. That's about 70 years after John was originally written.

More important than these papyrus scraps are the *codices*—plural for *codex*. A codex was not a scroll but a book—text on both sides of the page, stitched together at the edges. Like scrolls, they were hand-copied. The importance of the codices is that they "put it all together"—that is, they show the New Testament as a unit. The oldest codices are Codex Vaticanus and Codex Sinaiticus, both from about the mid-300s. (Interestingly, these ancient books lay buried until the 1800s.)

Take a Yawn Break and ask the obvious question: Why is this history lesson important? The simple answer is, we ought to have a Bible as close as possible to the original documents. Since we can't have the originals (if they even exist now), we ought to try to find the oldest copies. Logically, the older the Greek and Hebrew copies are, the closer they are to being like the originals.

Let's be honest here: copyists tried hard to copy things precisely. But not all the copyists were people of faith, dedicated to passing on the Bible without error. Some professional scribes who made New Testament copies were not Christians. Some were just hired help, working fast and hard (but not always accurately) to make a buck. In the ancient and medieval world there was nothing corresponding to a modern proofreader. To err is human, and so changes crept into the copies. Once a change or error crept in, there was a good chance it would be copied, and recopied, etc. None of the changes are extremely significant. (You won't find a copy that says Jesus was *not* the Son of God, for example.) But the many, many copies do show differences—*variants*, the scholars call them. Most of the changes are sentences or phrases added into the text—again, minor things.

For these reasons, the ideal that translators strive for is to produce a Bible based on the oldest manuscripts. The other test is not just how old the manuscripts are, but how much agreement is among them. This is a matter of majority rule: if one manuscript shows a variation from the hundreds of others, the scholars tend to side with the majority. After all, that one odd variation might have been caused by a drowsy copyist—or one trying to "improve" the text, or add his own opinion.

This, in short, is why Bible translators show such a passion for studying Greek and Hebrew—and for digging up dusty old scraps of papyrus. Well, modern translators are lucky: they have more ancient manuscripts available to them than any other translators in history.

●●●●●●●●●●●●●●●●●●

Imagine English without AEIOU

A language without vowels? The Greek of the New Testament has them, but not the Hebrew in the Old Testament. Ancient Hebrew was consonants, nothing more. So how did they know how to pronounce words? The same way we do: habit. (We learn that death is pronounced DETH, not DEE-ATH. How? From hearing it pronounced this way, not by looking in a dictionary.) The Hebrews passed on their pronunciations in the obvious way: word of mouth.

But as Hebrew gradually ceased to be a common, spoken language, the copyists raised a logical question: Future generations will be able to read the sacred Hebrew books, but will they know where the vowel sounds are? In other words, if they read the Hebrew text out loud, how will they know how to pronounce these words without vowels?

Along came the unsung heroes of Bible tradition: the Massoretes. (Massorah is the Hebrew word for "tradition.") This is the group name of the scribes who inserted marks called "vowel points" into the Hebrew text. These points indicated, as far as they could tell, the accurate vowel sounds in the words. Working from the sixth century on, the Massoretes did us a tremendous service. The texts they have bequeathed to us are the basis of Biblica Hebraica, the standard Hebrew text that translators use today.

●●●●●●●●●●●●●●●●●●●

There's an important reminder about errors in the text of the Bible: The key teachings of the Bible are found throughout its pages, not just in a few isolated passages. In spite of many variations among the old Greek and Hebrew manuscripts, none of the Bible's teachings is affected in any way. What the Bible teaches about God, creation, man, sin, salvation, Jesus, the Holy Spirit, heaven and hell, and morals is not changed in any way just because the old manuscripts disagree in spots.

FROM GREEK TO LATIN TO . . .

As the centuries passed, Greek ceased to be a universal language. Christians believed strongly that people should be able to read

THE ADULTERERS' BIBLE

AS ANY WRITER KNOWS, GOOD PROOF-READERS ARE A CRITICAL PART OF PUBLISHING. PERHAPS THE PRINTERS WHO PRODUCED THE ENGLISH BIBLE IN 1631 NEEDED A BETTER PROOFREADER. A THOUSAND COPIES OF THE BIBLE WERE PRINTED WITH A KEY WORD MISSING FROM ONE OF THE TEN COMMANDMENTS: NOT. THIS MISPRINTED BIBLE HAD THE VERSE "THOU SHALT COMMIT ADULTERY." THE PRINTERS WERE FINED 3,000 POUNDS.

the Bible in their own languages, so translations were made. The most famous one was by the great scholar named Jerome, who set up shop in the Holy Land. With his amazing knowledge of both Greek and Hebrew, Jerome single-handedly produced the Vulgate, an amazing translation into . . . Latin. Latin is a "dead language" now, but it wasn't at the time. It had replaced Greek as the international language. It was the common language of Rome, the grandest and most influential city in Europe at that time. Completed around the year 400, Jerome's Vulgate was superb. The churches of Rome adopted it, and churches throughout the Roman Empire followed suit. Unfortunately, the Vulgate was so well-liked

● ● ● ● ● ● ● ● ● ● ● ● ● ● ● ● ● ●

ARTISTS AND MODELS

For centuries artists loved to paint pictures of Jerome, the scholar who translated the entire Bible into Latin. So what makes a Bible translator such a good subject for a painting? Maybe his pet lion. According to an old legend, Jerome kindly extracted a thorn from the paw of a suffering lion. The lion, in eternal gratitude to the saintly man, became his docile pet from that point on. The next time you're in an art museum, check out the medieval and Renaissance galleries and you're likely to find at least one picture of St. Jerome—always with the lion nearby, gentle as a lamb.

● ● ● ● ● ● ● ● ● ● ● ● ● ● ● ● ● ●

that it "fossilized." Long after Latin had ceased to be a language of the people, Jerome's Vulgate was still the official Bible of the Catholic church. This created that painful situation in the Middle Ages: the Bible written, and preached from, in a language people didn't understand. Latin was the scholars' language, so they read Jerome's Vulgate and wrote commentaries on it—all in Latin.

From 366 to 385 a man named Damasus was bishop of Rome—pope, that is. The prestige of the bishop of Rome was on the rise, though at this time he was still not recognized as the head bishop. But Damasus liked power, and he wanted to free Christianity in Western Europe from the dominance of the East. Greek had long been the accepted language for the church, even while some translations were being made into other tongues. Damasus wanted the Western church to be clearly Latin. One way of accomplishing this was to make a solid translation of the Bible into Latin.

Damasus' secretary was a workaholic scholar by the name of Eusebius Hieronymus Sophronius—thankfully, known as Jerome. Trained in Latin and Greek classics, Jerome had also forced himself to study Hebrew. (Hebrew is a difficult language to learn, requiring intense study and concentration. Jerome believed that studying Hebrew kept his mind busy and free from sinful thoughts.) By the time he entered Damasus' service, Jerome was probably the most brilliant Christian scholar in the world.

Damasus asked Jerome to produce a new Latin translation of the Bible, one that would throw out the inaccuracies of older translations.

Jerome began in 382. After twenty-three years of labor, he finished his translation in 405. (If twenty-three years seems like a long time for a translation, consider that Jerome was working alone. Also, he was churning out volumes of Bible commentaries and other writings during these years.)

At first Jerome worked from the Greek Old Testament, the Septuagint. But then he established a precedent for all good translators: the Old Testament would have to be translated from the original Hebrew. In his quest for accuracy, Jerome consulted many Jewish rabbis.

In translating the Old Testament, something struck Jerome: the books the Jews regarded as Holy Scripture did not include the books we know as the Apocrypha. So Jerome did not wish to include them in his translation. However, they had been included in the Septuagint, the basis of most older translations, and Jerome was compelled by the Roman church authorities to include them. But he made it clear that in his opinion the Apocrypha could be read for enrichment—but not for establishing Christian doctrine. Hundreds of years later, the leaders of the Protestant Reformation would follow Jerome's advice and not include these books in Protestant Bibles. Due to Jerome's influence, Catholic and Protestant Bibles differ to this day.

"The Divine Library," as Jerome called the Bible, was finally available in a well-written, accurate translation in the language commonly used in the churches of Western Europe. Jerome had enormous clout as a scholar, and his translation became the standard. Known as the Vulgate (from the Latin word *vulgus*, meaning

THE MATERIAL CHURCH'S CRITIC

JEROME IS BEST KNOWN AS THE GREAT TRANSLATOR, THE CREATOR OF THE LATIN VULGATE BIBLE. BUT JEROME WAS A BUSY BEE, SOMEHOW FINDING TIME TO WRITE ON ALMOST EVERY SUBJECT OF THE TIMES. HE FREQUENTLY PLAYED THE ROLE OF CHRISTIAN CRITIC, SCOLDING THE CHURCH FOR BEING TOO MATERIALISTIC. IN JEROME'S VIEW, A WEALTHY CHURCH WITH LAVISH BUILDINGS WAS A FAR CRY FROM THE SIMPLE CHRISTIANITY OF THE NEW TESTAMENT. ACCORDING TO JEROME: "OUR WALLS GLITTER WITH GOLD, AND GOLD GLEAMS UPON OUR CEILINGS AND OUR PILLARS. YET CHRIST—IN THE FORM OF THE NAKED, HUNGRY, AND POOR—IS DYING AT OUR DOORS."

"common"), it was later used as the basis for translations into other languages.

This had some good—and bad—effects. On the good side, the Vulgate was a good translation. It was highly regarded by all scholars in the Middle Ages. Indeed, Martin Luther, though he knew Hebrew and Greek, quoted Jerome's Vulgate throughout his life. (When Luther translated the Bible into German, however, he used the Greek and Hebrew originals—just as Jerome had done.)

On the bad side, Jerome was a tough act to follow as a translator. His cherished translation had the church's seal of approval, and this put a damper on new translations being made from Hebrew and

Greek. Not for a thousand years did scholars again attempt translating from the Greek New Testament.

So why didn't some sensitive souls say, "Hey, let's gather together the Greek and Hebrew books of the Bible and translate them into our own language"? Actually, some people did. But the church authorities, who had become powerful people as time passed, frowned on this. They were afraid of what might happen if the average farmer or baker or merchant had access to the Bible. It might cause . . . what? Revolution? Perhaps what the church authorities feared was losing their own position as the official interpreters of the Bible. So long as the Bible was in Latin, it was a book for a privileged class, the "brain elite." Translated into laymen's language it was—well, common. And anyway, the common folk didn't need to read the Bible individually, since the church authorities would tell them all they needed to know about faith. The private, individual Christian had no need to read the Bible for himself.

The situation changed in the 1500s with the two overlapping movements we call the Renaissance and the Reformation. Both movements urged "getting back to basics," including a return to the real Bible, in Greek and Hebrew. The Reformation leaders went further and insisted that the Bible be in the people's language— English, German, Spanish, whatever. Latin was dead; the Bible was supposed to be a living document.

Technologically, the timing was perfect. Something amazing had been sprung on the world: the printing press. The Era of the Scribe was over. Any printed matter— and the Bible held the prize as the "Book of all books"—could be mass-produced. The Protestant leaders of the Reformation were quick to put the printing press to good use.

1456: JOHANN GUTENBERG PRODUCES THE FIRST PRINTED BIBLE

• • • • • • • • • • • • • • • • • • •

If you're in Mainz, Germany, you can visit the Gutenberg Museum and see not only a Gutenberg Bible but also a replica of Gutenberg's print shop. Looking at the massive mechanisms used in the world's first printing job, most visitors assume that Gutenberg (or his assistants) must have moonlighted as body-builders. Not only was the world's first printed Bible extremely bulky, but so was the press it was printed on.

• • • • • • • • • • • • • • • • • • •

In 1456, Gutenberg— or a group he was a part of—printed a book: the Bible. Specifically, it was the Latin translation by Jerome, the Vulgate. But this Latin book started a revolution that would affect people who had no knowledge of Latin.

First, a word about the Gutenberg Bible's appearance: It was stunning—a work of art that has never been equalled in the history of printing. Some book collectors say that the first printed book was also the most beautiful printed book. Gutenberg's typeface resembled the beautiful handwritten letters the scribes had used for ages. Later, in the interest of economy, more straightforward, less artsy, typefaces developed—easier to read, easier to cast in metal.

Here was a revolution: Books could be produced so that people besides the professional clergy could have access to them. The Bible could be available in large quantities—not only in scholarly Latin but, later, in translations people could understand. Martin Luther was one of the first to realize this. He translated the Bible into a readable German version that was used for centuries.

A major thrust of the Reformation was the desire to return to biblical faith and practice. Such a reform might have been impossible in the pre-Gutenberg age. An inaccessible Latin Bible would cause no major shake-up. Indeed, many Catholics argued that God meant for the Bible to be kept from the people's hands. (In fact, the official position was that the Latin translation was inspired just as the original Hebrew and Greek had been inspired.) Only the theologians, the Catholic authorities said, could interpret it properly. Luther and the other Reformers said no: Give the Scriptures to every plowboy and serving-maid. The Bible and the believer together are enough. No priest, no pope, no official church council needs to stand between us and the Word of God. Everything the Reformers said about the priesthood of all believers was rooted in the assumption that people could have access to the Bible in their own language.

As Bibles and other books were printed, a cycle began: more books were printed, more people became readers, and readers demanded more books. Even for the illiterate, the Bible became accessible because at least the pastor could read from, and preach about, a Bible that could be understood. And most households had at least one literate person who could read aloud to the family.

As the Reformers wished, the boundary between pastor and layman began to break down. The question for believers now

Crime: Reading an English Bible

Many people were eager to read the Bible in English, and John Wycliffe's version (done in the 1380s) circulated in manuscript form for 150 years. The church authorities in England decreed that reading an English Bible was a criminal offense. People read it anyway. With copies being rare and expensive, people would even pay a "rental fee" to study a copy of the Bible for an hour or so. Some common folk like farmers would pay for this privilege with produce. With so many people being illiterate, nonreaders would gather around while some brave soul read to them the Bible in their own language.

The next time you see your Bible sitting on the shelf gathering dust, remember: 600 years ago a poor man might pay a load of hay just for the privilege of reading the Bible for an hour.

Incidentally, Wycliffe was never in his lifetime punished for doing his English translation. He was put on trial postmortem, forty years after his death. Found guilty, his body was unearthed and burned, with his ashes scattered in a river.

became: "Is my life in keeping with the Bible?" instead of: "What will I have to confess to the priest?"

It is hard for us to fathom this revolution. The Bible is easily accessible to us—now, even on portable computer. But imagine how awesome it was to sixteenth-century laymen to have the words of the Lord spoken in their native tongue.

THE 1500S: ENGLISH VERSIONS OF THE BIBLE

Wherever the Protestant Reformation spread, Bible translations were made. In the history of the English Bible, King Henry VIII is both hero and villain. King Henry split the Church of England from the Roman Catholic Church in the 1500s. Such splits were taking place elsewhere in Europe, and the new churches were called Protestants. But Henry didn't see himself, or England's church, as Protestant. He still considered himself a good Catholic—but a Catholic without a pope. So while the Protestant churches in Germany and elsewhere were abandoning the Latin Bible and producing translations in their own national languages, Henry said, "Not in my country you don't." Henry was afraid that letting the people read the Bible in English might lead them to all sorts of revolutionary ideas. The Catholics at that time had the same belief.

William Tyndale and his helpers labored over an English translation of the Bible—the first to be produced on a printing press. In the new age of the press, Bibles could be mass-produced. But Tyndale had to work in another country. Henry VIII decreed that Tyndale's English Bible must be "clerely extermynated and exiled out of the realme of Englande for ever." Even so, courageous souls managed to smuggle in the new translation. But Tyndale paid the ultimate price: he was betrayed by a turncoat friend, arrested, strangled, and burned at the stake. His dying prayer was, "Lord, open the king of England's eyes!"

His prayer was answered. Henry joined Europe's Protestants—for political, not religious, reasons. To show them that he had really broken free from the Roman Catholic fold, he did a Protestant thing: he ordered a translation of the Bible into his national language. The new English Bible was—surprise!—the Tyndale version, completed by Tyndale's friend, Miles Coverdale. The new—and officially legal—English Bible

FAMOUS FIRSTS:

THE GENEVA BIBLE

THIS ENGLISH TRANSLATION, PUBLISHED IN 1560, BROKE SOME NEW GROUND. IT WAS THE FIRST BIBLE TO BE DIVIDED INTO VERSES AS WELL AS CHAPTERS. IT WAS THE FIRST TO USE STANDARD ROMAN TYPE, NOT THE ORNATE (BUT HARD-TO-READ) OLD ENGLISH TYPE. IT WAS THE FIRST BIBLE TO OMIT THE BOOKS KNOWN AS THE APOCRYPHA. AND IT WAS THE FIRST ENGLISH BIBLE TO BE READ WIDELY IN HOMES. UNTIL THE *KING JAMES VERSION* OF 1611, IT WAS THE "PEOPLE'S VERSION"—THE VERSION WILLIAM SHAKESPEARE WOULD HAVE READ, AND THE VERSION THE PILGRIMS BROUGHT TO AMERICA ON THE *MAYFLOWER*.

was completed in 1535 and dedicated to . . . King Henry VIII. So Henry, who had ordered Tyndale's execution, was the first English king to have a Bible dedicated to him.

Bitten by the Protestant bug, Henry later decreed that every English church possess the Bible in English. Within a hundred years of Henry's decree, more than one English Bible had appeared. One early English version was the *Great Bible*, officially authorized by King Henry VIII. In St. Paul's church in London, six copies were set up, and crowds gathered to hear the Bible being read in . . . English. It's hard for us to appreciate the shock and novelty of this. Readers—and illiterate people who wanted to hear the Bible being read aloud—came in droves. Some illiterates, including older adults, learned to read just so they could read the Bible themselves.

The *Great Bible* was a "pulpit Bible"—bulky and expensive. The next great innovation was the *Geneva Bible*, printed in clear Roman type, not the ornate Old English typeface. It was smaller, more portable, more suited to home use. First printed in 1560, it became England's "family Bible" for many years. You might say that the *Geneva Bible* was the first "household book" in the English language. If a family could afford to own only one book, it was the *Geneva Bible*.

1611: PUBLICATION OF THE *KING JAMES BIBLE*

● ● ● ● ● ● ● ● ● ● ● ●

Tobacco, Witchcraft, Kings, and So On

We are so used to hearing the phrase "King James Bible" that some people probably think King James wrote the Bible himself. He didn't, but King James I of England was an author. In 1604, a few years before the publication of the Bible that bears his name, James wrote Counterblaste to Tobacco. *It was directed against that strange new custom imported from America, smoking tobacco. James' book had little effect— the English, and later all Europeans, picked up the new habit and loved it. James also wrote the book* Demonologie, *a study of witchcraft published in a day when people took sorcery seriously.*

● ● ● ● ● ● ● ● ● ● ● ●

"To the most high and mighty Prince James by the Grace of God . . ." So begins the dedication at the front of the most popular English Bible of all time, the *Authorized Version*, better known as the *King James Version*. The much-loved KJV (as it is often abbreviated) has lost popularity in recent years as more readable modern translations speak to twentieth-century readers. But generations of English and American readers have absorbed its phrases. I doubt that any other translation will ever have such an effect on the English language.

Who was the "mighty Prince James" whose name has been stamped on millions of Bibles? He was the son of the colorful ruler Mary Queen of Scots, executed by England's Queen

LOOKING FOR A CATCHY TITLE FOR A BOOK?

Any author knows that you can't just write a good book. You have to give it a good title to help it sell. In the past, and even in the present, authors have found the Bible to be a great source of book titles. And inevitably the version they choose from is the old reliable one of 1611, the King James Version.

American novelist John Steinbeck's East of Eden:
"And Cain went out from the presence of the LORD, and dwelt in the land of Nod, on the east of Eden" (Gen. 4:16).

American novelist Ernest Hemingway's The Sun Also Rises:
"The sun also ariseth, and the sun goeth down, and hasteth to his place where he arose" (Ecc. 1:5).

American novelist William Faulkner's Absalom, Absalom:
"And the king [David] was much moved, and went up to the chamber over the gate, and wept: and as he went, thus he said, O my son Absalom, my son, my son Absalom! would God I had died for thee, O Absalom, my son, my son!" (2 Sam. 18:33)

Ben Ames Williams' 1947 Civil War novel A House Divided:
"But when the Pharisees heard it, they said, This fellow doth not cast out devils, but by Beelzebub the prince of the devils. And Jesus knew their thoughts, and said unto them, Every kingdom divided against itself is brought to desolation; and every city or house divided against itself shall not stand" (Matt. 12:24-25).

English poet Robert Browning's collection Bells and Pomegranates:
"Beneath upon the hem of it thou shalt make pomegranates of blue, and of purple, and of scarlet, round about the hem thereof; and bells of gold between them round about: A golden bell and a pomegranate, a golden bell and a pomegranate, upon the hem of the robe round about" (Ex. 28:33-34).

American novelist Winston Churchill's The Inside of the Cup:
"Woe unto you, scribes and Pharisees, hypocrites! for ye make clean the outside of the cup and of the platter, but within they are full of extortion and excess" (Matt. 23:25). (By the way, this isn't the same Winston Churchill who was England's Prime Minister.)

French novelist Marcel Proust's Cities of the Plain:
"Abram dwelled in the land of Canaan, and Lot dwelled in the cities of the plain, and pitched his tent toward Sodom" (Gen. 13:12). The cities are the immoral Sodom and Gomorrah, which are destroyed by God. The book's original French title is Sodome et Gomorrhe.

American novelist Edith Wharton's The Valley of Decision:
"Multitudes, multitudes in the valley of decision: for the day of the LORD is near in the valley of decision" (Joel 3:14).

Elizabeth I. Ironically, when the childless Elizabeth died, James was her successor, since he was the next male in the royal line. Already king in his native Scotland, James marched south to London to be crowned King of England too.

Under Elizabeth, the Church of England had assumed a definite form: It was not Catholic—that is, it did not bow to the pope, and certain elements of the Catholic mass had been discarded. But it wasn't as noticeably Protestant as the Lutheran and Calvinist churches in Europe. Many people felt that Elizabeth had created a "compromise" church that wasn't Protestant enough. Known as Puritans, they wanted to "purify" the church of anything that resembled Catholicism, including bishops, priestly garb, and too much ritual.

The Puritans hoped that James would push the English church in the right direction. After all, he had been raised in the very Protestant country of Scotland. Before the new king even reached London, they presented him with the Millenary Petition, so-called because it had a thousand signatures. They asked for moderate changes in the Church of England. James surprised them. He rather liked the Church of England with its pomp and ritual. In fact, he told the Puritans they must "conform themselves" or he would "harry them out of the land."

But the Puritans were a large group, and James couldn't push them aside so easily. In January 1604, a conference of bishops and Puritans met at the royal palace at Hampton Court, near London. On the whole, the conference was a failure for the Puritans—except on one point: James gave his approval to making a new trans-lation of the Bible.

James appointed fifty-four scholars. These were divided into companies of seven or eight men each, working both individually and in conference. Then the whole text was gone over by a committee of twelve. While the scholars used the original Hebrew and Greek, they also leaned on previous translations. In fact, it may be inappropriate to call the KJV a "translation." In some ways it is really a revision of earlier versions. The work of William Tyndale, the first major English translator, is evident in many passages. We should be glad that the revisers chose to retain some of the beautiful wording of the older versions.

Work began in 1607 (the same year the English colony of Jamestown was established in America) and ended in 1611. From that time on, it has been called the *Authorized Version*. Oddly, there is no proof that James ever formally "authorized" it.

Officially, the new version was "appointed to be read in churches," replacing the Bishop's Bible. It was a long time before it replaced the *Geneva Bible* as the Bible of the individual reader, particularly the Puritans. But once established, the KJV was unshakable. Even though some critics said that its language was already outdated the very year it appeared, later generations loved its "Bible English." As English evolved, becoming less and less like the language of James' day, English-speaking Christians continued to express themselves in terms echoing the KJV. (To name but one example, multitudes of Christians still address God as "Thee" and "Thou.")

And how the language has been affected!

HAVE YOU HEARD THESE EXPRESSIONS BEFORE?

Consider some everyday expressions from the King James Version of 1611:

* wolves in sheep's clothing
"Beware of false prophets, which come to you in sheep's clothing, but inwardly they are ravening wolves" (Matt. 7:15).

* salt of the earth
"Ye are the salt of the earth" (Matt. 5:13).

* drop in the bucket
"Behold, the nations are as a drop of a bucket" (Isa. 40:15).

* fat of the land
"I will give you the good of the land of Egypt, and ye shall eat the fat of the land" (Gen. 45:18).

* my brother's keeper
"The LORD said unto Cain, Where is Abel thy brother? And he said, I know not: Am I my brother's keeper?" (Gen. 4:9)

* spare the rod and spoil the child
"He that spareth his rod hateth his son" (Prov. 13:24)

* giving up the ghost
"Man dieth, and wasteth away: yea, man giveth up the ghost, and where is he?" (Job 14:10).

* the skin of my teeth
"I am escaped with the skin of my teeth" (Job 19:20).

* Woe is me!
"Then said I, Woe is me! for I am undone" (Isa. 6:5).

* Pride goes before a fall
"Pride goeth before destruction, and an haughty spirit before a fall" (Prov. 16:18).

* Eat, drink, and be merry
"A man hath no better thing under the sun, than to eat, and to drink, and to be merry" (Ecc. 8:15).
And also:
"Take thine ease, eat, drink, and be merry" (Luke 12:19).

* a lamb to the slaughter
"He is brought as a lamb to the slaughter" (Isa. 53:7).

* Can a leopard change his spots?
"Can the Ethiopian change his skin, or the leopard his spots?" (Jer. 13:23)

* holier than thou
"Come not near to me; for I am holier than thou" (Isa. 65:5).

Even if the KJV were to someday go out of print—which is unlikely—our language still bulges with such immortal *King James* expressions as "the skin of my teeth," "Woe is me!" "a drop in the bucket," "my brother's keeper," "holier than thou," and hundreds of others.

But the effect goes beyond phrases. There is a cadence, a sentence rhythm, in the KJV that has never been matched in English Bibles. It's true that the obvious beauty of the KJV's words has probably discouraged some readers from hearing the message. But the KJV, born in the age of Shakespeare and other brilliant authors, couldn't help but be incredibly memorable and memorizable. If learning Scripture is important, then committing it to memory is important, and we know that poetry—or poetic prose—is easier to memorize than flat prose. Even now in the last decade of this century, most people who can quote the Bible inevitably quote the version published in 1611.

KING JAMES ON THE MAP
IF YOU'RE TOURING THE EASTERN U.S., VIRGINIA IN PARTICULAR, YOU CAN'T GET AWAY FROM KING JAMES. THE OLDEST ENGLISH SETTLEMENT IN THE U.S. WAS JAMESTOWN, VIRGINIA, FOUNDED IN 1607. IT SITS ON THE JAMES RIVER, IN JAMES CITY COUNTY.

FROM KING JAMES TO TODAY

What happened between the 1611 *King James Version* and our own time? A lot. The Bible scholars have made some amazing discoveries (the Dead Sea Scrolls, for example), so today we have a better idea than the King James translators of what the original Bible was like. So some changes were made in the old *Textus Receptus* (Latin for "received text"). This was a standard version of the Greek New Testament, the one used by most New Testament translators. New discoveries—and an improved knowledge of Greek—required that the *Textus Receptus* be changed ("new and improved").

Why all this fuss about manuscripts and Greek and Hebrew? Consider an analogy: American author Washington Irving published *The Legend of Sleepy Hollow* in 1819. If someone chooses to translate that story into Swedish in, say, 2019, should he translate from an edition printed in 1990—or should he try to get his hands on an original edition of 1819? True, the differences might be minor. But a good translator would want to get as close as possible to the original. This is exactly the aim of Bible scholars.

So, the new finds in ancient manuscripts—plus the fact that people no longer spoke "King James English"—required new translations into English. The *King James Version* of Mark 10:14 has Jesus saying, "Suffer the little children to come unto Me, and forbid them not." Today's *New International Version* says, "Let the little children come to Me, and do not hinder them." Which is clearer? Isn't it obvious that the *King James Version* of 1611 used "suffer" in a way we no longer use it?

There was—and still is, to some degree—some resistance to contemporary translations. The affection people had for the *King James Version* (KJV, for short) has proved

Morphing: How the English Language Changes in Six Centuries

Psalm 23:1-4 in John Wycliffe's version, 1384: "The Lord governeth me, and no thing to me shal lacke; in the place os leswwe where he me ful sette. Ouer watir of fulfilling he nurshide me; my soule he convertide. He brogte doun me upon the sties of rigtwisnesse; for his name."

Psalm 23:1-4 in the *Coverdale Bible*, 1535: "The LORDE is my shepherde, I can wante nothinge. He fedeth me in a grene pasture, and ledeth me to a fresh water. He quickeneth my soule, & bringeth me forth in the waye of rightuousnes for his names sake."

Psalm 23:1-4 in the *King James Version*, 1611: "The LORD is my shepherd; I shall not want. He maketh me to lie down in green pastures: he leadeth me beside the still waters. He restoreth my soul: he leadeth me in the paths of righteousness for his name's sake."

Psalm 23:1-4 in the *New International Version*, 1978: "The LORD is my shepherd, I shall not be in want. He makes me lie down in green pastures, he leads me beside quiet waters, he restores my soul. He guides me in paths of righteousness for his name's sake."

very strong. But people need to know that the KJV itself was a "new and improved update" in its own time (1611). The KJV translators were aware that the English language had "outgrown" the older versions— just like a growing child can't keep wearing the same clothes.

People say they love the language of the *King James Version*. It is still impressive. And no wonder—this was the same era that produced William Shakespeare and other great authors. But the original Greek and Hebrew Bibles contained "everyday" vocabulary. They weren't designed as "artsy" or "classy" books for highbrows. They weren't even designed to be literary classics. They simply communicated in very direct, basic language. And when the KJV was published in 1611, it was in the very direct, basic English of the day. But almost 400 years later, that language is no longer everyday English. People say the KJV is "dignified" and "solemn" and "majestic." It does seem that way. But for every reader who likes (and

understands) the dignified language of the KJV, there are twenty other readers who can't grasp the language. The old-fashioned language makes the Bible seem distant, too "holy" to be read. A dignified English Bible doesn't reflect the Hebrew and Greek originals, which were in everyday language.

Another shortcoming of the older versions: They often reproduced the long, cumbersome sentences of the original Hebrew and Greek. So, while the translations were often accurate (they reflected the wording of the original languages), they were written in sentences that modern readers find hard to swallow at once.

One deficiency of older versions such as the *King James* is—well, a deficiency in ourselves, actually. Modern readers are no longer familiar with theological terms that were fairly well known in times past. For example, the *King James Version* of 1 John 2:2 says that Jesus is the "propitiation for our sins." Count on one hand the people you know who can define *propitiation*. (Can *you* define it?) One modern version, the *Jerusalem Bible*, does much better with "The sacrifice that takes our sins away." *Today's English Version* reads: "The means by which our sins are forgiven." Better, don't you think?

But people liked the KJV so much that translators hesitated. "Why not," they asked, "just revise the KJV, updating the language in places, and correcting it where necessary?" This was exactly how new versions were done in the 1800s and early 1900s. The popular *Revised Standard Version* (RSV) of 1957 was this type of version. All these revisions, by the way, added something noticeably missing from the KJV: quotation marks. This made it much easier to tell who was speaking to whom. (Some later editions of the KJV have added quotation marks.) Most of these versions eliminated the old "thees" and "thous"—except, curiously, when these referred to God Himself.

In the 1960s and 1970s something new happened: completely new translations from the Hebrew and Greek bypassed the KJV entirely. One was the 1970 *New English Bible*, which has been more popular in Britain than in the U.S. Another (generally considered easier to read) was the simple and straightforward *Today's English Version* (TEV, also called the *Good News Bible*). Published by the American Bible Society in 1976, the TEV has impressed people with its simplicity and directness. Kenneth Taylor's *The Living Bible* became a phenomenal best-seller. Readers loved it, but scholars have snubbed it because, as Taylor admits, it is a paraphrase (a rewording, that is) of the English version, not a translation from the Greek and Hebrew.

One interesting version that some people like is *The Amplified Bible*. Its name has nothing to do with sound or speakers, but with the interesting way that words are added [in brackets, like these] to help show the meaning of the text. This looks a bit odd when you first read it, but once you get used to the bracketed words, you'll find they serve the purpose of making the original Greek and Hebrew meanings clearer. (Don't try reading it aloud in a church service, though.)

Catholics may like two readable contemporary versions, the *New Jerusalem Bible* and the *New American Bible* (sometimes sold in stores as *The Catholic Bible*). These include the books of the Apocrypha. If you have the older Catholic version known as the *Confraternity of Christian Doctrine* version (CCD), you might want to get a newer version. The CCD is no longer considered a good translation, since it was a translation from Latin, not the original Hebrew and Greek.

One very popular translation—the one generally quoted in the book you are holding—is the NIV, the *New International Version*, published in 1978. Another popular version, for those who like the "flavor" of the KJV, is the *New King James Version* (or NKJV), which continues the tradition of updating the language of the KJV.

In the 1980s and 1990s, some new versions claiming to be "gender-inclusive" were published. These—the *New Revised Standard* (1989), the *Revised English Bible* (1989), and others—aim to eliminate language that some people consider "sexist." For example, they use *humanity* or *humankind* instead of the older generic term *man*. Some readers like this. Others feel that it leads to some clumsy wording. (The obvious advantage of the term *man* was that it could refer to one individual and to the entire human race. This was also true of the Greek word *anthropos* that we translate as "man.")

Which one is the "best" Bible in English? The obvious answer is, *the one you actually read*. If you can read, and really understand, the *King James Version*, then do so. If you enjoy *The Living Bible*, by all means read it. But most people do better with a good readable contemporary translation like the *New International Version* or *Today's English Version*. If you're new to the Bible, these two are excellent choices.

TRANSLATION: ACCURACY—OR CLARITY?

Sentences in the original Hebrew and Greek were often very long and complex. Older translations of the Bible were so faithful to the original languages that they not only translated the words (and ideas) but also the sentence structure. So the translations were accurate—but often difficult to read in English.

As an example, consider the first sentence in the Letter to the Hebrews. Here's how it reads (very accurately) in the *King James Version* of 1611):

God, who at sundry times and in divers manners spake in time past unto the

CANYOUREADTHIS

Would you care to read a New Testament passage as it was delivered to its original readers? Here's Matthew 5:3-5, with English words instead of Greek: BLESSEDARETHEPOORIN-SPIRITFORTHEIRSISTHEKINGDOMOFHEAVENBLESSEDARETHOSEWHOMOURNFORTHEYWILL-BECOMFORTEDBLESSEDARETHEMEEKFORTHEYWILLINHERITTHEEARTH.

Did you have any trouble following that? This is what the New Testament Greek text looked like—no punctuation, no spaces between words, no lowercase letters—just one long string of letters (all capitals), one after another.

So how could people read such material? To put it mildly, Greek is very different from English. In Greek, words change form based on the role they play in a sentence. Our word cat is always "cat," changing only when we add an "s" for plural or "'s" for a possessive. But a Greek noun would change form, depending on whether it was the sentence's object or subject, plural or singular. It could also change to indicate a preposition. What the Greeks lacked in punctuation marks, spaces, and lowercase letters they made up for in a rich variety of words.

Something else was missing: paragraphs. Your Bible is divided into paragraphs—and probably into sections with headings that indicate the subject of that particular block of text. (You might see a heading "The Beatitudes" over Matthew 5:3, for example.) These headings make for ease of reading because it's easy to see where one section begins and another ends.

fathers by the prophets, hath in these last days spoken unto us by his Son, whom he hath appointed heir of all things, by whom also he made the worlds; who being the brightness of his glory, and the express image of his person, and upholding all things by the word of his power, when he had by himself purged our sins, sat down on the right hand of the Majesty on high (Heb. 1:1-3).

Now, that is a *long* sentence—one that very accurately reflects the words of the original Greek. But all those commas and clauses—mercy! Maybe we contemporary readers have a bad case of Attention Deficit Disorder. It's just hard for us to read a sentence that long—accurate or not.

Compare the wording in *Today's English Version:*

In the past God spoke to our ancestors many times and in many ways through the prophets, but in these last days he has spoken to us through his Son. He is the one through whom God created the universe, the one whom God has chosen to possess all things at the end. He reflects the brightness of God's glory and is the exact likeness of God's own being, sustaining the universe with his powerful word. After achieving forgiveness for the sins of mankind, he sat down in heaven at the right hand of God, the Supreme Power.

The modern version actually runs a little longer than the *King James*. But the modern version contains three sentences, not one. Yet all the thoughts are there in both versions. Technically, the *King James* is closer to the Greek.

But which is easier to read? You choose.

THE BIBLE IN AMERICA: SOME CHOICE TIDBITS

1492 and the Bible

Christopher Columbus came to America guided by . . . the Book of Isaiah. Columbus, a very devout believer, claimed that his voyage across the Atlantic fulfilled a prophecy of Isaiah: "From a far-off land I summon a man to fulfill my purpose. What I have said, that will I bring about; what I have planned, that will I do."

After his third voyage to the New World, Columbus wrote A Book of Prophecies. In it he explained how his voyages had fulfilled numerous prophecies in the Bible. He was absolutely certain that "neither reason nor mathematics aided me. Rather, the prophecy of Isaiah was completely fulfilled."

English, Indian, Whatever

The first Bible printed in America was not in English but in the Algonquin Indian language. During the colonial era, all English Bibles had to be printed in England itself.

Cherry Trees and Bibles

Mason Weems, who concocted the tale of young George Washington chopping down the cherry tree, made a living as a Bible salesman. Around 1800 he wrote to his publisher, "This is the very season and age of the Bible. Bible dictionaries, Bible tales, Bible stories, Bibles plain or paraphrased—so wide is the crater of public appetite at this time!"

Jefferson the Cutup

President Thomas Jefferson produced his own version of the Gospels. He cut out all the miracles and had the Gospels end with Jesus' burial, not the resurrection.

A Proper Yankee Bible

Noah Webster, father of the American dictionary, published an "Americanized" King James Version in 1833. His version dropped British spellings and eliminated the old-fashioned wording of the KJV. This was a time period when Americans were trying hard to prove they were distinct from their former masters, the British.

Reed the Bye-bul?

The strangest spellings in a Bible must be those in Andrew Comstock's Filadelfia New Testament, published in 1848. Comstock concocted a "purfekt alfabet" so readers would know exactly how to pronounce every word.

The Woman's Touch

Julia E. Smith of Connecticut was the first woman to translate the entire Bible all by herself. Her translation was published in 1876.

New Age, 1880s Style

The Hare family of Philadelphia published the Christian Spiritual Bible in 1881. It differed from other Bibles in one notable way: it taught reincarnation, a belief that had some popularity in the 1880s (and in our own day).

Honest Abe's Sweaty Brow

Abraham Lincoln's second Inaugural Address given in 1865 quotes from the Bible twice. Here are the lines from Lincoln's speech:

"It may seem strange that any men should dare to ask a just God's assistance in wringing their bread from the sweat of other men's faces, but let us judge not, that we be not judged."

And here are the verses, from the 1611 King James Version, the version Lincoln would have read: "In the sweat of thy face shalt thou eat bread" (Gen. 3:19); "Judge not, that ye be not judged" (Matt. 7:1).

FDR and the Money Changers

Franklin D. Roosevelt's 1933 Inaugural Address contains these words: "The money changers have fled from the high seats in the temple of our civilization." Consider Matthew 21:12-13 in the King James Version: "Jesus entered the temple area and drove out all who were buying and selling there. He overturned the tables of the money changers and the benches of those selling doves."

JFK and Luke's Gospel

John F. Kennedy's 1961 Inaugural Address contains a quotation—or near-quotation—from Luke's Gospel. Kennedy said, "For of those to whom much is given, much is required." Here's the verse from Luke 12:48 (KJV): "For unto whomsoever much is given, of him shall be much required."

Before There Was Charlton Heston

Lew Wallace, a Union general in America's Civil War, set out to write a book proving that Christianity and the Bible are false. The more he studied, the more convinced he was that the Bible is true. Instead of writing an anti-Christian book, he ended up writing the novel Ben-Hur, which also became one of the most popular movies of all time. The novel's subtitle is "A Tale of the Christ."

Robots, Bibles, Etc.

Isaac Asimov, one of the world's most famous science fiction authors, also published Isaac Asimov's Guide to the Bible.

Webster and the Leaky Rock

The great American statesman Daniel Webster made a noted speech in 1831, praising Secretary of the Treasury Alexander Hamilton. In the speech Webster said, "He smote the rock of the national resources and abundant streams of revenue gushed forth. He touched the dead corpse of Public Credit, and it sprung upon its feet."

Consider these two Old Testament passages: "Moses lifted up his hand, and with his rod he smote the rock twice: and the water came out abundantly" (Num. 20:11). "It came to pass, as they were burying a man, that, behold, they spied a band of men; and they cast the man into the sepulcher of Elisha: and when the man was let down, and touched the bones of Elisha, he revived, and stood up on his feet" (2 Kings 13:21).

Abe's Divided House

Abraham Lincoln's speech at the 1858 Republican Convention in Springfield, Illinois included one of Lincoln's most quoted lines: "A house divided against itself cannot stand." (Lincoln was referring to the North-South division occurring in the country.) Lincoln borrowed his line from the Bible, Matthew 12:25: "Every kingdom divided against itself is brought to desolation; and every city or house divided against itself shall not stand." (This quote is from the King James Version, the version Lincoln knew so well.)

Revolutionary Bible-quoting

American Revolutionary leader Patrick Henry often quoted or alluded to the Bible in his great speeches. In a 1775 speech at the Virginia Convention, Henry said, "The battle, sir, is not to the strong alone." Consider Ecclesiastes 9:11: "I returned, and saw under the sun, that the race is not to the swift, nor the battle to the strong." In the same speech Henry said, "The gentlemen may cry, Peace, peace! but there is no peace." Consider Jeremiah 6:14: "They have healed also the hurt of the daughter of my people slightly, saying, Peace, peace; when there is no peace."

Ach!

The first American Bible in a European language was not in English. In 1743 Christopher Sauer of Pennsylvania published an edition of Martin Luther's German Bible. German Bibles did not fall under the British colonial law that said all English Bibles had to be printed in England.

Sing-song Bibles

The first book printed in America was not the Bible, but almost was. It was the Bay Psalm Book, a rhyming version of the Psalms, published in the 1600s in Massachusetts.

Best-sellers?

In 1961 the best-selling nonfiction book in the U.S. was The New English Bible. In both 1972 and 1973 the best-selling nonfiction book was The Living Bible. Oddly, best-seller lists in those years did not even mention these books. Why? Because most best-seller lists—like those in The New York Times—do not list religious books.

chapter 3

The Authority Problem: ◄···

Inspiration, Inerrancy, Infallibility, Etc.

Singer Bob Dylan had a hit with "You Gotta Serve Somebody." The song was about a pretty simple idea: each of us bows to some authority. We stake our lives on someone—or something—being reliable, dependable.

True, sometimes we claim to be self-reliant, looking no further than ourselves for guidance. But the bookstore shelves are full of books of advice. So are the airwaves, with their multitude of radio call-in "experts." (Odd that the books and radio hosts talk about *self-help*, isn't it? The fact that you're reading the book or calling the radio host means you want someone else's help.) The most self-reliant people around would, if they were honest, admit they aren't *totally* self-reliant. They will, at least in some areas of life, bow to someone else's authority.

WHAT DO YOU THINK OF THE BIBLE?

Your attitude toward the Bible is a measure of how you see its authority—or lack of authority. If you see the Bible as just a human document, a collection of fiction and people's hare-brained religious ideas, then you won't see the Bible as having any authority at all. It may be interesting—

> *We have never truly breathed air nor seen light until we have breathed in the God-inspired Bible and seen the world by the Bible's light.*
> —RUSSIAN NOVELIST FYODOR DOSTOYEVSKY, AUTHOR OF *THE BROTHERS KARAMAZOV, CRIME AND PUNISHMENT,* AND OTHER CLASSICS.

but not authoritative. You might even admit that it has a few good insights into human nature. But you'll probably say that, as a whole, it's just an interesting book, with no real importance for human life today. This is the same view many readers today have of classic Greek poems like *The Iliad* and

The Odyssey—interesting, and with some good insights into human life, but not really relevant for building our lives around.

> It is Christ Himself, not the Bible, who is the true word of God. The Bible, read in the right spirit and with the guidance of good teachers, will bring us to Him.
> —C.S. LEWIS, ENGLISH AUTHOR

At the other end of the spectrum is the person who believes the Bible is inspired. It is the word—the *ultimate* word—of God to man. It contains everything we need to know about our destiny as human beings—in this world and afterward. It adequately meets our deepest needs.

Between these two extremes are different shades of opinion. When ten people say "I believe in the Bible," they may mean ten very different things. (When you hear about recent polls that show that most Americans have positive feelings about the Bible, don't assume that their "belief" in it is all too clear.)

THE BIBLE AND THE KORAN: BOTH INSPIRED?

All the great world religions have their sacred writings. In our own day, none is perhaps as significant in world events as the Koran, the holy book of the Muslims. Any TV news broadcast or newspaper will convince you that the Koran is by no means a "dead" book. Millions of Muslims across the world take it very seriously. In fact, the devotion many Muslims feel for the Koran is intense compared to what many so-called Christians feel for the Bible.

In contrast to the Bible, the Koran (often spelled Quran, by the way) was a one-man production. The sole writer was the prophet Muhammad himself. According to Muslim belief, Muhammad was a sort of "channel" for the words of Allah (God). In the Muslim view, Allah simply used Muhammad as a secretary. Every word of the Koran was written by Muhammad, and so was written in the life span of one individual.

The Bible, compared to the Koran, seems like more of a hodgepodge—a mingling of history, law, poetry, prophecy, letters, parables. Its authors are numerous. It was written over a period of centuries. It is not only a group effort, but also a trans-historical effort.

Something else that contrasts the Bible with the Koran: the tendency to ask questions of the Almighty. The Bible is authoritative, presenting God as the world's law-giver and ruler. And parts of the Bible are direct commands. But the Bible also shows human beings in dialogue with God. The wonderful Book of Job shows a saintly man agonizing, asking God why He allows a good person to suffer. The Prophet Habakkuk raises similar questions. The Book of Ecclesiastes has its author wrestling with a universal question: Is life ultimately meaningless, or does our devotion to God give it meaning? God in the Bible is (like Allah in the Koran) the Almighty. He is also one who allows man to argue with him. In the Bible, it is OK to ask God "why?"

There is another contrast: The portrayal of saints who were also sinners. Their stories fascinate us. King David of Israel is a great man—musician, poet, warrior, devoted man of God. He is also adulterer, overly indulgent father, sometimes a downright rogue. Abraham is also a man of faith—and sometimes a phenomenal liar. Moses leads Israel out of its slavery in Egypt, aided by his devoted brother and sister—who then rebel against him.

Are these just amusing stories? Or is there some benefit of seeing God and man portrayed in stories? Instead of just laws and commands, the Bible also gives us pictures—pictures of human beings engaged in relationships with God. The Bible gives us statements—like "Do not murder" and "God is love." But it also tells us stories—showing us how God is love and how bad things result from murder. No wonder some people have called the Bible "the Book of the Acts of God."

So perhaps there is something to be said for a multitude of authors. They all witness, in their different ways, to the acts of God.

Let's consider the source of authority: God. The Bible is not supposed to be authoritative in itself. Like any book, it is ink on white paper. But it is authoritative because it represents the ultimate Authority, God. Jesus made this sort of claim. He acted, according to witnesses, with authority. But He claimed that the real authority was His Father, God: "The words I say to you are not just my own. Rather, it is the Father, living in me, who is doing His work" (John 14:10). Yet people believed that God had delegated power and authority to Jesus: "All the people were amazed and said to each other, 'What is this teaching? With authority and power He gives orders to evil spirits and they come out!'" (Luke 4:36).

The prophets of the Old Testament did not claim to act or speak on their own authority. They claimed to speak for God. The phrase "This is what the Lord says" (or "Thus says the Lord," in some versions) is spoken again and again by the prophets. But Jesus never used that expression. He *did* claim to receive His authority from God. But unlike the prophets, He never said, "This is what the Lord says." He spoke with *His own* authority—as if His words and God's word were the same. This is what the first Christians believed: that Jesus was, in some way beyond our understanding, God. His authority *is* God's authority. "I and the Father are one" (John 10:30).

No one has ever claimed that Jesus wrote the Bible. He didn't. But the New Testament is *about* Jesus. It claims to present, accurately, what He said and did. It claims to present what His earliest followers believed about Him. They must have believed very strongly because quite a few of them paid the ultimate price for their belief.

The Bible does not say much about its own authority. Why would it? Would you ask a gypsy fortune-teller or an astrologer or a psychologist, "Are you for real?" Of course not. A document might contain the words "Read me, I am inspired and authoritative." But what kind of witness is that? Wouldn't a fake document make the same claim? The Bible has four Gospels. There were plenty of other Gospels that didn't make it into the Bible. Many of these actually claimed to be the "real" story of the "real" Jesus. One of the fake Gospels was even called the Gospel of Truth. No one reads these anymore, except for historical curiosity. They're full of stories about Jesus working miracles in His boyhood, or they have Him mouthing some philosophical gibberish that sounds peculiarly close to today's New Age beliefs (which may explain why some of these are being read again).

But even though the Bible says little about its own authority, many people are

• • • • • • • • • • •

Ethan Allen, the leader of Vermont's Green Mountain Boys in the American Revolution, also wrote a book on religion. In his 1784 book Reason the Only Oracle of Man, *Allen claimed that the Bible is not divinely inspired and that reason alone can lead people to happiness. (Allen did not, by the way, start the furniture company that bears his name.)*

• • • • • • • • • • •

impressed by the Bible's seriousness. That formula "Thus says the Lord . . ." occurs throughout it. Even when those exact words aren't used, the idea is there. The writers seem

---

THE KING AND I, AND GENESIS

YOU MAY HAVE SEEN THE POPULAR MUSICAL *THE KING AND I*. IN THE PLAY, THE KING OF SIAM COMPLAINS TO ANNA, THE ENGLISH SCHOOLTEACHER, THAT ENGLISH BOOKS ARE INCONSISTENT. THE BOOKS OF SCIENCE SAY THE UNIVERSE TOOK MILLIONS OF YEARS TO FORM. BUT THE BIBLE CLAIMS CREATION TOOK ONLY SIX DAYS. WHICH IS CORRECT? ASKS THE KING. WHY DO ENGLISH BOOKS CONTRADICT EACH OTHER?

ANNA EXPLAINS, POLITELY AND FIRMLY, THAT THERE IS NO CONTRADICTION. THE MEN WHO WROTE THE BIBLE WERE NOT SCIENTISTS, SHE SAYS. THEY WERE MEN OF FAITH WHO EXPLAINED CREATION IN A SIMPLE AND POETIC WAY, COMMUNICATING THE BELIEF THAT GOD MADE EVERYTHING IN THE WORLD, AND MADE IT FOR A PURPOSE. THE SCIENTISTS HAVE NOT BEEN ABLE TO DISPROVE THIS.

---

to have been convinced that they were writing the dead-serious words God motivated them to write. You do not get the impression that the Bible authors were just trying to entertain or impress with their cleverness. It was as if the words they wrote down were marked "Take me seriously! Urgent!"

Still, the authority question can't be settled by the Bible itself. So what about human experience? Millions of people have, for centuries, believed the Bible was the Word of God . . . and millions have not. You can't settle a matter like this by discussing numbers. After all, most people in the past believed the world was flat, and they were wrong. But for what it's worth, many

people—intellectuals, simple folk, rulers, authors, military leaders, philosophers, merchants, doctors—have believed that the Bible has divine authority. Some believed it along with all the people they knew. Some went against the tide and believed it in spite of the belief being unpopular. Some became martyrs.

WHAT DOES INSPIRATION MEAN?

Let's consider the matter of *inspiration*. The word *inspire* literally means "breathe in." The New Testament in Greek uses an interesting word: *theopneustos*. It means "God-breathed." This doesn't mean God had a literal breath that created the Bible. It means the invisible, spiritual God is somehow "in" the Bible. The Bible came to exist because God was "in" the writing process. His power, His life, are represented by the figurative word "breath."

The Apostle Paul wrote to Timothy, a young Christian pastor: "All Scripture is God-breathed and is useful for teaching, rebuking, correcting and training in righteousness, so that the man of God may be thoroughly equipped for every good work" (2 Tim. 3:16-17). ("Scripture" means the same as "Bible.") Paul had a practical concept of the Bible. It was "God-breathed," but that didn't mean we should fall down and worship the book. It means the Bible's words are *useful*. They are God's way of training us to be the kind of people we're meant to be. Paul had no interest in "opening up sacred mysteries." He saw the Bible as God's manual for the good life. In another letter, Paul claimed that "everything that was written in the past was written to teach us, so that through endurance and the encouragement of the Scriptures we might have hope" (Rom. 15:4).

Peter, author of two New Testament letters, made a high claim for the Bible's authority: "You must understand that no prophecy of Scripture came about by the prophet's own interpretation. For prophecy never had its origin in the will of man, but men spoke from God as they were carried along by the Holy Spirit" (2 Peter 1:20-21). Again, the idea of "God-breathed." Who wrote the words in the Bible? Human beings. Who gives the "life," the "breath," the "spirit" to the Bible? God.

Generations ago, some people believed that God "dictated" the Bible. In this view, the human authors were nothing more than secretaries—writing robots, you might say. But the Bible—either in a translation or in the original Greek and Hebrew—shows that the authors had very different styles of writing. Paul's letters are unmistakably Paul's. He had his own personality and writing style. If the human authors were merely secretaries for God, wouldn't God have always used the same voice? God did not override or smother the individual's personality. The authors were moved by God. We might say they felt an "inward pressure" or "compulsion" to write the words that God wished to communicate to the world.

This is what we mean by inspiration—a hard concept to explain, as you may have noticed. It can't be proven scientifically. But many people—some simple, some brilliant—have believed it. They have believed that Jesus was, in some unexplainable way, both fully human and fully divine. They believed the same about the Bible. It was produced by living, breathing human beings. It was produced by the power of a God who wished to reveal Himself. Human and divine—both.

You can believe that Shakespeare's *Hamlet* is an "inspired" work. You can believe that God gave Shakespeare his talent, his genius. You can believe that there is truth in *Hamlet.* But this isn't the same as "God-breathed." Believing the Bible is "God-breathed" means believing that it—the whole Bible, not just portions we enjoy, or portions that fit well with contemporary thought—is God's Word to the entire human race.

WHAT DOES INERRANCY MEAN?

Bible scholars have been quarreling for years over the matter of inspiration. They argue about something else called *inerrancy.* If something is *inerrant*, it is without error. No mistakes. None.

I personally believe the Bible is inerrant. By this I mean that, in terms of spiritual and eternal matters, it is always correct. But I will be honest: it contains difficulties. It disagrees with itself about some things. For example, the four Gospels report different things about the women who find Jesus' grave empty. Mark's Gospel says, "As they entered the tomb, they saw a young man dressed in a white robe sitting on the right side, and they were alarmed" (Mark 16:5). Luke's Gospel says: "While they were wondering about this, suddenly two men in clothes that gleamed like lightning stood beside them" (Luke 24:4). Which is right? One man inside the tomb or two men near the tomb? The Gospels are apparently describing angels—but one angel or two?

These kinds of discrepancies bother some people. They shouldn't. Think of four people you deeply trust, and ask all four to report something that they all witnessed. You will hear the same story—but not exactly. (You may gain more from hearing four witnesses than just one.)

We have to consider the copying process: we learn from the Bible scholars that the ancient manuscripts agree on most things—but not all. In the process of making thousands of copies, changes occur. Those old pieces of papyrus agree on all the important things. They do disagree about minor things. Looking at how similar all the copies are, you might conclude that God was overseeing the process. You might also conclude that, yes, human beings do make mistakes.

Do such "errors" mean the Bible is untrustworthy? Why would it? If your spouse leaves a mess in the kitchen and runs off to play tennis, do you conclude that he or she is completely selfish and unloving? No—not if you have a lot of other evidence to the contrary.

Besides these minor discrepancies, there is something you need to know about the Bible: it isn't a science textbook. Its authors weren't physicists or biologists. They described natural phenomena in language that was available to them. They weren't lying—they just had limitations on how to describe things that science can now describe and explain easily. We ourselves use an untrue phrase all the time: we say the sun rises and sets. We know full well it doesn't. Genesis 7:11 describes the great flood in Noah's day and says "the floodgates of the heavens were opened." Did the author really believe the sky has gates? Probably not. But his words give us the main idea: it *really* rained.

Jesus is portrayed as being divine, the Son of God. But He was not a scientist. In Mark 4:31, Jesus compares the kingdom of God to the mustard seed, "which is the smallest seed you plant in the ground." Strictly speaking, He was wrong. We know now that many plants have seeds smaller than the mustard seed. Put this into the So What? file. Was Jesus speaking as a botanical expert, or was He simply using the mustard seed as an example of a very small seed (which it is)?

Does anybody really take the whole Bible *literally?* Of course not. All of it wasn't meant to be taken that way. Some of it is poetic. When Jesus said "I am the bread of life," no one believed He could be cut up and spread with butter. When He told His disciples, "I am the vine, you are the branches," none of them expected to grow leaves. The New Testament says many times that the resurrected Jesus is now "seated at the right hand of God." Literally? No. The Bible makes it clear that God is a spirit, not a body with a right hand. The authors meant that Jesus is with God—and not just with Him, but in close fellowship with Him—God's "right-hand man," to use our modern phrase. (When we call George Washington "the father of our country," everyone knows we don't mean it literally, right?)

Sometimes the poetic element got misunderstood. Jesus told the inquisitive Nicodemus, "no one can see the kingdom of God unless he is born again." Poor

Nicodemus! He asked Jesus just how that was literally possible. We chuckle. Nicodemus was too literal-minded. Didn't he know Jesus was talking about a spiritual rebirth?

But, take note: Most parts of the Bible *were* meant to be taken literally. When the Old Testament says that the Assyrian king Sennacherib made war on Judah, it means just that. In fact, the Old and New Testaments refer to lots of hard, historical facts. The archaeologists continually find new evidence that the Bible authors had their facts straight. There was a real Assyrian King Sennacherib, and he really did make war on Judah. Most of the Bible takes place in this literal, historical world. Saying the Bible is a "spiritual" book is true. But it is full of history too—hard data, real events. The Old and New Testaments are about God acting in history.

Other things were also meant to be taken literally. That includes the miracles. And it includes the great miracle of Jesus being raised from the dead. This miracle is mentioned again and again in the New Testament. There is not a hint that anyone understood it "figuratively." The writers themselves did not believe this was a legend. Jesus' followers really did believe that, somehow, the body that had died and was buried was alive again. It was somehow like His old body, but different too. You may not believe this. But if you read the New Testament, you have to conclude that the early Christians really did believe it. Some paid the price of their lives for believing it. Would they have died for an illusion, for a figurative resurrection? No. They believed that a real historical event had occurred: Jesus had been raised from the dead.

WHAT ABOUT INFALLIBILITY?

Believing the Bible is error-free means that *in all matters of faith, the Bible is true.* To be concise, we call this *infallibility.* The early Christians believed that Jesus' resurrection was a key point of faith. They believed He really had died, been raised, and been taken into heaven. They believed that if they trusted Him, they would spend eternity with Him, with their own new, resurrected bodies. These things can't be scientifically proven—nor disproven. It comes down to faith. Accept the Bible as the inspired, authoritative Word of God—or don't. If you do accept this, you don't have to accept it as a science text. Nor do you have to say that all its parts completely agree in every detail (because they don't). All you have to accept is that "the holy Scriptures . . . are able to make you wise for salvation through faith in Christ Jesus" (2 Tim. 3:15). In the Bible's view, salvation is Priority Number 1. And we need to remember this: People are not saved by the Bible. People are saved by God.

One very old statement of faith claims that the Bible "contains all things necessary for salvation." That's a nice summary. It does not say the Bible is a science textbook or an encyclopedia, but a "salvation handbook." The one thing it is supposed to do—reveal the saving truth of God—it does perfectly well.

IF YOU BASE YOUR BELIEFS ON THE BIBLE . . .

Christians believe that the Bible—the sixty-six inspired books—sets the boundaries of belief. Any belief that is truly *Christian* has to be based on the clear teachings in the Bible. Unlike Hinduism and that wide group of beliefs called New Age, the faith presented in the Bible isn't open to any idea that seems vaguely "spiritual." So if you base your beliefs on the Bible, you can be environmentally conscious, but you can't worship nature. You can't practice channeling, dabble in the occult, try to get in touch with your past incarnations, worship Mother Earth, call yourself a pagan or neo-pagan, or believe that you yourself are God. The Bible sets a wall around belief. This isn't a wall to keep you from anything good. It's a wall to keep out garbage.

INSPIRATION AND THE CANON

Canon is the word the scholars use to refer to the sixty-six books included in the Bible. It means "rule" or "standard," and the idea is that the sixty-six books of the Bible are the definitive holy writings for believers. The canon—the Bible as a whole—is God's word to man. Other writings besides the Bible may seem "inspired," but only the Bible itself is "holy," separate and distinct from all other writings.

If the whole Bible is *inspired*, that does not mean every part of it is *inspiring*. Millions of readers throughout the centuries have been touched by Jesus' wonderful Sermon on the Mount (Matt. 5–7). Not many people will admit to being inspired by the laws for animal sacrifices (Lev. 5–6). The Book of Job is beautiful and touching, sensitive in its exploration of human questions about suffering and justice. The Book of Esther is . . . well, an interesting (but violent and vindictive) story about a particular incident in Jewish history.

So people have their own "canon within the canon." Entire books have been written on Matthew's Gospel, the Psalms, and Paul's Letter to the Romans. Pastors have preached great series of sermons on the Book of Isaiah and the Book of Acts. But it's hard to find much inspiration from the Song of Songs or from the tiny Book of Obadiah. Most readers just don't find material there that is useful in their lives. The Bible as a whole is a useful book. But not all parts seem equally useful. So each person finds parts that seem worth reading—and re-reading, while other parts are neglected.

This is normal. But it can lead to danger. Since the very beginnings of Christianity, people have been tempted to "cut and paste" their own Bible, tossing out parts they don't find appealing. Thomas Jefferson, for example, was a highly moral man, but he couldn't swallow the miracle stories in the Gospels. So he put together his own New Testament, editing out the miracles. (That left a crucified, buried, but not risen Jesus.) Early in Christian history a man named Marcion edited his own Bible. He threw out the entire Old Testament and some of the New. Why? He didn't like the "angry" God, the God as Judge depicted in some parts of the Bible. He liked the images of God as a loving Father (don't we all?) but felt that they didn't jibe with the "darker" images of God. He thought Christianity was an easier sell if it threw out the "bad God" and left only the "good God." But Christians as a whole said, "No. You can't just pick and choose the parts you like. You can't create a god of your own liking. You have to accept the God of the whole Bible."

And, as it happened, Marcion is one of the main reasons we have a Bible with sixty-six books. Radical individualists like Marcion prodded Christians to put their heads together and decide, once and for all, just what writings were "holy Scripture."

When the New Testament mentions *Scripture* (as in 2 Tim. 3:16— "All Scripture is God-breathed"), it refers to the Old Testament, which the church honored as God's Word for mankind. But while the young church was growing, the New Testament as we know it was not considered Holy Scripture—not yet anyway, for it was still being written.

The New Testament itself indicates that early Christians were starting to regard the Gospels and Paul's epistles as special in some way. In 2 Peter 3:16 there is a notable reference to Paul's writings. Peter's epistle says that Paul's epistles are sometimes "hard to understand." But nevertheless Paul's wisdom is described as God-given, and Peter chides the "ignorant and unstable people" who distort Paul's words—as they distort *other* Scriptures. So by the time 2 Peter was written, there was already awareness among Christians that holy writings other than the Old Testament were available for inspiring the faithful.

The idea of a *canon—canon* is the Greek word for *standard*—began to develop. The Jews had established that some books—the Old Testament—were clearly inspired by God. Christians felt the same need to distinguish between truly inspired writings and those that were questionable. What were the guidelines the Christians had in mind as they began to formulate the New Testament canon?

One was *apostolic origin.* Among the first Christians, apostles were highly honored. The apostles—Jesus' appointed "ambassadors"—were key figures in the Book of Acts. As the new faith spread, writings from the hands of the apostles were especially honored. The bulk of the writings in our New Testament were authored by apostles— Paul (his many letters), Matthew (his Gospel), Peter (two letters), and John (his Gospel, three letters, and possibly Revelation). Surprisingly, two of our four Gospels were not written by apostles. But the authors had "connections." Mark, mentioned several times in the New Testament, was supposed to have been a fellow worker with the Apostle Peter. So Mark's Gospel is not by an apostle but is based on the testimony of one of the key apostles, Peter. Likewise, Luke's Gospel. Luke was not an apostle but was a close associate of the Apostle Paul. Luke wrote not only his Gospel, but also Acts. The "we" passages

. . . .

BIBLE AND STATE

Most people know that the U.S. Constitution forbids Congress to establish a national religion. Yet Pennsylvania's first state constitution required legislators to "acknowledge the Scriptures of the Old and New Testaments to be given by divine inspiration." A few Jews protested—but only because the requirement specifically mentioned the New Testament, which they did not believe was divinely inspired.

. . . .

of Acts are written by Luke as eyewitness accounts.

The books that now make up our New Testament passed the apostolic authorship test. They were written by Jesus' apostles, or by people who knew the apostles well, people who could say, "I know about this, because I was there."

Another guideline for what books should be included in the New Testament was *the writing's use in the churches*. An operating principle seemed to be, "If a lot of churches use this writing and it continues to enlighten them, it must be inspired." In other words, if something is inspired by God, it will, no doubt, inspire many people. So a writing that God had not inspired would inevitably, over time, fall out of use.

But these concerns did not settle the issue of which books would finally be established as the canon. For one thing, many books were attributed to apostles, and some of these writings were blatantly heretical—that is, not in keeping with the true gospel. And churches in some locales used writings that other churches did not care to use.

Yet there was some consistency in the churches. By the end of the second century, the four Gospels, Acts, and Paul's epistles were honored almost everywhere. There was no "official" list but, rather, an unofficial grass-roots consensus that these writings had spiritual authority. But while these were generally seen as inspired, there was much dispute over Revelation, James, 2 Peter, 2 and 3 John, Jude, and Hebrews.

Heresy has a way of making orthodox believers clarify their position. The necessity of an official canon became clear as notable heretics established their own canons. As far as we know, the first attempt at a canon was that of the heretic Marcion, whom I mentioned earlier. His canon included only ten epistles of Paul and a heavily edited Gospel of Luke. Later heretical groups cherished their own special "secret books" (usually circulated with an apostle's name attached, so as to lend authority).

In 367, the influential bishop of Alexandria, Athanasius, penned a widely circulated Easter letter. In it he listed the twenty-seven books that we now have in our New Testament. The list was intended to be exclusive. Athanasius, hoping to guard his flock from heresy, stated that no other books could be regarded as Christian Scripture, though he allowed that some others might be useful for private devotions.

Athanasius' letter did not settle the matter completely. There was still dispute over certain books—Hebrews, James, Jude, 2 Peter, and 2 and 3 John. But eventually the Christian world did accept all twenty-seven books, excluding all others. Scattered groups of heretics continued to cherish their pet writings, but these heretical writings did not gain universal acceptance. Athanasius' list has indeed become the canon—the standard.

BROWS HIGH AND LOW

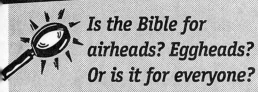 *Is the Bible for airheads? Eggheads? Or is it for everyone?*

In the New Testament, the Apostle Paul (an educated man, a thinker) said to some of the Christians: "Brothers, think of what you were when you were called. Not many of you were wise by human standards; not many were influential; not many were of noble birth" (1 Cor. 1:26).

Paul (who was not being unkind, just honest) was aware that the first Christians were not intellectuals—not many of them, anyway. In fact, in the first few years of the new faith, very few intellectuals were attracted to it. (One early Christian, Apollos, is called "a learned man" in Acts 18:24.) Most intellectuals then saw Christianity as just another silly superstition—and the Roman Empire was full of them at that time. This rejection by the "brain elite" did not bother the early Christians at all. They believed the faith was real—and if the highbrows rejected it, well, what did it matter?

But the intellectuals' attitude changed. Some were won over to the new faith. They were attracted not only by its morals and its belief in an afterlife, but by its teachings. Some of them tossed aside the pagan philosophies they had been teaching and embraced the Bible. This was, they thought, the real Ultimate Truth they had been pursuing so long. This new belief system seemed to "hang together" in a way their old philosophies didn't. By the year 300 (around the time that Emperor Constantine made Christianity a legal religion), most of the great intellects in the Roman Empire were Christians.

Has anything changed in 1,700 years? Are there uneducated, semi-literate people today who claim to believe in the Bible? Of course—and why not, since the Bible never makes any claim to being a book just for intellectuals? But are there intellectuals in our own day who believe the Bible? Or is the old Book past its prime?

The Bible is definitely not past its prime, and yes, there are plenty of intelligent, well-educated people who believe the Bible.

chapter 4

Meaning What? ◀···

Interpreting the Bible

Reading the Bible is like reading someone else's mail. In the case of the many letters in the New Testament, this is literally true. As in the case of reading someone else's mail, we may not understand everything we read. We have some obvious questions: Who sent this? Who received it? What was the purpose of the letter? What incidents caused the letter to be sent? How is the recipient expected to respond?

This last question is the key one. You see, the books of the Old and New Testaments weren't sent to us . . . and yet they were. Christians know that Paul sent the original Letter to the Romans to the Christians at Rome in the first century A.D. Yet Christians believe that this letter, like all parts of the Bible, is addressed to us also. If it is not, then we study the Bible only out of curiosity (which is a valid reason, but not one that many people choose). If the Book of Exodus was written for the ancient Hebrews—and

only for them—why study it today? If we read the Bible only for curiosity, wouldn't we get as much (or more) pleasure from reading a Tom Clancy novel or a Dave Barry humor column?

So Bible readers have a two-pronged task: interpret the Bible (What does it mean?) and apply the Bible (What does it mean to me and how I live my life?). This is what makes the Bible different from other ancient writings, like Homer's *Odyssey* or Sophocles' *Oedipus Rex*. We can read and try to interpret the *Odyssey*. But we don't follow up by asking, "How will this now affect my life?" Homer and Sophocles never included the words "Thus says the Lord" or "Thus say the gods" in their writings. But the Bible in many, many places uses the phrase "Thus says the Lord." It is clear that the Bible authors believed they were saying something with a divine origin. And if it is divine, it must affect human life. We can't read the Bible and then reply, "So what?"

AN AGE OF CONFUSION

You don't have to be brilliant or well-educated to read and understand the Bible. Jesus Himself made this clear: "I praise you, Father, Lord of heaven and earth, because you have hidden these things from the wise and learned, and revealed them to little children" (Matt. 11:25). Jesus didn't mean that the truth was off-limits to the wise. He meant that it was possible for anyone with an open mind—even a child—to understand the truth.

In the early days of Christianity, most people could read. They had access to the books we now call the Old Testament, and also to the writings that eventually were collected as the New Testament. But after about the year 500, literacy declined. This was the period historians called the Dark Ages—not literally dark, but a bad period for learning and literacy. During this period the Bible continued to be read and copied. But the average Christian (who probably could not read anyway) had no access to the Bible. The people who had Bibles were priests and the monks who lived a secluded life in monasteries. Here they did something important: copied Bibles so that future generations would have them. (See chap. 2 for a more detailed account.)

But they did something else: wrote commentaries on the Bible. They weren't writing these commentaries for the Average Reader (and remember, the Average Person couldn't read anyway), but for themselves. There was a sort of "Bible elite," the sheltered monks who spent their days studying and copying the Bible and writing books about it.

Some of their commentaries dazzle us. They weren't satisfied just to read the Bible and discover what it meant and how to apply it to life. They wanted to go "beyond the surface"—to discover the *hidden* meanings of the Bible.

An example: the word *water*. When you run across this word in the Bible, you probably assume it means just what it says: water—that wet, clear stuff we drink and bathe in. But the Bible elite of the Dark Ages said, "No, that's only the literal meaning. It must mean more than that. They interpreted the word *allegorically* and said that it meant baptism. They interpreted it *morally* and said it meant sorrow (or wisdom, or heresy, or prosperity). They interpreted it *spiritually* and said it meant eternal happiness. These three "senses" were the "real" meaning of the word, a meaning much more interesting than the *literal* one (the fourth "sense"). And you thought water was just water.

• • • • • • • • • • • • • • • • • •

DOES GOD HAVE FINGERS?

God is an invisible spirit, true. But the Bible sometimes speaks—perhaps figuratively —of God's bodily parts. "When the LORD finished speaking to Moses on Mount Sinai, He gave him the two tablets of the Testimony, the tablets of stone inscribed by the finger of God" (Ex. 31:18). So the mysterious "fiery finger" depicted in the movie The Ten Commandments is perhaps not as farfetched as we might think.

• • • • • • • • • • • • • • • • • •

Here is another example: Genesis 1:3 records God saying, "Let there be light." Literally, this means God created light. Allegorically, it means "let Christ be love." Morally, it means "let us be illuminated by Christ." Spiritually, it means "let us be led to heaven by Christ." (And you thought it meant just that God had created light.)

In some passages, where the name "Jerusalem" occurred, these were the four interpretations: literally, the old city named Jerusalem; allegorically, the church; morally, the human soul; spiritually, heaven.

The Bible experts were especially devoted to applying this four-way interpretation to the Old Testament. With so many stories of tribal wars, rebellions, and other unpleasant subjects, the interpreters couldn't take these violent tales at face value. They reasoned, "There has to be a deeper meaning, an allegorical-moral-spiritual meaning." The literal meaning of Joshua's armies invading Canaan was not important. Nor were the blatantly sensuous poems in the Song of Songs. (This book was a particular favorite of interpreters, who firmly believed that these poems about male-female attraction just *had* to have a spiritual meaning. Consider something: All the Bible experts in the Middle Ages were men who had taken a vow of celibacy. No wonder they couldn't take the Song of Songs at face value!)

There was one advantage of interpreting the Bible in these fantastic ways: none of the Bible went to waste. By assuming that every verse in the Bible had a "deeper" meaning, the Bible elite could find meanings in the most unlikely places—the laws of sacrifice in Leviticus, the measurements of the temple in Ezekiel, the censuses of Israel in Numbers. Taken literally, these passages don't seem to have much meaning for us today. But the Bible elite of the Middle Ages could find *lots* of meanings—even if those meanings really had nothing to do with the passage! Yet by finding meaning in every verse, they were able to use the whole Bible—no "leftovers," no verse without some importance.

Does all this sound like a sort of intellectual word game? It was. But to give these men credit, some of them were probably trying to find real spiritual meaning in the Bible. Believing that the whole Bible had real meaning for people in every time and place, these interpreters sought to find that meaning. They assumed (probably correctly) that most readers want to know about God and themselves, but are not terribly interested in the Canaanites or the Prophet Ezekiel.

But most of these scholars were caught up in their own cleverness, eager to put a new spin on some Bible verse that had been interpreted cleverly before. It was a case of "Can you top this?" Common folk might read a Bible passage and accept it "as is." But if you were an "egghead," you believed that this literal reading was a "surface" reading. One noted Bible commentator of this period said, "The sense of God's Word is infinitely varied, and like a peacock's feather, it glows with many colors." (A modern comparison: Literary critics today talk about "feminist themes in Shakespeare" or "social beliefs in the novels of Charles Dickens." They are trying to make the old writings relevant to a new age. But they are missing the real point—and real beauty—of Shakespeare and Dickens.)

In the meantime, while these clever Bible scholars were finding new colors in the peacock's feather, the people in the churches were not benefiting. If they even heard the Bible being read in church, it was read in Latin, a language only the scholars understood. An odd situation: in the Middle Ages everyone in Europe was a baptized Christian. Yet the average person lived and died without much exposure to the words and teachings of the Bible. The Bible elites found lots of meanings in the Bible. But the average Christian really had no knowledge of *any* meaning of the Bible. The people in the pews depended on the priests and bishops and monks to do their thinking for them. The priests rarely preached sermons on the Bible.

Change came with the Protestant Reformation in the 1500s. The Protestant leaders emphasized translating the Bible into people's own languages. (See chap. 2 for more details.) They insisted that pastors preach sermons that explained the Bible to the people. And that amazing new invention, the printing press, helped make the Bible more available to everyone. With more books available, more people learned to read—often for the sole purpose of being able to read the Bible. For the first time in centuries, laymen—farmers, merchants, housewives, laborers—could read the Bible themselves. Living in "the real world," not the world of professional scholars, they took a commonsense approach to the Bible: "What does this literally mean?" they asked. That question has—thank heaven—dominated Bible study ever since.

THE LITERAL MEANING

Even during those centuries when interpreters were finding all kinds of fantastic meanings in the Bible, some voices of sense prevailed. "Emphasize the literal meaning," they said. "Try to discern what the author was trying to communicate."

But can we take the whole Bible *literally?* Consider these verses, which are God speaking to the patriarch Abraham:

> *He [God] took him [Abraham] outside and said, "Look up at the heavens and count the stars—if indeed you can count them." Then He said to him, "So shall your offspring be"* (Gen. 15:5).

> *[God said:] "I will surely bless you and make your descendants as numerous as the stars in the sky and as the sand on the seashore"* (Gen. 22:17).

Now, if God is truly the all-knowing One, He would know the number of the stars in the sky and the grains of sand on the seashore. Abraham didn't, and neither do we. Based on what scientists tell us, the sands on the seashore are a huge number—and definitely larger than Abraham's descendants, the Hebrews/Israelites/Jews.

So was God amiss in His promise to Abraham? Of course not. Literally, the promise isn't true. Abraham's descendants haven't been as numerous as the stars or the grains of sand. But neither Abraham nor we are expected to take the promise literally. The message of the promise was this: *I will give you many, many descendants—so many that you would think of them as innumerable.* In other words, it is poetic exaggeration, done to make a valid point. It is more memorable than if God had simply said, "I will give you lots and lots of descendants." (We say "It's raining cats and dogs," and no one takes it literally. It sounds more interesting than "It's really raining hard.")

Other parts of the Bible are obviously not meant to be taken literally. Jesus made several statements about Himself that were not meant literally: "I am the bread of life"; "I am the light of the world"; "I am the gate for the sheep"; "I am the true vine, and my Father is the gardener." Did He mean He was literally bread, or a gate, or a vine? Of course not. He meant something deeper—a figurative, spiritual meaning. But it is usually very obvious in the Bible when you are dealing with a passage like these. (When you read about the Confederate General "Stonewall" Jackson, you probably do not assume he was actually made of stone. Why? Because our mental habits make us aware that it was a figurative name. He was "Stonewall" because of his grit and determination.)

Consider some other examples: God's "body." The Bible makes it clear that God is a spiritual being, without a body. Yet many times, especially in the Old Testament, we read about the "hand of the Lord," "eyes of the Lord," "ears of the Lord," even the Lord's "nostrils." The Bible writers knew that God has none of these literal body parts. They were expressing as best they could some important ideas: God knows things ("eyes" and "ears") and He has power to act ("hand" and "arm"). In describing an indescribable spiritual Being, we have to use words people understand—even if those words are poetic or symbolic, not literal.

Let's take another example: hell. Jesus said,

The Son of Man will send out His angels, and they will weed out of His kingdom everything that causes sin and all who do evil. They will throw them into the fiery furnace, where there will be weeping and gnashing of teeth (Matt. 13:41-42).

Let's interpret. Jesus spoke of Himself as "the Son of Man," so there's no confusion about this. What about the "fiery furnace" and the "weeping and gnashing of teeth"? He is apparently talking about the fate of people who are not part of His kingdom. Will they be in a literal fire, grinding their literal teeth? Probably not. If you say, "Joe's wife left him, and she broke his heart," did his literal heart crack open? No. You're saying, figuratively, that his wife caused him a great deal of inward pain. His literal heart didn't break—but something equally serious happened. The same with the "fiery furnace." Jesus was communicating that sinners would be disposed of—like something tossed away in a trash-burner. "Weeping and gnashing of teeth" are what people in agony would do, of course. If hell isn't literally a place of fire, it is something equally serious: human beings who have ended up being separated from God. For Jesus, this was real, even if His image of a fiery furnace was only figurative. It is no less true for being figurative.

When we talk about finding the literal meaning of the Bible, this doesn't mean that every verse is meant to be taken literally—as the above examples indicate. Searching for the Bible's literal meaning means going for the obvious: finding out what the original writers intended to communicate to their readers. That's the first step. Finding out how that applies to us today is the second step. We must take the first before we take the second.

BUT IS THERE REALLY A HIDDEN MEANING?

The last few paragraphs have been driving home a key point of this book: Try to read the Bible "as is," finding the most obvious meaning, the meaning that its writers intended.

But we have to be honest: the Bible writers themselves found "hidden" or "spiritual" meanings. You will notice this if you spend any time with the New Testament. The writers were quite capable of reading the Old Testament "as is." But they also found deeper meanings in it—meanings that the original Old Testament authors probably did not intend. Quite often, the New Testament writers found that parts of the Old Testament applied to the life of Jesus. If your Bible has footnotes, you will notice this in the New Testament. On practically every page you'll see notes referring you to places in the Old Testament. Why? Either the author is quoting the Old Testament directly, or at least making a passing reference to it.

Take an example: Matthew's Gospel (2:18) quotes this passage from the Old Testament's Book of Jeremiah: "A voice is heard in Ramah, weeping and great mourning, Rachel weeping for her children and refusing to be comforted, because her children are no more." The footnote tells you this is found in Jeremiah 31:15. If you look up that passage in Jeremiah, you'll find it in the middle of a passage about the Jews being abused by the Babylonians. Rachel was the wife of Jacob (also named Israel, father of the twelve tribes of Israel). In the Jeremiah passage, "weeping for her children" meant she was mourning for her descendants who had been cruelly treated by the Babylonians. (See page 21 for more information on footnotes in the Bible.)

But Matthew uses Jeremiah's words to refer to evil King Herod, who slaughtered all the male infants of Bethlehem in an effort to kill the newborn Jesus. Matthew probably knew the literal meaning of Jeremiah 31:15. But when he told the story of Herod and the children, it struck him that the words of Jeremiah had a new meaning. Jeremiah's words had been "fulfilled" by an incident in the life of Jesus. Another way of looking at this: the slaughter of the infants by Herod *reminded* Matthew (painfully, we assume) of the verse in Jeremiah. It was as if Matthew remembered the verse and said, "Ah, that horrible incident concerning Herod certainly gives a new meaning to those words of Jeremiah."

Consider another example. In Luke's Gospel (22:37), Jesus quotes Isaiah 53:12: "He was numbered with the transgressors." Jesus goes on to say, "What is written about Me is reaching its fulfillment." In short, Jesus Himself read new meanings into the words of the Old Testament. Isaiah's words are part of what is called the "Suffering Servant Song," a poem about someone who suffers on other people's behalf. Was Isaiah making a prophecy, or just speaking about how an innocent person often suffers for others? We don't know. But apparently Jesus believed that Isaiah's words applied to Him. Words that had been only words were now "fulfilled."

Here is one more example. The Apostle Paul's sermon in Acts 13:35 quotes Psalm 16:10: "You will not let your Holy One see decay." If you look up Psalm 16, it isn't really a prophecy. It is the song of a moral person saying to God, "You will not let me die right now." It did not mean—so far as we can tell—that God would actually raise the man from the dead. But that is exactly what Paul means in Acts 13:35. He takes the verse from Psalm 16 and claims it has a deeper meaning—is "fulfilled"—because Jesus, who is God's "Holy One," actually did not see decay but was raised from the dead.

This occurs repeatedly in the New Testament. People familiar with the Old Testament could not help noticing all these coincidences. They believed that many passages from the Old Testament could now be read in a new light, since the life and work of Jesus had given them a new meaning.

So, when you read the Bible, try to find the most obvious literal meaning in any passage. But be prepared. Its own authors often found spiritual meanings. More about that later.

THE "FISH BONE" THEORY

When you read the Bible, you will find that most of it—let's say 80 percent—is pretty self-explanatory. You may stumble a bit over archaic-sounding names (like Sennacherib or Nebuchadnezzar or Zedekiah), but these don't really affect your understanding of the text. (If you read about Mexican history, you aren't surprised that people are named

Francisco and Antonio and Diego, are you? Nor are you surprised that the towns have names you aren't accustomed to.)

Let's say you are reading the Book of Exodus. Beginning at chapter 1, you read of the Israelites being slaves in Egypt. The Lord calls Moses, a shepherd, to lead the Israelites out of Egypt. Moses accepts the assignment and is on his way to Egypt. So far, so good—a pretty straightforward story.

But then you reach this odd passage: "At a lodging place on the way, the LORD met Moses and was about to kill him" (Ex. 4:24). Say what? Moses just faithfully accepted God's assignment, and now God tries to kill him. Why? You read on. "But Zipporah [Moses' wife] took a flint knife, cut off her son's foreskin and touched Moses' feet with it. 'Surely you are a bridegroom of blood to me,' she said. So the LORD let him alone. (At that time she said 'bridegroom of blood,' referring to circumcision)" (Ex. 4:25-26).

You can look up this passage in a Bible commentary if you have one. But even the Bible scholars have trouble explaining this. We are faced with a rather obvious fact: in stories that were written down thousands of years ago, *we cannot hope to understand every detail*. It's just not possible. Human nature is the same, and God is the same. But social customs and historical circumstances do change. Many centuries separate us from Moses and his wife Zipporah. Most of Moses' story is perfectly clear. But Exodus 4:24-26 isn't—not even to the Bible pros. The original writers must have understood it. We don't.

So here's an option: Take a passage like

this and put it aside. Treat it as you would a bone you find in a piece of fish. Lay it to the side of your plate and keep eating. Finding the bone in the fish shouldn't stop you from enjoying the rest of your dinner.

It is human nature to want to understand what you read. If you read a Stephen King or John Grisham novel, you can probably grasp just about everything in it. Of course you can. Stephen King knows how to write for people who think and speak the same as he does. You can't expect such complete clarity from something more than 2,000 years old. (Does Stephen King expect his words to be selling well in 3,000 years?)

So reading the Bible means putting aside the urge to understand every word. The old song says "accentuate the positive." In reading the Bible, you should "accentuate the understandable," the parts you can grasp. A basic rule in Bible reading is to judge the unclear passages by the clear. You could, if you were new to the Bible, read Exodus 4:24-26 and conclude "God is cruel. He calls Moses to serve Him, then tries to kill him. God is unpredictable and mean!" You could conclude that—but it disagrees with the rest of the Bible, which shows God as faithful and loving. The Bible as a whole agrees with James 1:17, which speaks of God as "the Father of the heavenly lights, who does not change like shifting shadows." The best idea is, *judge the individual piece of the Bible by the whole Bible.* This won't help you understand Exodus 4:24-26, but it will

help you to "push it to the side of the plate."

A word of warning: Don't apply the "fish bone" rule to passages that you happen not to *like.* If you happen to be committing adultery, or considering it, you might not like Exodus 20:14, "You shall not commit adultery." But *not liking* and *not understanding* are two different things. This commandment seems perfectly clear. So do Jesus' words about the "fiery furnace," mentioned above. They make it clear that hell is a real possibility for human beings. You may not like that idea. But the idea is clear and understandable. You can't treat it like a fish bone.

• • • • • • • • • • • • • • • • • • •

American author Mark Twain claimed that "Most people are bothered by those Scripture passages which they cannot understand. But for me, the passages in Scripture which trouble me most are those which I do understand."

• • • • • • • • • • • • • • • • • • •

That brings us to an important point. The gap between us and the Bible's original audience is not as big as we might think. The fact is, the prophets of the Old Testament and Jesus and His apostles of the New Testament were not always accepted or understood. Some people heard them gladly and responded with joy. But the majority did not. The faith of the Bible has always been a minority faith—not because people can't fathom it, but more often because they can fathom it and simply can't accept it. The Bible writers always taught a higher morality than most people actually practiced. Some people responded to this by saying, "Yes, that's for me!" Others responded with "Killjoys! Fanatics! Puritans!" Some things never change.

A "BOWL OF FISH BONES," THE BOOK OF PSALMS

I admit that Psalms is my favorite book of the Old Testament. Many people across the centuries have agreed with me. Besides being the longest (150 psalms altogether), it is also the richest emotionally. The 150 poems run the gamut of spiritual feeling—dejection, joy, doubt, ecstasy, anger, sorrow, gratitude. In all these poems the key character is the same: the God of Israel. The authors of the Psalms didn't just wallow in their own feelings. They always came back to a higher reality: the God who is in control of everything. Behind all the psalms—even the ones that express doubt or anger—is a strong belief in a God who is both just and merciful.

The Israelites and their descendants, the Jews, loved and still love the Psalms. More than any other book of the Old Testament it brings together the people's beliefs—and feelings—about their God. It was so well-loved by the Jews that the New Testament authors (most of whom were Jews) quoted it frequently. Jesus Himself quoted from it many, many times. The early Christians accepted the Psalms as their own. They had no doubts that the Psalms were holy and sacred, and they took them a step further than the Jews had—they saw many of the psalms as predictions of events in the life of Jesus. So they made the Psalms a Christian book, and it was and is a favorite book for Christians.

In the process of adopting the book as their own, the Christians often read meanings into the psalms that the original authors may not have intended. Take for example, the ending of the popular "Shepherd Psalm,"

Psalm 23: "I will dwell in the house of the LORD forever." As far as we can tell, the ending of the psalm in its original Hebrew meant "I will live in the Lord's temple the rest of my life." The psalm did not seem to be talking about the afterlife, heaven. (You'll find that that is actually a rare idea in the Old Testament.) But when Christians read this verse, they couldn't help but find an "enriched" meaning in it. After all, the first Christians believed strongly in eternal life with God in heaven. So, they believed this verse in Psalm 23 had a new "fulfilled" meaning. They believed that "dwell in the house of the LORD forever" meant "live with God in heaven forever." You can argue whether it is right to "read in" a new meaning to part of the Old Testament. But Christians did it for centuries. It has probably not done any harm.

Unfortunately, the Psalms are full of "fish bones" that cause some readers to choke. Since you probably will—and definitely should—read the Psalms, let's point out some of the things that cause readers problems.

A. Vindictiveness

The New Testament emphasizes loving our enemies, forgiving people who are cruel to us. Mercy is supposed to be a Christian trait. But many of the psalms have a very different spirit. Some are even called "songs of vengeance." Consider this example from Psalm 137:8-9: "O Daughter of Babylon, doomed to destruction, happy is he who repays you for what you have done to us—he who seizes your infants and dashes them against the rocks." Here is another example, from Psalm 35:3-4: "Brandish spear and javelin against those who pursue me.... May those who seek my

TWO THOUSAND YEARS AGO, BUT FEELS LIKE NOW

In your mind's eye, picture a society undergoing significant changes. This society had been founded by people dedicated to freedom and equality. These people emphasized simple living and sneered at pomp and aristocracy. They wanted a society based on individual achievement, not inherited wealth. As this society grew and expanded, new lands were added. But all were included in this vision of freedom and equality.

Things changed. As time passed, the government began to promise the citizens more and more things. Most people still preferred to manage their own lives and create the good life by their own efforts. But an ever-expanding government became more eager to hand out "benefits." And the more benefits handed out, the greater the number of people willing to accept them. This society became a magnet for the lazy and idle. This was especially true in the cities, which became miniature welfare states.

Art and literature changed. In the old days the authors and artists had been restrained, hoping to inspire and entertain people in ways that would make no one blush. But decay set in. Many authors and artists chose to shock and titillate rather than to enlighten. Many sensitive people lamented the changes in literature and art. But some government officials and wealthy people applauded the degraded "art," and even bestowed government support on it.

The government could afford to be generous. As the society had grown, it had more people to tax. It could tax more and spend more. The beneficiaries of the spending applauded—and begged for more. After all, wasn't the government like a doting parent with limitless resources?

Entertainment was an obsession. The society in its young days had leisure time, but it emphasized hard work too. The society in decay emphasized play. Professional sports were on everyone's mind, and egotistical pro athletes became overpaid heroes. This went along with a general focus on the body. People became fanatical about what they ate. On the one hand, people gorged themselves when they could. On the other hand, they went to great lengths to have youthful figures.

In the area of morals, relativism became the rule. The old rules governing business ethics and sexual morals seemed to break down. Some protradition voices were heard, but as time passed the rule was . . . no rule. A "do your own thing" attitude pervaded moral choices. The ideas of restraint and self-denial seemed old-fashioned. The old norm of a close-knit family that passed on the traditional morals fell by the wayside.

And religion? There were lots of them, scattered across a wide spectrum of beliefs and moralities. The society had no one religion that bound it together, and no longer even a system of core beliefs that everyone accepted. Any new teacher of religion or philosophy could get a hearing in the marketplace of ideas. Some would not be accepted, but most could find a loyal following. So across the society, and especially in the urban centers, every form of religion prospered—goddess worship, nature worship, astrology, channeling, reincarnation, pantheism and, perhaps most popular, a glorified self-centeredness that cast a halo around every individual's desires. If you read polls, you would believe the people were very religious. Probing deeper, you would find that their beliefs were all over the map.

One rule held true in the sphere of religion: ABTOR—Anything But the Old Religion. People were confused about religion, but they weren't confused about one thing: the old religious orthodoxy of the society's founders was boring, old-fashioned, not worth considering. A few tradition-minded people said, "No, the old beliefs are still valid." But they were a tiny minority. Around them swirled a sea of strange and conflicting beliefs and moral attitudes.

What society is—or was—this? Our own today—or the Roman Empire of the New Testament period. You see, after 2,000 years, *we still live in the New Testament world.* The world of the Old Testament is like our own—but in some ways so radically different. But in the New Testament world we can feel right at home. Lay aside the differences in technology, and we're basically the same people.

One key difference between our world and the New Testament world is that in their day, the scorned Old Religion was the old belief system of the Roman republic. In our day, the Old Religion is . . . Christianity. True, Christianity is alive and well—and making great strides in Latin America and Africa. But in the U.S. and Europe, Christianity is . . . well, the unfashionable religion of a bygone era. In the New Testament period Christianity had an advantage: it was a new thing, so many people gave it a hearing.

Despite the times, Christianity has proved amazingly durable. It is, as one historian noted, "an anvil that has worn out many hammers."

life be disgraced and put to shame; may those who plot my ruin be turned back in dismay." These are only two of many, many psalms that express the author's rage. Instead of saying,"Lord, bless our enemies," these vengeful psalms say, "Crush them, Lord!"

From psalms like these we get the idea of vengeful authors. Even worse, they portray God as vengeful also. Some of the psalm writers speak as if God's purpose in the universe was to let loose His wrath on the writers' enemies.

A sensitive reader asks, "What do we have to gain from reading these mean-spirited, un-Christian poems?" One answer is to put them aside—like fish bones. You could do that, then go on to concentrate on the other psalms that are more inspiring.

But you can learn something from the vengeful psalms. First, you learn that hate was socially acceptable in ancient times. In our civilization we try to keep our strong feelings to ourselves. (That may be changing, if you've followed politics in recent years.) In the ancient world, people were very blunt about their hatred for an enemy. And most often, the enemies in the Psalms are not individuals, but whole nations— Egyptians, Babylonians, etc. From the vengeful psalms you can learn something about these nations. They were amazingly cruel (something the archaeologists have confirmed). They were not only cruel as enemies, but even their worship services were primitive and cruel (some of them sacrificed children, for example). So it was natural, when Israel was threatened by these cruel nations, to say, "Smash them!" We may say this sounds cruel. Looked at another way, it meant that the Israelites had a deep sense of justice. They took right and wrong seriously, and that in itself is a very good thing.

We don't like the image of God as Judge. In our day we think that judgmental is one of the nastiest things we can say about someone. But the Hebrews didn't see it this way. God the Divine Judge was the one who would bring justice—punishing the wicked, releasing the good and rewarding them, righting all wrongs. As a small nation surrounded by larger (and crueler) nations, Israel had good reason to want this kind of justice. To an oppressed people, stripped of their possessions, the news that the Judge is coming is wonderful news.

B. Self-righteousness

This is heartily condemned in the New Testament, notably by Jesus. It has no place in the Christian life. But it definitely has a place in some of the psalms. Consider three examples: (1)"I have kept the ways of the LORD; I have not done evil by turning from my God" (18:21); (2)"Look upon my suffering and deliver me, for I have not forgotten Your law" (119:153); (3)"Judge me, O LORD, according to my righteousness, according to my integrity, O Most High" (7:8). Isn't this self-righteous boasting? Could a Christian pray these words? Didn't Jesus warn against such an attitude?

Yes, He did. We have to think of these self-righteous passages as fish bones. This is easy to do because so many other psalms are quite the opposite: heartfelt confessions of sin. Psalm 51 is one of the greatest confessions in all the world's writings. It and several others (notably 32 and 38) remind us that the true follower of God should be conscious of his own failings.

But, for the record, we can sympathize with the self-righteousness in some of the psalms. Remember, the psalms weren't really meant for one person's solitary reading. They were hymns, things used in group worship, usually at the temple in Jerusalem. When the self-righteous psalms speak of "my righteousness" and "my integrity," the people were actually thinking of "our righteousness." There was a strong "us" feeling in Israel, particularly since they saw themselves as God's chosen nation. Think of the self-righteousness this way: the nation of Israel, with all its faults, still compared well to the immoral and cruel nations around.

C. Absence of belief in an afterlife

As noted earlier, the whole Old Testament comes up short in this area. Only a handful of verses—none of them in the Psalms—

hint at a happy afterlife with God.

What you will find in Psalms are clear indications that there is no afterlife at all:

No one remembers you when he is dead. Who praises you from the grave? (6:5)

He will join the generation of his fathers, who will never see the light of life (49:19).

Do you show your wonders to the dead? Do those who are dead rise up and praise you?(88:10)

What man can live and not see death, or save himself from the power of the grave? (89:48)

It is not the dead who praise the LORD, those who go down to silence (115:17).

These are typical. You will find psalms that express a belief that God will "save me from death" or "deliver them from death." But these refer to deliverance in this life, not complete deliverance after death. Does this shock you? It shouldn't. The Old Testament hints at an afterlife, but does not show a strong belief in it. When the Israelites thought of God rewarding or punishing people, they thought of this life only, not the next.

But sometime before the New Testament period, belief began to change. Jesus was not unusual in believing in heaven and hell. Most of His fellow Jews shared the belief, and the Christians followed Jesus' lead. When did the belief creep in? Why hadn't God made the belief clear to the earlier people of Israel? Simply put, we don't know. Consider this a fish bone. Be thankful that the New Testament does contain a powerful belief in eternity.

chapter 5

Life of the Heart: ◄
Devotional Reading of the Bible

SOME BASIC RULES FOR STUDY

Below I've listed several different approaches to studying the Bible. All of them are useful for either Bible beginners or longtime readers. All of them work best if you follow obvious guidelines.

A. Do it regularly

This seems obvious enough. We exercise our bodies regularly, work regular hours at our jobs, watch a favorite TV show at a reg-

Scripture does not aim at imparting scientific knowledge, and therefore it demands from men nothing but obedience.
—BARUCH SPINOZA, PHILOSOPHER (1632–1677)

ular time, eat regularly (oh, yes!), read the newspaper regularly. In short, most significant acts in our lives are done regularly. If you plan to become familiar with the Bible, you should count on doing it regularly—and *daily* is the best choice for most people. A

time in your day when you can have the fewest distractions is best, naturally. This might be just after waking, just before bedtime, during a bus or train commute, during a coffee break—whenever allows you to give it your undivided attention.

B. Set a reasonable goal of time you can commit

Assuming you can study daily, set a general goal of time—say, fifteen minutes, twenty minutes, whatever you feel is both reasonable and adequate. Anything less than fifteen minutes probably won't allow the material to sink in very deeply. If the time commitment seems like a burden, consider the amount of time you spend exercising (for some people, an hour or more a day) or reading mindless drivel or listening to people talk trash on radio and TV. (Don't get the idea that "quality time" with the Bible can mean three quick minutes. Quality is important, but give some thought to *quantity* too.)

C. Use a Bible you're comfortable with

Comfortable means two things. One, we mean literally comfortable—a typeface you can read easily. A pocket-size Bible can be handy, but if it's hard to read, you probably won't read it. Two, comfortable means a translation you can easily understand. (See pages 49–52 for a discussion of some good contemporary translations.)

D. Learn to underline

Many people (this author included) are firm believers in underlining. I firmly believe that your basic tool in Bible study is an underliner—either a regular pen or, even better, a highlighter. You can underline for different purposes. A passage or verse may inspire you, puzzle you, even irritate you. You might choose to mark passages in different colors—yellow for verses that inspire you, green for those that puzzle you, etc. The point is underlining lets you interact with the Bible. As you study more, you'll find yourself coming back to places you've underlined— re-experiencing the glow you felt when you first underlined, or perhaps pausing to think why that passage impressed you at an earlier time.

E. Take notes

Let's not underestimate the hand-brain connection. Many people can study material closely and absorb it all—without ever writing anything down. But most of us can't. The fact is "putting it in writing" is good for us, mentally speaking. Reading a Bible passage and asking yourself "How do

I respond to this?" is good. Writing down your response to that question is much better. Writing has a way of clarifying. Thoughts can be vague, shapeless, badly defined. Put on paper, they make more sense. Or, to put it another way, if our thoughts are badly defined, putting them on paper will make us see just how badly defined they are.

A technological note: This book does not assume that you have a computer. But you might have one, so when I say "write down" or "take notes," assume I'm referring to either the old method (pen and paper) or the new method (your fingers on a computer keyboard). The computer has been delightfully liberating for people like me whose handwriting is so atrocious that writing notes would be pointless, since I often can't decipher my own scribbling. In front of a computer, many people's fingers can function almost as fast as their brains can. And it's all nice and legible. A resounding "Hallelujah!" for the advancement of computer technology. If you're so inclined, use your computer. It can make note-taking on the Bible and your own spiritual life a pleasant experience.

F. Don't be afraid to ask questions

No one is an expert about every subject. You aren't an expert in the Bible (or you probably wouldn't be reading this book). One nice thing about studying the Bible is that it levels the playing field: a Ph.D. in physics may know as little (or as much) about the Bible as a clerk in a shoe store. So don't feel stupid if you need help.

The book you're holding in your hands anticipates some of the basic questions you may have as you study the Bible. In chapter 14 you'll find a useful glossary, Bridging the Culture Gap, with key words and ideas that pop up again and again in the Bible. This section explains those in a clear, concise, nonacademic way. It won't answer every question, but it will answer some of the most common ones.

Don't be afraid to avail yourself of Bible dictionaries and other helps. You'll find these explained in chapter 15.

Don't be afraid to call on a friend, either. If you know someone who seems very much "at home" with the Bible, he or she can probably answer a lot of the questions you have.

APPROACH 1:
A SINGLE BOOK

The sixty-six books of the Bible range in length from one chapter (Obadiah, Philemon, Jude, and others) to the very long Book of Psalms. Most of the books could be read through in one sitting. This is one way to approach the Bible if you're new to it or want to become reacquainted.

Since Christians see Jesus as the key figure of the Bible, it makes sense to start with one of the four Gospels, the four New Testament books that tell Jesus' story. These are not full-length biographies—certainly not as long as modern-day book-length biographies of famous people. Any of the four Gospels could be read in one sitting—say, two hours or less. Let's say you want to start with the first Gospel, Matthew.

A. Read it through

Simply put, read the whole thing from beginning to end, without writing anything down and without consulting any reference books. Just read the entire Gospel of Matthew. The biggest "snag" in Matthew is at the very beginning—Jesus' genealogy, tracing His ancestry from the Hebrew patriarch Abraham. The genealogy runs from Matthew 1:1 to 1:17. Breeze through this long list of names and start the real story at 1:18. This is familiar turf: the Christmas story—Mary, Joseph, the wise men, the star of Bethlehem. For the rest of the book you'll find Jesus as teacher and miracle-worker. He teaches people, He heals people. The main segment of teaching is chapters 5–7, known as the Sermon on the Mount. As you read this section, you'll probably note that some of these wise sayings sound familiar. Toward the end of the

> *We ought to listen to the Scriptures with the greatest caution, for as far as our understanding of them goes, we are like little children.*
> —AUGUSTINE, A THEOLOGIAN (354–430)

Gospel of Matthew, it becomes clear that Jesus is facing opposition. He riles up the Jewish religious establishment, and they, in cahoots with the Roman Empire's officials, arrange to have Jesus executed by crucifixion. He dies but after being buried is miraculously raised to life. He commissions His followers to preach His message to the whole world.

With this first reading, don't write anything down. That can be done in a later step. But do make some mental notes. Ask yourself these questions:

• What are the main themes here?

• Who are the main characters?

• What words or phrases crop up again and again in the book?

• What does the book teach about morals and behavior?

• What does the book communicate about the nature of God?

• What is my immediate, gut-level response to the book?

> *You can learn more about human nature by reading the Bible than by living in New York.*
> —WILLIAM LYON PHELPS, AMERICAN LITERARY CRITIC (1865–1943)

B. Read it again, with pen in hand

This step doesn't have to immediately follow the first reading. But don't wait too long, or you may forget much of what you read the first time. Try to time the second reading to within 72 hours of the first one.

This time, read the book with a notepad and pen handy. As you read, take time to pause and answer the questions listed in the previous section. Also write down:

• Chapter and verse numbers of sections you don't understand.

• Words and names you don't understand.

• Chapter and verse numbers of sections you find particularly impressive.

• Chapter and verse numbers of sections you are skeptical about.

This second reading should take a good bit longer than the first. You might not even finish it in one sitting. In this reading you can pause, move back and forth from your notes to the text, flip back to a part of Matthew you've already read.

C. Review your notes and write an outline of the book

Have your Bible open to Matthew, but focus on your notes. What have you learned after two readings of the Gospel of Matthew? If your notes actually list the main themes of Matthew, its main characters, its key words and phrases, its moral teachings, and its view of God—well, then you're way ahead of where you were when you started. If you wrote down chapter and verses of sections that really impressed you, you might reread those sections.

Then, do an outline of the book. This does not have to be as neat and organized as an outline you would do for a term paper. But, with your notes and the Gospel of Matthew open in front of you, write down a rough outline of the book's content. Write it as if you were doing a table of contents for the book, so that another person could read the table and get a good idea of what Matthew contains.

D. If your Bible has study notes, read the notes on Matthew

Some Bibles are straight Bible text, nothing more. But most have some form of notes and study aids. At the bare minimum, most have a few introductory paragraphs at the beginning of Matthew, plus footnotes that explain things. (See pages 20–21 for an explanation of the different types of Bible footnotes.) If your Bible has notes, read through the notes on Matthew, taking time to read the notes and any introductory paragraphs. These study aids are not the Bible, and they aren't sacred or holy —

meaning, Christians don't consider anything authoritative except the Bible text itself. But the notes and other study aids in most Bibles are reliable and helpful. Chances are they will answer any questions you had during your second reading. If you find those questions answered, write the answers down in your notepad.

E. If your Bible has no study notes, consult a Bible dictionary or a one-volume Bible commentary

In your notes you wrote down chapter and verse numbers of sections that you didn't understand or names and terms that puzzled you. For names and terms, use a handy-size Bible dictionary (*Young's Bible Dictionary* from Tyndale House is a good choice). For sections of Matthew that puzzled you, use a one-volume Bible commentary. A good commentary can usually explain passages that are troubling.

Let's take an example, Matthew 6:22-23:

The eye is the lamp of the body. If your eyes are good, your whole body will be full of light. But if your eyes are bad, your whole body will be full of darkness. If then the light within you is darkness, how great is that darkness!

These are Jesus' words. What do they mean? Even longtime Bible readers puzzle over this passage. In fact, the scholars aren't 100 percent sure of this passage's meaning. It isn't, we gather, concerned with any physical eye problem—something an optometrist would treat. You'll find that commentaries don't explain the pas-

sage very well. This is a case of the fish bone problem we discussed on pages 75–76—something you can't "eat," so push it to the side of the plate for the time being. Matthew 6:22-23 occurs in the middle of a long section that most people find simple and straightforward. So, don't hesitate to push Matthew 6:22-23 to the side of the plate. Your commentary or your Bible's footnotes may do better at explaining other puzzling passages. Don't let your puzzlement over a few passages keep you from enjoying the rest of the book.

(Consider an analogy here. You're reading a Tom Clancy novel, and you come to a paragraph with a lot of techno-jargon in it. Clancy knows what he's talking about, but do you understand every word? Probably not. But chances are you keep reading, emphasizing the parts you *do* understand.)

Let's take another example: the term *Pharisees*. Matthew's Gospel says a lot about these people, particularly in chapter 23. If you're not sure you understand just who they were, or if you just want to know more about them, you could look up *Pharisees* in a Bible dictionary (preferably a smaller one, since the large ones get overly technical).

F. Read Matthew a third time, focusing on how to apply it to your own life

The first two readings were get-acquainted times. Now you can get more serious, more in-depth. Keep in mind that the Bible is never aimed at someone else. It is always directed at whoever reads it. It always confronts the reader—not with a threat, but with the question, "How do you respond to all this?" A related question is, "How does this book apply to the world I'm living in?" After a third reading of Matthew, you could respond to these questions in a number of ways.

• You might admire Jesus' ethical teaching, believe you should apply it to your own life, and attempt to do so.

• You might be in awe (or in doubt) of Jesus' miracles, resulting in a deeper appreciation of divine power (or in more doubt about it).

• You might be in awe (or in doubt) about Jesus' resurrection, resulting in a deeper conviction that Jesus was the Son of God (or in continued doubt about it).

• You might desire to focus not just on appearing religious outwardly, but on being right on the inside—a key theme of Matthew.

G. Try to memorize a key verse that particularly impressed you

Matthew's Gospel is extremely quotable, so it overflows with words that stick in the mind. You might choose, for example, "Come to me, all you who are weary and burdened, and I will give you rest" (11:28). Memorize this passage (writing it down a couple of times always helps), along with the chapter and verse number. For the next week, repeat it to yourself at regular intervals—say, after breakfast, or just before going to sleep. (See chap. 8 for some tips on memorizing.)

What you've just read is an uncomplicated method to read—*study*, rather—one book of the Bible. This method will not turn you into a scholar or expert. It will, however, ensure that you are familiar with at least one book of the Bible—one of the most important, in the case of Matthew.

You could work through all the steps listed earlier, not just with Matthew but with any book of the Bible. If you're fairly new to the Bible, I recommend studying the following books (after you've studied Matthew):

NEW TESTAMENT
Acts
Luke
John
Mark
James
Romans
1 Corinthians
Ephesians
1 Peter
1 John
Hebrews

Any of the New Testament books can be read with profit. The ones listed here are generally the easiest to grasp. The sequence they are listed in is deliberate—that is, most people find Acts easier to grasp than the last book on the list, Hebrews. I generally recommend that people avoid the last New Testament book, Revelation, until they are more familiar with the Bible.

OLD TESTAMENT
Genesis
Exodus
Psalms
Proverbs
Job
1 and 2 Samuel
1 and 2 Kings
Daniel (chaps. 1–6)
Hosea
Amos
Micah

Jonah

Isaiah

Jeremiah

You don't have to read the entire New Testament before studying the Old, but I recommend with the single-book approach that you read at least three New Testament books before moving on to the Old Testament. The sequence of books I've listed here is just a suggestion, based on how most people react to Old Testament books. The easier books to grasp are the first ones listed—that is, Genesis is easier for most readers than Jeremiah is. The Old Testament books not listed here are not bad or unreadable—they are just less readable than the ones listed here. Most people who have read the Bible through will assure you that Job is more rewarding to read than Leviticus.

Turn to chapters 12–13 for summaries of

The Bible is a book of faith, and a book of doctrine, and a book of morals, and a book of special revelation from God.
—AMERICAN STATESMAN DANIEL WEBSTER (1782–1852)

each book of the Bible. This might help you decide which to study.

A special note to those readers who may be getting reacquainted with the Bible after a few years: An excellent place to begin is the Book of Acts. It's a good action book, one that shows how the new faith (Christianity) spread in a culture that had as much diversity as our own.

APPROACH 2:
A SINGLE PASSAGE

A *passage* is a connected unit of the Bible—say, Matthew 5–7, known as Jesus' Sermon on the Mount. Another well-loved passage is 1 Corinthians 13, the Bible's famous chapter on love. In chapter 11 you'll find a list of great sections of the Bible—"Great Stories," "Great Passages," "Old Testament Highlights," "New Testament Highlights," etc. Studying any of these is a good introduction to the Bible's main teachings and key characters.

Choose a passage from that list and read it straight through without stopping. Any of them can be read through in 15 minutes or less.

Then read the passage again, slowly, and this time make some notes.

• Summarize the passage in a paragraph or two. If the passage tells a story, summarize the story and characters. If the passage is teaching, summarize the main ideas.

• Give the passage a title. This could be a short summary of the summary you just wrote. Or you could phrase it in some catchy, clever way—as if you were packaging it to advertise.

• Write down what the passage seems to say about what God is like. Loving? Just? Holy? Angry at sin? Forgiving?

• Write down what the passage says about human nature.

• Write down any moral commands that the passage contains. You might quote these exactly, or restate them in your own words.

• Write down any promises from God in the passage. Again, you can quote these or restate them in your own words.

• Write down any contemporary situations

that you think the passage applies to. For example, if you're studying 1 Corinthians 13, the "love chapter," it might strike you that the contemporary divorce rate would be different if married couples remembered these words from the passage: "Love does not delight in evil but rejoices with the truth. It always protects, always trusts, always hopes, always perseveres."

• Write down anything about the passage you don't understand. You can look these up in a Bible dictionary or commentary. If you still don't understand the parts that

> *What you bring away from the Bible depends to some extent to what you carry to it.*
> —OLIVER WENDELL HOLMES, AMERICAN AUTHOR (1809–1894)

puzzle you, don't despair. The Bible has fish bones, parts that puzzle us but shouldn't keep us from reading and enjoying the parts that we do understand. Lay the fish bones to the side of the plate and keep reading.

If you applied this approach to all the passages listed in chapter 11 (and this would take a while), you would have a very good exposure to the high points of the Bible.

APPROACH 3: PURSUE A TOPIC

You may have a subject that is eating at you—divorce, child-rearing, money, heaven and hell, whatever. If you knew the Bible by heart, you could probably call to mind what the Bible says on these subjects. But hardly anyone knows the Bible by heart, not even people who have read it for years. So it's OK to get a little help as you trace a topic through the Bible.

Here, two study aids can help you greatly: a concordance and a topical Bible. (See chap. 15 for more about these.) The concordance lists words in alphabetical order, showing where they occur in the Bible. A topical Bible actually shows the passages where the topic is covered.

Let's say you're interested in what the Bible says about money. You could look up "money" in a topical Bible and it would show you the most important Bible passages on that subject. It would also refer you to related sections—say, "wealth" or "riches" or "possessions."

You could also look up "money" in a concordance. It would point you to every Bible verse that contains that word. (You'd have to look up each verse yourself, of course.) To really cover the topic, though, you'd need to look under all related words—again, "wealth," "riches," "possessions," and even "gold" and "silver." If you're really interested in the topic or word, look up each verse in the Bible. Write each verse down, or at least the ones that say something significant.

A good Bible dictionary (like *Young's Bible Dictionary*) can be useful when studying a topic. So can a very useful book called *A Theological Word Book of the Bible*. In spite of its title, it looks at most topics of interest, not just ones that are "theological."

When you've worked through all the verses (including ones with related words like "wealth"), look back through what you've written down. Try to summarize in a paragraph or two what the Bible says—

as a whole—on this topic. If a few of the verses seem to contradict each other, look beyond that and ask: "What is the teaching of most of these verses on the subject?"

Then write down what these verses mean in terms of behavior. In other words, if you take all these verses seriously, what impact will they have (if any) on your own behavior? Are there any changes you would—or should—make? What are they? What effect do they have on your attitude toward God? Toward other people? What major changes (if any) have occurred in your life as a result of studying this particular topic?

Many people enjoy the topical approach. One thing you need to beware of is choosing a topic that is too big. "Love," for example, is an excellent topic—but so broad that you could be looking up verses for days. Narrow a broad topic. Instead of pursuing the broad topic of love, focus on God's love for us, or our love for God, or love for other people. Each of these is also a broad topic, but more manageable than just love in general. One suggestion: focus on "love of neighbor." Use a concordance to find where "neighbor" occurs in the Bible. You'll find it refers not just to the person living next door, but to people we encounter in life—not always pleasant people, but people that the Bible instructs us to show compassion to anyway. You can have some interesting discussions about the Bible's instruction not to love mankind in general, but to love the actual flesh-and-blood "neighbors" we encounter every day—quite a challenge!

One other hazard to guard against: You may choose a subject you like, such as "Jesus' sayings about God's love." This is a great topic, one worthy of study. *But,* realize that when you study a particular topic, you ought to balance it with its "flip side." No one in the Bible said more about God's love than Jesus did. But the flip side is that Jesus had a lot to say about hell and damnation—the consequence of ignoring God's love. We tend to choose topics we feel comfortable with, such as God's love. But if you want a good and balanced view of the Bible, try choosing a subject that challenges you and makes you uncomfortable—like judgment or hell, for example. If you really want to challenge yourself and make yourself uncomfortable, do a study of that unsettling topic "the human tongue and the evils it is capable of." The Bible has a lot to say about this subject—and the subject is still relevant, don't you think?

APPROACH 4: A SINGLE VERSE

Call this "micro-study" of the Bible. It involves study—"up-close and personal"—of a single verse of the Bible.

Let's make it clear that this should not be the only approach you use to the Bible. To know the Bible well, you need the "big picture," and to get that you need to read through some entire books, as suggested in Approach 1.

A comparison is in order here. If you wanted to be an expert on Steven Spielberg movies, you would see all the movies he's directed. Doing that would give you an idea of his approach to movie-making. And you'd become familiar with the variety of movies he's done. To really get to know his style well, you might concentrate on one of his movies—say *Raiders of the Lost Ark*. And if you really wanted to study his style in detail, you might pick one scene from *Raiders*, watch it again and again on videotape, closely observing the camera angles, use of sound, acting, lighting, costumes, the set, etc. This kind of close study is enriching. So is watching all his movies. The two approaches are both rewarding, in different ways.

Well, the Bible writers might feel this analogy was appropriate, but they would quickly tell us that the Bible is more important (and even more interesting) than a Spielberg movie. I agree, or else this book you are holding would never have been written.

A. Choose a verse

Don't do this at random (for instance, by opening the Bible and letting your finger fall on the page). That method might select a good verse for study, or it might fall on some law in Leviticus about sacrificing sheep. So choose a verse that you have already run across—say, when you read an entire book or a passage (Approaches 1 and 2) or studied a topic throughout the Bible (Approach 3).

Let's say you read through the entire First Letter of John (known as 1 John, for short). This short letter is "dense"—that is, it's packed full of important teaching about living the Christian life. Let's pick a verse from this letter, "The world and its desires pass away, but the man who does the will of God lives forever" (2:17). This is a good verse to choose because you don't scratch your head wondering what it means, but it is also full of meaning so you can benefit by studying it closely.

B. Read the verse in context

Most Bibles are divided into paragraphs. You might read the whole chapter 2 of 1 John, but definitely read the paragraph that contains 2:17. Ask yourself what the meaning of the entire paragraph is. You'll find that 2:17 is part of a paragraph on the subject of loving the world. The paragraph contrasts the love of the world and its pleasures with the love of God the Father. So 2:17 sort of sums up the paragraph.

C. If you have a commentary, look up the verse

A good commentary can give you additional insights into the verse, getting to the meaning of the original languages. You don't have to know Hebrew and Greek to enjoy and understand the Bible. But be glad that the Bible scholars can explain some of the meanings of Greek and Hebrew words that don't always come through in the English translations.

D. If the verse has footnotes that refer you to other Bible verses, read them

This verse, 1 John 2:17, doesn't have any. Lots of Bible verses do. In the New Testament, many verses have footnotes indicating that the verse is quoting or referring to an Old Testament verse. For example, 1 John 3:12, which mentions Cain and Abel, has a footnote that reads "Genesis 4:8." That footnote refers you to the part of Genesis where Cain, Adam and Eve's son, murders his brother Abel. You might already be familiar with that story. If not, the footnote referring you to Genesis 4:8 would be very helpful.

E. Rewrite the verse in your own words

Try to restate it without using many of the words from the verse. You might restate it by personalizing it. For example, "If I am obedient to the Lord, I live eternally—but everything around me, the things people pursue, aren't made to last."

> The true hero of the Bible is God. All the other men in it are his aides and foot soldiers.
> —THOMAS "STONEWALL" JACKSON, CONFEDERATE GENERAL

F. Apply the verse to your life

First John 2:17 could have several applications. State them in a personal way.

1. Remember that I am made to live eternally.

2. Subordinating my will to God's will is critical.

3. The things in the world that seem so attractive aren't made to last.

APPROACH 5: BIOGRAPHY

Would you rather read a biography or a book of theology? Most people would quickly reply, "A biography." Thankfully, the Bible is much more biography than theology. But in fact, it is both. Instead of giving its theology in the form of dry propositions, it gives theology-in-action—that is, you learn about God and man by watching God interact with people.

The key person for study is, of course, Jesus. His four brief biographies in the New Testament are known as the Gospels. You can, and should, study all four.

But the Bible abounds with fascinating people, and the Bible has no hesitancy about showing them warts and all. Except for Jesus Himself, there are no super-heroes in the Bible. Heroes, yes—but people with flaws and weaknesses, which make them more interesting and also remind the reader again and again that we ought to worship God, not human beings.

If you choose to study a particular person, you will need a concordance. This will show you where to find the Bible passages that concern that person. Or, for the people listed below, you can follow the Bible passages listed in parentheses.

A. Paul the apostle

(Acts 7:58–8:3; 9:1-31; 13–28; 1 Cor. 16; 2 Cor. 6; 10–12; Phil. 1:12-30; 2:19-29; 3:1-11; 2 Tim. 4:9-22; Phile.) In Acts, Paul is the chief character. Combining Acts with some personal passages from Paul's letters, we have a vivid portrait of this fascinating man of faith—missionary, pastor, theologian.

B. David

(1 Sam. 16–31; 2 Sam.; 1 Kings 1–2:12) No Old Testament man's life is shown in such vivid detail as David's. We see him as shepherd boy, giant-killer, musician and poet, warrior, king, bosom friend, husband, adulterer, father, subject of a conspiracy, old man. Most importantly, he is shown as a man of deep and exuberant faith.

C. Samuel

(1 Sam. 1–10; 12–13; 15–16; 25:1, 28) Samuel is prophet, judge, and king-maker.

His story intertwines with those of David and Saul.

D. Saul
(1 Sam. 8–2 Sam. 1) Israel's first king is an inspiring but tragic figure. You could easily spend a long time studying Samuel, Saul, and David together.

E. Abraham
(Gen. 12–25) The "father of the faithful," Abraham is a great role model, even with some noted character flaws. The Israelites looked on Abraham as the nation's true spiritual father. Study him and find out why.

F. Jacob and his twelve sons
(Gen. 27–50) Jacob, also named Israel, is both cunning trickster and man of God. His relations with his twin brother Esau are sometimes amusing, sometimes touching. His favoritism toward a particular son is an object lesson in how *not* to handle one's children.

G. Joseph
(Gen. 37; 39–50) He is the most interesting of Jacob's twelve sons, and the best role model. Some parts of his tale are heart-wrenching. The story never grows old, as proven by the popularity of the musical *Joseph and the Amazing Technicolor Dreamcoat.*

H. Moses
(Ex. 1–20; 32–34; Num. 10:11–14:45; 16:1–17:13; 20–25; Deut. 34) As proven by the ever-popular movie *The Ten Commandments*, Moses' story is never boring. Israel's liberator and law-giver is the most important Old Testament figure (other than God, that is).

I. Gideon
(Jud. 6–8) The great judge (champion) of Israel makes a good short study, with his life occupying only three chapters in Judges.

J. Samson
(Jud. 13–16) The Israelite strongman is both hulk and man of God. No one has ever gotten bored with this story. Samson and the wily Delilah are known even by people who have never opened a Bible.

K. Ruth
(The Book of Ruth, naturally) This sweet story touches everyone who reads it. Ruth is a great role model of faith and womanly devotion.

L. Solomon
(1 Kings 1–11) Son of David and Israel's "golden boy," Solomon is both majestic and, at the end, tragic. Find out why he became the symbol of both wisdom and luxury in Israel.

M. Elijah
(1 Kings 17–19; 21; 2 Kings 1–2) The fiery prophet of the Lord is preacher, miracle-worker, and scolder of the mighty. His confrontations with wicked Queen Jezebel are fascinating.

N. Elisha
(1 Kings 19:16–21; 2 Kings 2–9:13; 13:14-21) Elijah's successor is another miracle-worker and confronter of kings.

O. Hezekiah

(2 Kings 18–20) This man was a rarity—a highly moral king of Israel! His story intertwines with that of the Prophet Isaiah.

P. Josiah

(2 Kings 22:1–23:30) Israel's last king with any moral fiber, Josiah is not only king but reformer, one who meets a tragic end.

Q. Stephen

(Acts 6–7) The first martyr for the Christian faith, and an eloquent speaker to boot, Stephen's final speech to an angry mob makes good reading.

R. Peter

(Acts 1–5; 9:32–12:19; 15:1-21) Peter is the most interesting of Jesus' twelve apostles. Before you study his life in Acts, become familiar with how he is presented in the Gospels.

The Bible is never content to record raw history. It draws morals, so you don't have to guess at what the character's life means. But as you study the life of one of these people, jot down your answers to these questions:

• What are this character's chief virtues?

• What are his or her chief weaknesses?

• How does my own life resemble this person's?

• Is my own life moving in a good (or bad) direction that is similar to this person's life? Can that direction be changed? How?

• What is a key verse or passage from this person's story that is worth memorizing? (You might choose one that in some way summarizes the person's character.)

• What is the one incident in the person's story that sticks in my mind? (This could be something that shows the person at his or her best or worst.)

APPROACH 6: FROM BEGINNING TO END

My feeling about this approach can be summed up in one word: *Don't.* This was a common practice in my grandmother's generation. She readily admits that this practice often became more of a duty than a pleasure—or is there some pleasure in the sacrificial laws of Leviticus that we have not yet discovered? Or in the long genealogies in 1 Chronicles?

This approach seems neat and tidy. If you followed it, you would end up having read the whole Bible, every word. A good idea—except that, if you begin at Genesis 1 and try to get to Revelation, you probably won't make it. Not many people do.

There is an alternative. Try *The One-Year Bible*, published by Tyndale House. This is available in several translations, including the *New International Version*. It neatly divides the Bible into 365 readings for each day of the year. (You can take a break on February 29 in Leap Year, obviously.) *The One-Year Bible* begins on January 1 with the beginning of the Old Testament (Genesis 1) and the New (Matthew 1), plus the Psalms and Proverbs. The beauty of this is that when you're working through some of the less interesting parts of the Old Testament (say, Leviticus, Numbers, 1 Chronicles), you'll still have a good New Testament reading each day. For a read-the-whole-Bible through approach, you probably can't do better than *The One-Year Bible*.

Even if you're using *The One-Year Bible*, I strongly suggest you turn to chapters 12–13 of this book and use the summaries of the Bible's books as a guide. You'll be particularly interested in the sections about **For Those Who Skip . . .** There's no use pretending that the laws of sacrifice in the Book of Leviticus deserve as much of your attention as the Gospel of Luke.

APPROACH 7: PURSUE A CONTEMPORARY ISSUE

This can be very rewarding. It also involves more effort on your part. Many contemporary topics—marriage, money, children, for example—can be studied through Approach 3 mentioned earlier. You might also check to see if your local religious bookstore has a Bible-based study guide to the particular subject that interests you.

APPROACH 8: ALTERNATE THE OTHER SEVEN APPROACHES

Of the eight methods listed in this chapter, is there a "best"? Yes—any of the eight is best compared with the usual approach (not studying the Bible at all). And no—none of the eight is better than the other seven. All eight have their advantages and disadvantages. But all eight will get you deeper into the Bible.

Forgive me for stating the obvious, but people are creatures of habit. If you are willing to break the habit of not reading the Bible (or of reading it very haphazardly, or with no sense of purpose), fine. But most people easily slip into a new habit. So for the sake of variety, change your Bible study habit from time to time. If you've just finished studying the whole Book of Luke, try a topical study of, say, money or marriage. Or, if you've finished a biographical study of Paul, try a micro-study of some selected verses—maybe some verses from Paul's letters, just to reinforce what you've already learned about Paul.

THE FAMILY PLAN

All the approaches discussed in this chapter are suitable for your individual use. All are also suitable for a group. We include some advice on group study in chapter 9. But studying with your family is another matter. It can be done. In fact, if you take the Bible seriously, you should do it.

A. For couples without kids

If your spouse has no interest in studying the Bible, don't try to force it. Marriages are difficult enough without deliberately introducing conflict. On the other hand, do at least throw out the option of studying as a couple. Couples often surprise each other.

"Hon, this may sound crazy, but I'm thinking about studying the Bible for a few minutes each day."

There are several possible responses to this:

"Fine."

"Hrmph."

"So what?"

"What a waste of time. Don't expect to get me involved!"

"Why?"

But one other possible response is:

"Really? I think that might be interesting. . . ."

Or even:

"Really? Maybe that's something we could do together."

Scheduling a regular study time for yourself can be a challenge. Setting aside time for two can be even more of a challenge. On the other hand, if two people can't spare 15 minutes a day of togetherness, what

> Nobody ever outgrows Scripture; the Book widens and deepens with our years.
> —C.H. SPURGEON, THE MOST FAMOUS PREACHER IN VICTORIAN ENGLAND

kind of marriage are we talking about?

Again, you can use any of the approaches described in this chapter. But as a couple, you can introduce some other elements.

1. Read to each other. That is, one reads, the other listens—maybe taking turns on alternate days. The listener can also be the note-taker.

2. Answer all the questions described in the Approach sections earlier in this chapter, but discuss them together. You will probably agree and disagree. One spouse may see something the other didn't.

3. Discuss how the text you're studying applies to your marriage (if indeed it does). If you're studying alone, this is a good question to ask yourself also. But you can certainly have some interesting discussions with your spouse about how the Bible applies to the two of you as a couple.

If the two of you are interested in using the topical method (Approach 3), one logical topic to study is marriage, while anoth-

er is men and women. The Bible has a lot to say about both these topics. Not all of it is appealing to contemporary couples. I can guarantee that a study of Paul's teachings on marriage will definitely generate a lively discussion.

One other suggestion if you study the Bible with your spouse: Be honest with each other about how you react to the material. In a group Bible study, a person is often reluctant to say "This passage is offensive!" or "Oh, come on!" or "I don't grasp this at all!" With your spouse, you don't have to appear pious or wise. The Bible has been around for centuries, so there's nothing you can say about it that hasn't been said before, no criticism that someone else hasn't said already. Don't expect that every sentence in the Bible will be understandable, or that it will square with your own beliefs about God and human behavior. Be willing to wrestle with the Bible—and be willing to change your own opinions too. (You might want to reread the section on the Bible's fish bones in chap. 4).

B. Bringing the kids on board

Children have a built-in advantage over adults: they don't approach the Bible with any prior assumptions. They don't know it's supposed to be dull or boring or old-fashioned—or even holy. So they can do something that too many adults don't allow themselves to do: enjoy it, get lost in it, frolic in its good stories. Kids can enjoy Samson, Noah, David, Paul, Moses, and, yes, Jesus. They probably won't enjoy the long teaching passages in Paul's letters or the laws in parts of the Old Testament. Kids enjoy—and learn—through stories.

A question arises: Aren't parts of the Bible violent—and downright smutty? Answering bluntly, yes, definitely. A book whose central character dies on a cross with nails through His wrists is not, we admit, shy about violence. The violence is there—wars, murders, executions, child sacrifice, you name it. Sex is there too—adultery, prostitution, homosexuality, the whole nine yards. (Mark Twain snickered that some libraries banned

> The greatest source of material for motion pictures is the Bible, and almost any chapter would serve as a basic idea for a motion picture.
> —MOVIE DIRECTOR CECIL B. DEMILLE, FAMOUS FOR *THE TEN COMMANDMENTS*

his "scandalous" books while they kept the Bible on their shelves. It's true that the Bible is more "scandalous" than *Huckleberry Finn*.)

Parents are right to be concerned about their kids' exposure to violence and sex. TV and movies give them enough of it. The Bible has both—but with a radical difference from the sex and violence on TV. In the Bible, sex is not romanticized—unless you count the Song of Songs. The Bible presents marriage as the only moral option. Sex outside marriage is bad—as vividly portrayed in David's adultery with Bathsheba, in the shocking story of the homosexual men of Sodom, in the painful tale of Amnon raping his half sister Tamar. Unlike TV sitcoms, the Bible doesn't snicker at immorality. It is never treated as something to amuse people. So the Bible's frankness about sex is a good antidote to the usual immorality in the media. Be aware that the Old Testament

does seem to take polygamy in stride. The Israelite men who have more than one wife (or concubine) are not condemned for this. The New Testament, however, presents the one-spouse situation as normal (and, incidentally, has a strict view of divorce).

You'll have to judge your own kids' capacity to deal with sexual matters. The older they are, obviously, the more frank you can be. But even with very small children (who probably can't grasp the physical meaning of "adultery"), you can point out the Bible's emphasis on marital fidelity.

In regard to violence, the Bible is a good antidote to the images in the media. TV and movies make violence look like a game. People are shot, blown up, dismembered—then the camera focuses on something else. The Bible shows violence as horrible, not entertaining. Some parts (notably Joshua and Judges) present the troubling picture of God's nation, Israel, slaughtering other people. But generally the Bible—particularly the New Testament—teaches a love ethic that has no place for physical cruelty. Remember that Jesus was the victim of violence, but He made it clear that His followers could not respond with violence.

If your kids are twelve or under, you may not be able to use all the Approaches described earlier. Because kids are interested in stories and characters, you could choose to focus on a character (Approach 5) or on a single book (Approach 1) if the book has enough action (the Gospels, Acts, 1 and 2 Samuel). You can use all the discussion questions listed in this chapter, but you may need to (pardon the expression) "dumb them down" some.

Another option might be for you (either individually or with your spouse) to pursue your own Bible study plan, *and* another with your kids. These could be on totally different tracks or on the same one. For example, you might be studying the Book of 1 Samuel. You study separately for twenty minutes per day, then you read your children a Bible storybook about Samuel, Saul, and David. Because you're studying those characters yourself, there's no harm in reinforcing your learning by sharing their stories with the kids. In fact, as all teachers know, there's a lot to be said for having to retell a story for kids. For one thing, it forces you to use your imagination. Instead of just reading through a story (say, David and Goliath, or Daniel in the lions' den) without giving much thought to it, retelling the story for your kids forces you to visualize it, dramatize it, focus on some visual details, verbalize what the characters' thoughts and feelings were. Retelling a story for kids also forces you to get to the "meat" of it. What's important here? What's the bottom line? Dumbing down a Bible story isn't a bad thing—it means you're making a story simple enough and clear enough for a child to understand. Generations of people who were exposed to the Bible as children prove that it can be done.

Every bookstore in America can supply you with Bible storybooks for every age level of child. These are good—especially if you're not too familiar with the Bible yourself. (There's also a well-kept secret about Bible storybooks for kids: because they present material simply and directly, they're often more appealing to adults than guides written for adults.)

But don't pass up a chance to have fun with your kids—and exercise your own mind and imagination at the same time. If your kids are willing, share a Bible story time together, with you (or you and your spouse together) as both storyteller and actor. Have fun with it, even ham it up if you like. Parents forget that they themselves can amuse their own kids—a nice alternative to the Mighty Morphin Power Rangers and the Teenage Mutant Ninja Turtles. You can have a good time, bond with your kids, reinforce your own learning of the Bible, and teach some moral lessons.

Let's state the obvious: the earlier you start this with your children, the better. Teach them that the Bible is "user-friendly." It can be enjoyed. It can teach life lessons. It can be enjoyed by the whole family. It does not have to be just a "church book."

Your children may even learn that Dad and Mom are good entertainment, not just the purchasers of TVs and VCRs.

C. The teen factor

If you have children above age fourteen—or if you *are* a teen yourself—you can use any of the Approaches listed earlier. A teen who willingly engages in Bible reading with his family is . . . well, remarkable and rare. A teen who chooses to study the Bible on his own is probably more common. At the age when the teen is "finding himself," the desire to study the Bible alone is something you should encourage, not discourage.

Sometime around age eleven or so, children discover they can say no to parents. (Actually, they discover this much earlier, but it becomes more pleasant to them sometime around age eleven.) Even if they have been in the habit of sharing family activities (including Bible reading), they may try to opt out. It does not mean they've forever turned against the Bible. It means they're being kids. Some come back to it eventually, some don't. If you want your kids to like the Bible, don't feel guilty about that desire. If they have seen you studying it, enjoying it, even living by its teachings, and if you have exposed them to it in early childhood, you have done all you can do. They do reach an age when too much effort by you is perceived as "ramming it down their throats." Just what constitutes "ramming"? No one agrees on this. Many adults claim they detest the Bible because their parents "rammed it down their throats." Other adults glow as they talk about how their parents taught them the Bible. If you think you can predict which of those groups your own children will fall into, you are probably overestimating your predictive powers. Hope for the best, and don't beat yourself if your children won't share your feeling for the Bible.

READ-ALOUD TIME?

In the ancient world, reading always meant reading aloud—never silently to oneself. (None of this "Shhh!" or "Quiet, please" in libraries.) People just assumed that the written word had to be "brought to life" by speech. In our own day, a subway car might be filled with readers, each person reading something by himself, silently. This wouldn't happen in Bible times. A scroll—the ancient version of book—was a public, not private, message. It was intended to be shared. There was a "community" feeling about literature. Only a few rich people had private libraries, so most of the scrolls that circulated were shared. In other words, it was highly unusual for one person to read the Bible by himself. Chances are someone else would be within hearing distance.

What would those ancient folks have thought about a Walkman playing a book-on-tape? Maybe they'd ask, "Hey, if that book's good, why are you keeping it to yourself?"

chapter 6

Yes? No? Maybe?
Decision-Making and the Bible

Should I marry Chris?"

"Should I have an abortion?"

"Should I take the kids to Disney World or the mountains?"

"Should I wear my blue or gray suit today?"

"Should I return this wallet I found to its owner?"

"Should I stick with my old job or look for something new?"

"Should I have waffles or pancakes for breakfast?"

"Should I . . . ?" Every day you make decisions, which means you make choices—some of them moral choices, some mere matters of taste. Some major, some minor. Some can affect your whole future. Some will have no effect beyond the next five minutes.

This is the way God designed us—so the Bible tells us. He made us free, capable of choosing the good or the bad. Under the name of *sin* are the bad choices, the things that (according to God) are bad for us and for everyone. The Bible never assumes

that you will escape making bad choices. In fact, the only person presented as sinless in the Bible is Jesus. Everyone else—even great heroes like David and Moses—made bad choices. That's the bad news. The good news is that God is always willing to forgive. The other good news is that we can be guided so that we make fewer mistakes. This is a combination that attracts many people to the Bible: guidance to keep us from failing, but a God who forgives our failures.

Of course, if you want guidance in life, you don't have to go to the Bible. Guidance is easy to find elsewhere. The bookstore shelves are bulging with books about "taking control of your own life." The airwaves are also full of advice. Psychologists and other self-appointed "experts" pour out their free advice via radio every day. Some of their advice seems sound, some seems ridiculous. The same goes for the advice of friends, coworkers, and family members. Many people are eager to give advice (even if their own lives are in shambles). If you're wise, you probably take most of it with a grain of salt. But the world is so confusing and so full of choices that most of us do feel a powerful urge to get help of some kind.

Because you're reading this chapter, I assume you believe the Bible can give us moral guidance. In all the history of Christianity (and Judaism also), believers have assumed that the Bible was more than a book of history or theology. They believe that the Bible shows us what God wants for human life. They believe that God's will for us is not that we be strangled by thousands of rules, but that we have some plain, basic guidelines that make us better human beings—if we follow them.

WAYS PEOPLE USE THE BIBLE IN DECISION-MAKING

I can think of several ways to approach the Bible as a basis for decision-making.

A. The Bible has commandments for leading a moral life

Some people like to emphasize the parts of the Bible that have clear-cut moral commands. The Ten Commandments are an example: "Do not murder." "Do not steal." "Do not commit adultery." It is quite clear that some things are definitely and completely prohibited in the Bible. Where it speaks clearly, there is no argument. You cannot steal

Some Things Never Change

The ancient world was a violent place—no assault rifles or nuclear weapons, but plenty of swords, knives, spears, and such. The Book of Psalms contains songs directed against the cruel enemies of Israel. Naturally, these poems contain references to weapons of war and destruction.

But in fact the authors of the Psalms spent a lot more time talking about a really dangerous weapon:

You destroy those who tell lies; bloodthirsty and deceitful men the LORD abhors (5:6).

Not a word from their mouth can be trusted; their heart is filled with destruction. Their throat is an open grave; with their tongue they speak deceit (5:9).

Everyone lies to his neighbor; their flattering lips speak with deception (12:2).

Your tongue plots destruction; it is like a sharpened razor, you who practice deceit (52:2).

They sharpen their tongues like swords and aim their words like deadly arrows (64:3).

They make their tongues as sharp as a serpent's; the poison of vipers is on their lips (140:3).

These are the tip of the iceberg. There are many more similar verses from the Psalms. The Book of Psalms has been called many things. It could be called "The Book of God's Contempt for Cruel Speech." The psalm writers were apparently well-acquainted with the weapon that did more harm than all the swords of the Babylonians and Assyrians.

The Psalms' view of the lethal power of the tongue reflects the whole Bible's view. Both Old and New Testaments make it clear that God has a low view of people who use their tongues to do harm.

The next time you hear of Christians joining in an antinuclear rally, ask yourself: Has anyone ever staged an anti-tongue rally?

Maybe someone should. (Publicize it by word of mouth . . .)

your neighbor's lawn mower and hope that you'll find part of the Bible that will condone what you did. On some issues the Bible is refreshingly clear.

The problem is, it doesn't issue direct commandments about everything. A married man knows that the Bible commands him not to cheat on his wife. But does it forbid him from paging through *Playboy?* In terms of direct commandments, no, it doesn't. The Bible makes it clear that we shouldn't engage in cheating and swindling on the job. But it gives no command regarding changing careers, or how to know if a particular job is "right" for us. We are told not to murder—clear enough, but if someone is attacking your spouse or children, what if you kill that person? Commandments are simple; life is complex.

B. The Bible gives us moral direction by showing us role models of faith

In addition to seeing the Bible as a book of moral rules, we can find moral guidance by looking at the lives of faithful men and women in the Bible. By studying the words and acts of Moses, Paul, David, Ruth and, above all, Jesus Himself, we learn about moral responsibility and the life of faith. Rather than just focusing on rules, we can focus on people who embody the moral life.

Role models can work in reverse, too. King David is shown as being, generally, a good man, a real man of God. But his moral failures are depicted in painful detail in the Bible. We see David warts and all—David the loyal friend, the joyous lover of God, the forgiving king, but also David the adulterer,

the overindulgent father, the all-too-human human. We can learn a lot by reading about David's forgiveness toward his enemy Saul (1 Sam. 24), but also by reading about his adultery with Bathsheba (2 Sam. 11–12). Morally, David shows us what to do and what to avoid.

We all face situations that may not correspond to any faced by the people in the Bible. Many of their problems and quandaries were similar to ours—but not all. The issue of abortion, for example, is never directly addressed in the Bible.

C. The Bible's moral guidance comes to us when we focus on God

The Bible tells us a lot about God. He is Creator of everything, the Savior who rescues us from our selfishness and sins, and the Spirit who lives within our own hearts and consciences to guide us daily. Beyond focusing on rules or on role models of faith, we can also focus on God Himself. When we know more about Him, we have a clearer idea of how He wishes us to live. Reading the Bible, we see that God is holy, just, merciful, forgiving, caring. He wants our freely given love and fellowship.

The Bible tells us not to try to be God, but to imitate Him: "Be imitators of God, therefore, as dearly loved children" (Eph. 5:1). We are to be "chips off the old block," trying to be what God is (except Almighty, of course). To do this we must know what He is like. We learn more about Him by reading the Bible, and also by getting to know Him up close and personal. And the more we know Him the more guidelines we have for making moral decisions.

D. The Bible teaches us to love

Jesus proclaimed that there were really only two commandments: "'Love the Lord your God with all your heart and with all your soul and with all your strength and with all your mind' and, 'Love your neighbor as yourself'" (Luke 10:27). He also told His followers, "A new command I give you: Love one another. As I have loved you, so you must love one another" (John 13:34). Doesn't this sound much better (and perhaps easier) than following a set of rules? The whole New Testament emphasizes this theme: love is more important than rules.

The difficulty with love, as the Bible pictures it, is that love for others and for God may involve self-denial. It may lead us to do things that go against our natural instincts. As wonderful as love sounds, the self-giving love that the Bible talks about may be far different from the love spoken of in pop songs and movies. Paul's description of love in 1 Corinthians 13 is radically different from the selfish love in Top Forty songs. It is clear in the Bible that "love" is not a synonym for temporary lust. It is clear that love doesn't necessarily involve physical attraction to a person—or even liking him very much. It involves seeking another's welfare, not just satisfying our own urges. Most of us learn about this kind of love in our families, where we are often angry or irritated with our parents, siblings, and children. So many times we feel we really don't *like* our relatives. But we love them anyway because . . . well, because it seems the right thing to do.

All four views of the Bible listed above are perfectly valid. Actually, a person could hold more than one view—perhaps even all four. We should know the Bible's direct commandments. We should know its

> *This great Book is the best gift God has given to man. But for it, we could not know right from wrong.*
> —ABRAHAM LINCOLN, SIXTEENTH U.S. PRESIDENT

stories of people of faith. We should know how it portrays the character of God. And we should know what it says about love (including ways that real love differs from love as most people define it).

TEN RULES OF THUMB WHEN YOU'RE LOOKING FOR GUIDANCE

A. Learn the Bible's direct commands

Oddly, there aren't too many of these. But they do cover a lot of life situations. The fundamental ones are in the Ten Commandments (Ex. 20). These are basic morality, found not only in the Bible but around the world in every time and place. The Ten Commandments include respect for others' property ("You shall not steal"), for honesty ("You shall not give false testimony against your neighbor"), for marriage and sexual morality ("You shall not commit adultery"), reverence for human life ("You shall not murder"), respect for authority ("Honor your father and your mother"). These are so basic that most people would agree on them even if they weren't in the Bible. Most people know instinctively that they shouldn't cheat on their spouses, lie about a fellow worker, verbally abuse a parent, or kill someone. Most of people's moral decisions are, if they thought about it, clear-cut. Should you cheat on your income tax? No, that's stealing, even if you are irked at how the government spends your money. Should you have an extramarital affair? No, that's adultery, even if your spouse does get on your nerves sometimes.

Interestingly, the Ten Commandments also include "You shall have no other gods," "You shall not make for yourself an idol," and "You shall not covet." Most people won't see how they apply to life today. Ah, but they do. The first one ("You shall have no other gods") means we aren't supposed to worship anything except the true God. Do we? Of course. People worship lots of things—their careers, their homes, their status, their own gratification, even their own bodies (or someone else's). The second commandment is similar: "You shall not make for yourself an idol." People do, though—everything from clothing to home decor to the airbrushed images in *Penthouse*. The Bible makes it clear that this is wrong. Not only do the Ten Commandments forbid it, but the whole history of Israel is a story of a nation that forgot the true God and worshiped something else.

What about the command "You shall not covet"? Here is a direct command that concerns our hearts, not our actions. We could actually conceal our envy of other people. No one need ever know—except God. This commandment lets us know that even if we look moral on the outside, we can still be wrong on the inside.

At the end of this chapter you'll find a list of the key "command" passages in the Bible. These are not (to many people's surprise) a very large part of the Bible. If

you think the whole Bible is a "rule book," you may be pleasantly surprised.

By the way, you'll feel better about the Bible's commands if you understand that they were designed to help you lead a happy, constructive life. God, who is a Father, didn't issue His decrees just to keep us from having fun, or to show us He's the Boss. The rules are there for the same reason all good rules exist: to make life bet-

BIBLIOMANCY IS THE NAME GIVEN TO THE PRACTICE OF OPENING THE BIBLE AND READING A PASSAGE AT RANDOM. SOME PEOPLE DO THIS WHEN THEY'RE LOOKING FOR GUIDANCE IN LIFE. I DON'T RECOMMEND THIS. AFTER ALL, A PERSON CONSIDERING SUICIDE MIGHT OPEN TO THE PASSAGE THAT SAYS, "JUDAS WENT AWAY AND HANGED HIMSELF."

ter. Most of us dislike the speed limits on interstate highways. (We especially dislike it when we're caught breaking the limit.) But we'll usually admit, if we're pressed, that the limits serve the purpose of getting us where we're going in relative safety. As with most rules, we sincerely believe that other people should obey the rules, even if we ourselves grumble about them. After all, why is that guy on the highway in such a hurry? Isn't 65 a reasonable speed limit for him? Then it probably is for us, as well.

B. Learn to apply the direct commands to other situations

Intelligence, as we all know, is more than just knowing facts. It involves dealing creatively with what happens to us. A kid in an urban ghetto may not be "book smart," but he may learn to use his wits to survive in the city jungle. In the same way, each of us—regardless of how much formal education we have—has a brain that we can use to live intelligently. The brain is something God gives us. The willingness to use it is our own choice.

This is the people's book of revelation, revelation not of themselves alone, but revelation of life and of peace.
—WOODROW WILSON, TWENTY-EIGHTH U.S. PRESIDENT

The brain can absorb rules such as "You shall not murder" and "You shall not commit adultery." These are understandable. These and the other direct commandments in the Bible would (if people obeyed them) make the world a better place. Society would be better. Individual lives would be better.

But not all moral decisions are covered by the Bible's commandments. What does the Bible say about smoking? About abortion? About nuclear weapons? Not a word. If you don't care to think creatively, you could say, "Well, I looked through the Bible and didn't find a word about pornography, so I guess it's OK to read smutty books." Well, in fact, the Bible doesn't say anything about pornography—not *directly*, anyway. It does say, "You shall not commit adultery." The married man might reply, "Well, I'm not committing adultery—I'm just looking at pictures, and isn't that much better than having an affair?"

This is a point where people should read Jesus' Sermon on the Mount (Matt. 5–7). This is one of the key sections on morality in the Bible. In it, Jesus looks at the moral commandments and tells His lis-

teners that they ought to go beyond the obvious meanings of the commands. Consider His words in Matthew 5:27-28: "You have heard that it was said, 'Do not commit adultery.' But I tell you that anyone who looks at a woman lustfully has already committed adultery with her in his heart." Meaning what? That a man can never be pleased at the sight of an attractive woman, other than his wife? No. The key idea is that our minds can sin—not just our bodies. Jesus was telling people that literal adultery was wrong, but so was adultery in the mind. In other words, you can be unfaithful from the neck up. And most people know, deep down, when an appreciative look at an attractive person has progressed into heavy-duty fantasy—or, as Jesus put it, looking "lustfully."

So does this apply to pornography? Probably. Certainly the Bible makes it clear that a married person has no business with magazines or videos that lead to mental unfaithfulness. What about an unmarried person? Let's look at that in the next section.

C. Learn about the type of life the Bible intends us to live

It bears repeating that the rules in the Bible aren't there to deny us pleasure, but to keep us from harm and to make us better people. Good parents make rules for their children to protect them, in the hope they'll grow up to be good people. God is the same way.

So the Bible gives us more than just rules. It gives us pictures of what the good life would be like. We see the good life portrayed in the lives of certain characters, notably Jesus. What did Jesus do? Healed the sick, raised the dead, showed forgiveness to enemies, showed love to both rich and poor, didn't gossip or slander, showed little concern for material things, gave Himself up for the happiness of others. His entire life was an illustration of the famous description of love in 1 Corinthians 13. If you read about Jesus in the Gospels, you don't get the impression of a repressed, frustrated person who was so bound up by rules that His life was lacking something. You get the impression of a fulfilled person, a man with a sense of purpose in life, a man whose joy is giving to others. This is what makes it all the more tragic that such a person ends up being executed. The Bible makes it clear that good people often do suffer persecution. We know this instinctively, and we see it every day in the news. Yet deep down, we also know that being good is just . . . well, good itself. It is its own reward.

In the previous section we were dealing with one moral problem—pornography— and how we could apply the Bible to it. Strictly speaking, the Bible says nothing about pornography. It does have a lot to say about keeping our minds out of the gutter. If you study the Bible, particularly the life of Jesus, you will never find a rule saying, "You shall not watch X-rated videos." You will find an image of life that allows no place for something like pornography. The Bible does not say, "Don't watch that video." The Bible simply reminds us, "Haven't you got something better to do with your life?"

You may face a choice in life when you will want to turn to the Bible and ask, "What can it tell me about this situation?" This is a valid way to use the Bible. But another valid way is to study it on a regular basis so that you'll already have an idea of the kind of life God wants us to lead.

Put another way, the best way you can use the Bible in moral decision-making is to know the Bible well. That can't come overnight. It does not need to.

Remember that God doesn't want a bunch of robots, slavishly following rules because we have to. God knows that things done strictly out of duty are not very fulfilling—either to Him or to us. Doing things because we want to—or, even better, *because we love someone*—is fulfilling. God's rule—a very good one—instructs us

> *Scripture is the school of the Holy Spirit.*
> —JOHN CALVIN (1509–1564), PROTESTANT LEADER

not to murder an enemy. But love can go beyond that, telling us to aid a wounded enemy. God is pleased when we don't murder. He is even more pleased when we go beyond the rules and act lovingly.

If you think back to your early childhood (or the early years of your own children), you might recall times when you were eager to please a parent. A question like "Sandy, would you like to help me set the table?" was greeted with "Sure thing!" Why was this so? Because small children seem to have the natural desire to please their parents, to be with them in any way they can. As the years pass, this goes away. How many teenagers have that wide-eyed eagerness?

If you read the Bible (especially the New Testament) closely, you can see some of that childhood innocence recaptured. The first Christians felt it—that amazing desire to please God. That desire, more than any set of rules, was what guided their behavior. People can still feel that today—but not so long as they have a negative attitude toward rules—or toward the One who is the final authority.

D. Learn to pray

You'll find a section on prayer in chapter 7. I won't cover all that material here, except to say that it is perfectly right for you to pray to God for guidance in life. Again and again the Bible shows people pouring out their hearts to God. Even if our prayers aren't clever or eloquent, God listens. He is pleased to have us coming to Him for guidance.

One problem people face is, how will they know God answers? In a few places the Bible tells of God actually speaking in an audible voice. Some people today claim this has happened to them. But more often people hear an "inner voice"—God speaking through their minds. Can they be 100 percent sure this is God—or maybe just their own wishful thinking?

One way to know is to ask, "Does this message from God contradict what the Bible teaches about God?" If it does, it can't be right. God, as the Bible shows, is consistent. He doesn't contradict Himself. If a man prays, "God, should I leave my wife and marry my secretary?" he might think he hears God saying to him, "Yes, your present marriage isn't so great, and you owe yourself some pleasure now." The man's own mind might be telling him that, but God wouldn't. What if a woman prayed, "Lord, I'm facing a career choice. This new job has more pay and prestige, but I'd do a lot of traveling and spend a lot of time away from my family. Should I take the job?" The woman's own inner voice might say, "Sure, everyone is entitled to a fulfilling career." But if she knows the Bible's view of self-giving love, she would know that God would not urge someone to take a job that would cause her to neglect her family.

Praying and expecting an answer from God are not shortcuts to knowing His clear will revealed in the Bible. People have believed for centuries that the Bible reveals God to us. We need to know that revelation well. We also need to pray so that the God of the Bible can also communicate with us personally. But we need to realize that, in the area of decision-making, the Bible is "home base." It is the foundation for decision-making, and we ought to consult it before deciding whether we ought to pray about a particular decision.

Let's consider an analogy: you make a rule that your children can't have sweets before meals. It's a sensible rule, and your children hear it enough that they ought to know it. So if one of your children comes to you just before dinner and asks, "Can I have some ice cream now?" how would you respond? You'd probably say, "Haven't I told you before that you can't do that?"

But some major decisions in our lives aren't covered in the Bible. For example, a childless couple has learned that they can adopt three siblings—all three, or none. The couple faces a choice: (1) Adopt all three (which means going from a two-person household to a five-person household overnight); (2) wait, and hope that later on they will have an opportunity to adopt just one child; or (3) risk the possibility that they might never again have the chance to adopt. The Bible gives no direct guidance in this matter. Wanting children is a moral thing. So is living without children. So is adopting—either one child or three. There are no "wrong" choices, strictly speaking. But the couple prays, hoping that God will guide them toward the *best* decision. It is perfectly right to pray in this way. The couple might believe that God gave them an answer—maybe an audible voice, or maybe an inward one. Or they might believe that they prayed but received no answer at all. The Bible does not promise us that God will give an answer in all situations like these. He sometimes does, sometimes doesn't. What matters is that the couple studied the matter carefully, made sure that none of their choices went against God's clear commands, then made a choice. We can do no more than that, except to ask God to give us courage to live with the consequences of what we choose.

E. Ask advice of people you respect

Moral decision-making is more than just "me, the Bible, and God." Wisdom comes through other people, notably through parents. Of course, many people have parents who aren't particularly wise or moral. If they haven't made a success (morally speaking) of their own lives, you aren't bound to follow their advice. But if you look around, you probably know at least a few people who have managed to live a moral (and happy) life. What is their secret? Have they struggled with some of the same moral dilemmas that you have? If so, give them a listen.

In times past, people often turned to their pastor for advice. If you don't attend church, you probably don't know any pastors, and I can't really recommend that you choose one at random from the Yellow Pages. If you do attend church, and your pastor is someone whose opinion you respect, consider him as one possible source of guidance. But don't assume that all pastors have a particularly high opinion of the Bible. Many do; some don't. There are plenty of pastors around more interested in advancing some social agenda than in help-

> *In all my perplexities and distresses the Bible has never failed to give me light and strength.*
> —ROBERT E. LEE, CONFEDERATE GENERAL

ing people find personal guidance through the Bible.

Don't assume that education has any effect on morals. I knew professors in undergraduate and graduate school who were shining lights of morality and good sense. But I knew some who were quite the opposite. Educated people tend to assume that, having "gotten their smarts" after years of education, they know how to lead moral lives. Some of them are more than happy to pass on their wisdom (or lack of it) to others. And some of them are so good with words and so good at appearing knowledgeable that they can always get someone to listen to them. Yet there are intellectuals who have no morals—just as there are cleaning women and garbage collectors who do have morals. If you're seeking some wisdom to live by, don't let a college degree (or lack of it) influence whom you listen to. Remember that the Nazi torturers who designed and ran concentration camps in Germany in the 1940s were all intelligent, well-educated, and cultured. And they were evil.

> *It is impossible mentally or socially to enslave a Bible-reading people.*
> —AMERICAN JOURNALIST HORACE GREELEY (FAMOUS FOR COINING THE PHRASE "GO WEST, YOUNG MAN"

F. Don't agonize when you don't have to

God likes people who have consciences that work. In a world where so many people seem to throw morality to the winds, God is pleased that people take morals seriously. A man who agonizes over his extra-marital fling is more pleasing to God than a man who has a fling and feels no guilt at all. (Of course, the man who resists the temptation to have the fling is even more pleasing to God.) Morals matter. We don't need to feel ashamed that we are aiming for a better life than many people aim for.

But we also don't need to agonize over things that aren't important. I have known some very moral people who, alas, agonized over everything. I knew a pastor who prayed every Sunday about which color suit he should wear into the pulpit. Did it matter? He believed it did because he believed that God cares about every aspect of our lives. Well, he was right there. He was right in believing that God wants us to honor Him

with everything we do. But when you read the Bible, you'll see that God is deeply concerned with our *hearts*, who we are on the inside. Our hearts deserve our attention more than anything else. We can wear ourselves out worrying about every tiny aspect of our lives, but God made us for something better than anxiety and worry.

The more familiar you are with the Bible, the more you notice that *respect* is a key theme. You won't actually find that word very often, but the idea is there, loud and clear. The usual synonym for it is *love*—which, unfortunately, is a word we associate with being "in love." But in the Bible it can mean "respect" and "concern." We are supposed to respect God by worshiping only Him. We are supposed to respect authority figures (like our parents). We are supposed to respect other people's property (by not stealing or swindling) and life (by not killing or injuring). We are supposed to respect the truth by not lying to benefit ourselves or harm other people. The Bible indicates that we can enjoy life immensely and have a fine time—*so long as we give the proper respect to others.* Our "wants" and "needs" and "rights" are not a problem—unless they infringe on what we owe others. Most people, if they give their situations some thought, could decide what to do if they asked themselves, "Am I showing the respect I owe to God and to other people?" If the answer is a clear no, then you need to give the dilemma some more thought.

Asking this question can also save you a lot of grief over unimportant things. Shall I wear my blue suit or my gray? Shall I have coffee or tea with breakfast? Shall I take the kids to Disney World or camping? If neither choice shows disrespect for God or others, don't agonize over the decision.

G. Learn to enjoy your freedom

Should you cheat on your income tax? No. Should you have a glass of wine with dinner? Well . . . the Bible does not answer that. It does show people (including Jesus) taking wine for granted. It also shows the abuse that drunkenness leads to. For this reason, some people choose not to drink at all. But they can't, strictly speaking, claim that the Bible tells them to do so. It doesn't. It is each person's own choice. We should respect someone who can enjoy a glass of wine with dinner. We should also respect someone who chooses not to. Neither person is doing anything immoral.

But it is immoral to create rules that we don't need. You'll find this idea coming up again and again in the letters of Paul. The early Christians believed that Jesus was their Savior, the One who blotted out their sins and made them right with God. Because they had a Savior, they were not bound by all the Jewish laws concerning kosher food, animal sacrifice, working on the Sabbath, etc. But Paul discovered something that is still true: people like to create rules for themselves. We hate rules—yet we like them too. Why? Because if we create rules of our own (rules we can obey, obviously), we can look down on other people who don't obey those rules. Sound silly? Think of contemporary food fanatics, who would like to turn everyone into vegetarians, or tell others to cut out all sugar, fat, cholesterol, etc. If they choose to eat that way themselves, fine. But many want to make their own dietary rules the norm.

People were the same way in the New Testament period. Paul gave a resounding "No!" to this. Again and again he talks about *freedom*—not freedom from all moral laws, but freedom from silly regulations that have no importance to God. Paul's Letter to the Galatians is concerned with this. He told the Christians of Galatia that they had been "bewitched" by the "rule-makers" who were trying to impose manmade restrictions.

In 1 Corinthians, Paul dealt with the same problem: people claiming to be more "spiritual" because they follow certain rules. Paul advised them to respect each other's differences over nonessentials. There are too many things that really matter for us to waste time bickering over things that don't matter. But at the same time, we aren't to sneer at people who choose to avoid things that we ourselves can enjoy. Nor are they supposed to sneer at us. It is possible for us to have morals and at the same time to say, regarding some minor matters,

> *We are not at liberty to pick and choose out of its [the Bible's] contents, but must receive it all as we find it.*
> —JOHN HENRY NEWMAN (1801–1890), ENGLISH CATHOLIC LEADER

"Do your own thing." The more we study the Bible, the more we understand what those minor matters are.

A word about the "new morality": We're talking about the new "social consciousness," particularly in the form of environmental concern. The Bible shows a deep appreciation for the natural world—but not for worshiping it. In our day, when the "Love Your Mother" (earth, that is) slogan is on bumper stickers everywhere, it is easy to be sucked in by the new morality of earth worship. How can we be a "concerned" person? Recycle, don't use your car unless you have to, give money to environmentalist causes, etc. If you do any of those things, fine. But don't be too proud of your "enlightened consciousness." The Bible doesn't present environmental concern as one of the marks of a moral person. But it does have a lot to say (all bad) about people who are spiritually proud.

H. Remember God

The first words of the Bible are "In the beginning, God. . . ." God is the main character from beginning to end. The Bible is saturated with God, and you can't read more than a few pages without realizing that the Bible authors believed firmly that God was watching them. This is a pleasant thought (since God watches over us with love), but also intimidating (God is aware of everything we do). Like the carnival fortuneteller, God "sees all, knows all"—except that, unlike the fortuneteller, God really *does* know all. In the words of Jesus, "There is nothing concealed that will not be disclosed, or hidden

OLD TESTAMENT VS. NEW

Many people have the impression that the two parts of the Bible are radically different—particularly in their moral teaching. You might have heard that the Old Testament teaches "an eye for an eye," while the New Testament teaches mercy, kindness, forgiveness.

Well, this is a good reason to study the Old Testament more closely. It's true that some parts of the Old Testament—some of the Psalms, for example—sound vengeful. They call on God to punish Israel's enemies. The idea of "getting even" is definitely present in the Old Testament. This is natural, considering that the nation of Israel was constantly harassed by more powerful nations.

But there's more to the Old Testament. Consider these ethical statements:

Do not hate your brother in your heart. Rebuke your neighbor frankly so you will not share in his guilt. Do not seek revenge or bear a grudge against one of your people, but love your neighbor as yourself. I am the LORD (Lev. 19:17-18).

If you come across your enemy's ox or donkey wandering off, be sure to take it back to him. If you see the donkey of someone who hates you fallen down under its load, do not leave it there; be sure you help him with it (Ex. 23:4-5).

Do not gloat when your enemy falls; when he stumbles, do not let your heart rejoice (Prov. 24:17).

If your enemy is hungry, give him food to eat; if he is thirsty, give him water to drink. In doing this, you will heap burning coals on his head, and the LORD will reward you (Prov. 25:21-22).

This last verse is quoted by Paul, the Christian apostle, in his Letter to the Romans (12:20). He was only quoting Proverbs, but many people think that Romans 12:20 was an original Christian ethical teaching from the mind of Paul. Many people also believe that Jesus was the first to say "Love your neighbor as yourself," when in fact He was quoting Leviticus 19:18.

The more we read the Old Testament, the more of these pleasant little surprises we find.

that will not be made known. What you have said in the dark will be heard in the daylight, and what you have whispered in the ear in the inner rooms will be proclaimed from the housetops" (Luke 12:2-3). Every page of the Bible assumes this belief. No matter where we are or what we do, God sees.

It is easy to forget this in our contemporary situation. In an earlier time, when people lived in smaller towns and could observe each other more closely, it was natural to believe that someone was watching— because someone probably was. Today, with sprawling cities and people moving frequently, we can be surrounded by strangers who don't give two hoots whether we're moral people or not. (In fact, we're likely to live among people who would be happy to encourage us in immoral behavior.) Given this situation, it is easy to forget that someone—or Someone—is watching over us. We can deceive ourselves into thinking that our actions don't matter, for no one will confront us.

Reading the Bible often is a healthful corrective to this. The more you read the Bible and the more seriously you take it, the more likely you are to ask yourself, "What does God think about what I'm doing right now?" Sometimes we may rightly conclude that God wouldn't mind at all. Does God mind if you walk your dog in the park? No. Does God mind if you pay for your girlfriend to have an abortion? Maybe so. Who knows how many wrongs would cease if people asked themselves, "Does God really want me to do this?" It's such a simple, childlike question—but one that is very basic to morals and decision-making. It is the idea behind the part of the Lord's

Prayer that prays to God, "Your will be done."

I. Remember God's forgiveness

God is not a cosmic killjoy. He is a Father, according to the Bible, so His rules for us are for our own benefit. He is not an *indulgent* Father. Instead, He punishes us. Or, looked at another way, He sometimes lets us suffer the consequences of our failings. But above all, He is a forgiving Father, a "God of new beginnings" who is always willing to receive us when we want to change. The story of the Prodigal Son and the forgiving father in Luke 15 is a touching illustration of just how merciful God is.

On the practical level, this means two things. First, because God is a loving Father, we ought to live to please Him. This—not fear of breaking the rules—is to be the motivating force in our lives. God loves us. When we love Him, morality is easier, because we *want* to do the right thing.

Second, because God forgives, we are free to fail. You probably remember your parents or teachers using that tired old analogy about learning to ride a horse: "When you fall off that horse, get right back on again till you get it right." This is exactly how we ought to approach our own morals. We fail, inevitably. It's tempting to get discouraged. After all, we've made so many mistakes that we're sure we're going to make others. But according to the Bible, God is pleased that we try. Our efforts aren't wasted because the efforts are themselves a gift to God.

J. Emphasize the small things

For most people in most situations, living a moral life involves dozens of little daily decisions, not big ones. In our daily, humdrum lives we seldom face the biggies like murder, adultery, and theft. We make little choices—gossiping over a fellow worker, buying a certain type of magazine, watching a particular TV show, showing our crankiness to the other drivers on the freeway, joining gleefully in a gripe session. In most of these situations, we are not facing great moral dilemmas—just little choices about how we spend our time and mental energy.

More often than not, these small moral choices involve that vicious organ of the body, the tongue. Interestingly, though people think of the Bible as being too concerned with sexual morals, it has a great deal to say about our words and the harm they can do. The authors of the Bible understood that basic human need of "information compulsion"— that desire to pass on information we know to someone else. If this is merely a matter of telling your neighbor how well your new car runs, fine. But sometimes information compulsion can do a great deal of harm to others. James 3 is the Bible's chapter par excellence on the harm we can do with our speech.

KEY ETHICAL PASSAGES IN THE BIBLE

The passages listed here are not the only parts of the Bible that relate to morals and decision-making. They are the "cream," and they contain the essence of what the Bible teaches about our moral life.

The Ten Commandments
Exodus 20:1-17
Deuteronomy 5:1-21

Jesus' Sermon on the Mount
Matthew 5–7

Love
Matthew 22:34-40
John 14:15-21; 15:9-17
1 Corinthians 13
Galatians 5:22-23
Ephesians 5:1-2
Colossians 3:12-14
1 John 2:5-17; 3:7-24

Advice on everyday living
The Book of Proverbs

Priorities in life
Matthew 4:1-11; 6:25-34
Mark 8:34-38
Luke 10:25-37; 12:13-34
Romans 12:1-2
1 Corinthians 1:20-31
1 Timothy 6:3-10
1 John 2:15-17

Injustice and oppression
Amos 5–6
Micah 6:8

Husbands and wives
Proverbs 5:20; 12:4; 18:22; 31:10-31
Matthew 5:27-32
1 Corinthians 7
Ephesians 5:22-33
Colossians 3:18-19
Hebrews 13:4
1 Peter 3:1-7

Parents and children
Proverbs 13:1; 17:6; 19:26; 22:6; 23:13
Ephesians 6:1-4
Colossians 3:20-21

Sexual morality

Matthew 5:27-32
Matthew 15:19
Romans 1:18-32
Romans 13:12-14
1 Corinthians 5–7
Galatians 5:19-26
Colossians 3:1-17
1 Thessalonians 4:3-8
Revelation 21:8

Gossip, criticism, judgment

Matthew 7:1-2; 15:19-20
Romans 1:28-31
Ephesians 4:31
Colossians 3:8
James 3:1-12; 4:11-12

Freedom from legalism

1 Corinthians 8:1–11:1
Galatians
Colossians 2:6-23

Dealing with temptation

Proverbs 2:10-12
1 Corinthians 10:12-13
Hebrews 2:14-18
James 1:2-15

Note: If you have a reference book called a *topical Bible*, you can look up topics alphabetically and find all the Bible passages that relate to that topic. You could look up, for example, "marriage," "career," "friendship," "temptation," "children," whatever.

Another note: In chapter 5 you'll find information on different ways to approach Bible study. You'll note that in the different approaches *application* is important—that is, in any Bible study you'll be asking yourself, "How does this apply to my life?" Doing this on a regular basis is the best means for getting the Bible into you so that, when you need to make important decisions, you'll already have the Bible in your mind and heart.

And one more note: On pages 155–159 you'll find the section "Facing Life's Crises, Challenges, and Changes." This is a comprehensive list of just about any major life subject, along with Bible passages that relate to it. This is part of the "Pathway through the Bible" chapter. One of the enduring realities of human beings is that we often ignore God and the Bible until some crisis sends us begging for help. At least the Bible assures us that God doesn't mind this, since crises at least remind us we aren't as self-reliant and independent as we thought.

chapter 7

Conversing with God: ◄⋯

Learning to Pray with the Bible

To an unbeliever, prayer may seem like talking to oneself. This is never the case in the Bible. Prayer is always conversing with God, addressing the Almighty. This conversation can take place anywhere, anytime. There are no "sacred places," since God is everywhere and can hear prayer anywhere. The Bible shows people praying in the temple, outdoors, indoors, standing, lying down, whatever. Prayer can take the form of praise, adoration, thanksgiving, requests—even questioning, tears, anguish, anger. In the Bible's view, the worst kind of prayer is no prayer. Not praying means, in practice, atheism. If we don't pray, we're acting as if God, the Ruler of the universe and of us, didn't exist. Not praying at all is like entering a house and ignoring the person who owns it.

The Bible is full of prayer. The longest book of the Bible, Psalms, consists of 150 poems that are mainly addressed to God. They run the gamut of human emotions. There is probably nothing you've ever thought about saying to God that is not somewhere expressed in the Psalms. They are the "prayer book" of God's people. The first Christians inherited the book from the Jews and accepted it as their own. Psalms is the most quoted Old Testament book in the New Testament. Throughout the world, Christians every Sunday read, chant, or sing a psalm during their worship. One long prayer, Psalm 119, is the longest prayer in the Bible and also the longest chapter.

But prayers are scattered elsewhere throughout the Bible. Smack in the middle of the historical books are prayers of thanksgiving, requests, even cries of anguish and despair. All the important Bible characters prayed, some very eloquently. Some, like the reluctant Prophet Jonah, found themselves praying in odd places (the belly of a "great fish" in Jonah's case). The Prophet Elijah, on the run from wicked Queen Jezebel, prayed that God would take his life. (Happily, God did not grant that anguished request.) Jesus taught the importance of prayer and gave the famous Lord's Prayer as a role model.

Churches that are *liturgical*—Catholic, Episcopalian, Orthodox, and some others—use books of prayer. These printed prayers often use language straight from the Bible, and they cover a wide range of subjects—prayers for healing, prayers for rain, prayers of thanksgiving, etc. These "fixed" prayers serve a purpose: people can look up an appropriate prayer for almost any occasion. But the problem with this practice is that a person may never learn to pray on his own. And it is clear in the Bible that each individual can and must address himself to God. Eloquence and cleverness are not important. The important thing is expressing honestly to God our feelings and thoughts, both good and bad.

But we don't learn to pray out of the blue, do we? Our parents or someone taught us how to pray our first prayers. Maybe it was the Lord's Prayer, or maybe the one beginning "Now I lay me down to sleep. . . ." Someone guided us in how to address God. The Bible can do that. It can do this very well, since its prayers cover so many topics.

JUST WHAT IS AN "AMEN" ANYWAY?

Amen is a permanent part of our language, even among people who have no religious feeling at all. An older generation remembers when a pastor's sermon would be punctuated with an approving "Amen!" from individuals in the church. Today, *Amen* is more likely to be used in a joking way.

It isn't a joking matter in the Bible. *Amen* is a Hebrew word, used often in the Old Testament. Loosely translated (although no one ever translates it), it means "so be it" or "yes, indeed." (The hip, contemporary "For sure!" is not a bad translation.) The New Testament, written in Greek, used the old Hebrew word, and with the same meaning. The people of the Bible used it exactly as we do. It implied a hearty "Yes!" to something that was said—roughly the same as saying "I do" in the wedding ceremony. When Moses read the divine Law to the Israelites, they said "Amen" at various times. The word occurs several times in the praise songs of the Psalms. In a few places the psalm writers got so caught up in their enthusiasm for God that they doubled the praise—"Amen and Amen!" The Jews came to use it as a good "praise word," and in the New Testament, Paul (a devout Jew before he became a Christian) uses the word many times when he speaks of God.

A bit of trivia: Who is called "the Amen"? Jesus is. In Revelation 3:14 He refers to Himself as "the Amen, the faithful and true witness, the ruler of God's creation." The key word here is "witness." As the faithful witness of God, Jesus Himself is a "Yes!" to God.

We think of "Amen" as an "ending word," since we're taught to end prayers that way. Not all prayers in the Bible end with an "Amen," although the most famous one (the Lord's Prayer) does. Several of the New Testament books end with an "Amen"—notably the last one, Revelation. In fact, it ends with a sort of "double Amen."

"Amen. Come, Lord Jesus. The grace of the Lord Jesus be with God's people. Amen" (Rev. 22:20-21).

PRAYER 101: THE LORD'S PRAYER

Consider the great model for prayers, the Lord's Prayer. The version found in Matthew's Gospel reads this way:

Our Father in heaven, hallowed be Your name, Your kingdom come, Your will be done on earth as it is in heaven. Give us today our daily bread. Forgive us our debts, as we also have forgiven our debtors. And lead us not into temptation, but deliver us from the evil one. For Yours is the kingdom and the power and the glory forever. Amen (Matt. 6:9-13).

Jesus prefaced this prayer by saying "Pray in this way," not "This is the exact prayer you should repeat every day." In other words, the prayer was a model—a pattern, a sort of "skeleton" that we flesh out with our own individual words.

What does the model consist of? It acknowledges God as "our Father." So the God being addressed is not some distant, cold Being. He is Father, meaning that a close relationship exists between Him and the one praying. He is in heaven—meaning not the sky or outer space, but "above us," spiritually speaking. (If He is not, why bother praying to Him at all?) The word "Father" conveys the idea of authority; in the Bible's view, a child is duty-bound to obey his father. So calling God "Father" carries the message "I'm here in an attitude of respect, willing to obey you."

"Hallowed be Your name" is simple enough. God is holy, sacred, so calling on Him by name involves reverence on our part. Even though we have just called Him

"Father," this Father is one that we "hallow"—that is, we respect Him and honor Him greatly. In our own day, when so many people don't take the Bible or religion seriously, it is easy to forget that in

THE STRANGEST PLACE TO PRAY

THEY TOOK JONAH AND THREW HIM OVERBOARD. . . . BUT THE LORD PROVIDED A GREAT FISH TO SWALLOW JONAH, AND JONAH WAS INSIDE THE FISH THREE DAYS AND THREE NIGHTS. FROM INSIDE THE FISH JONAH PRAYED TO THE LORD HIS GOD (JONAH 1:15, 17, 2:1).

ages past people had an awe of God. Even if they saw Him as loving and kind, they remembered that He was the Almighty— a powerful Father, not a cream puff daddy. Jesus was telling His disciples that when they approached their Father, they needed to recall that He was a power to be reckoned with. All the prayers in the Bible assume this, even prayers that complain to God.

"Your kingdom come" means "I desire Your rule (including Your rule over myself)." Notice that before the prayer mentions any of our own needs, it first expresses a wish for God's rule. (In Jesus' day, it was assumed that the ruler's will could—and should— override anyone else's.)

"Your will be done" acknowledges that we desire God to accomplish what He wills. It is a way of saying that our desires are aligned with His, or that we want them to be. It also means that we accept that God's desire has priority over our own. That seems appropriate, if He truly is the Almighty and All-knowing One. "Your will be done" isn't just a general way of saying, "I hope the universe is going the way You like it." More specifically, it is saying, "May Your will be done *in me*." In all prayers in the Bible, the praying person is willing to hold up his own life for God's inspection and use.

"Give us today our daily bread" means we ask for what we need—not what we *want* (which might not be good for us). The Bible never says we can pray for a Lexus and get one. If we really *needed* a Lexus (which is unlikely), that would be a different

> To forgive for the moment is not difficult. But to go on forgiving, to forgive the same offense again every time it recurs to the memory— there's the real tussle.
> —C.S. LEWIS

story. But Jesus made it clear in many of His sayings that God the Father would supply His children with what they really needed in this life. This part of the prayer makes it clear that praying for riches, fame, worldly power, etc., is wrong. We may *want* those things, but we have no business asking God to provide us with them. (At the same time, it is perfectly right to thank God for letting us have good things to enjoy—even the Lexus.)

"Give us today our daily bread" reminds us of something else: we are needy creatures. Nothing in the Bible indicates that we *deserve* anything. So the prayer says "Give us"—a polite request, not a demand. God does not owe us anything, but the Bible makes it clear that He does supply us with what we need anyway.

"Forgive us our debts" isn't referring to financial debts. It refers to wrongs we've done. (The version of the Lord's Prayer in Luke's Gospel uses "sins" instead of "debts," which makes the meaning more obvious.) The prayer is saying, "Forgive our wrongs to others, and we forgive people's wrongs to us." Forgiving others because God forgives you is a key idea in the New Testament. Be kind, because Someone has been kind to you. God is a God of mercy. To be near Him, we have to show mercy also. (If we believe this, we also must believe that we should never pray for something bad to happen to someone else, not even someone who has hurt us deeply.)

"Lead us not into temptation" confuses some people. Would a loving Father really lead His children into a bad situation? *Today's English Version* is a little clearer: "Do not lead us to hard testing." The prayer continues "but deliver us from the evil one." This refers to Satan, of course. Satan, the evil one, is also the "tester"—the one who "shows us what we're made of."

"For Yours is the kingdom and the power and the glory forever. Amen." The prayer ends up where it started by acknowledging God as great. So the model prayer is a kind of sandwich that states our needs and requests to God, sandwiched between our praise of God, our testifying to His authority. The model indicates that the right kind of prayer is polite—that is, we don't come storming in to God like a spoiled brat, making ridiculous requests. First, we acknowledge who we're dealing with, and only then do we ask for things. (A comparison: If you had a problem you wanted to discuss with your boss, you wouldn't just

barge into his office. First you would ask, politely, if you could discuss something. And once you had finished the discussion, you would politely leave the office, not go stomping out—not if you're smart, anyway, since you know your boss is in control of the situation. God deserves as much consideration as a human boss.)

Every prayer in the Bible does not follow the Lord's Prayer model exactly. But in general, they do. Throughout the Bible, people approach God as the Almighty King—in their prayer they bow (mentally, if not physically) before making a request. Perhaps our contemporary sloppiness about manners keeps us from appreciating this. And perhaps the flippancy that children use with their parents now keeps us from grasping that, in the Bible, a father (and *the* Father, God) was an authority figure, not just a breadwinner. If father was "dear old Dad," he was also "monarch of all he surveyed." If that sounds sexist and outdated, remember that the head of the household was also the protector, the guide, and the nurturer—a big load of responsibility, but a task that God is up to.

• • • • • • • • • • • • • • • • • •

The word Hallelujah *(or* Alleluia*) is often used in Christian worship and prayer. The only book of the Bible to use it is the Book of Revelation (19:1, 3-4, 6). But the Hebrew word* Hallelujah *occurs many times in the Book of Psalms. It is translated as "praise the Lord."*

• • • • • • • • • • • • • • • • • •

"PRAYING IN JESUS' NAME" (WHATEVER THAT MEANS . . .)

You may have heard people end a prayer with "We ask these things in Jesus' name. Amen." Like the "Amen," the "asking in Jesus' name" is a habit, one so ingrained that most people have no idea what it means. It is a habit, much like asking someone "How are you?" when we aren't really concerned about his answer. But the habit of "praying in Jesus' name" is based on a promise Jesus made: "My Father will give you whatever you ask in My name" (John 16:23). This is just one of several "My name" promises Jesus made.

Where two or three come together in My name, there am I with them (Matt. 18:20).

I will do whatever you ask in My name, so that the Son may bring glory to the Father. You may ask Me for anything in My name, and I will do it (John 14:13-14).

People are inclined to misinterpret this. After all, it sounds like a blank check—just ask God for something, and you get it. But this is a case where you have to measure a part of the Bible against the whole. Does the Bible *as a whole* tell us God will give us anything we want? (Like a Lexus, maybe?) No, indeed. So just what was Jesus promising then?

"In My name" doesn't just mean "using My name." It means "on My behalf." If you work for the mayor and rent a car "in his name" (on his behalf, that is) you better be using it for his official business, not for your own joy ride. When Jesus said, "My Father will give you whatever you ask in My name," those last three words are the key. If we are asking "in His name" —on His behalf—we aren't asking for a Caribbean cruise or a BMW. We know full well those aren't things He would ask for Himself. But we could in His name ask for strength to get through a difficult situation, or we could ask for more energy to do things we need to do, or for wisdom in managing our family. An easy way to understand "in His name" is this: If Jesus were standing next to you, would you be ashamed to make this request? If so, then it isn't something you should request on His behalf.

So, when you or someone else ends a prayer with "in Jesus' name," realize that the words are more than just a formula, the "magic words" that you have to end a prayer with. In fact, according to the Bible, you are under no compulsion to ever say those words. You are asked to pray *on Jesus' behalf.* Paul caught the idea pretty well when he told the Corinthian Christians, "We are therefore Christ's ambassadors" (2 Cor. 5:20).

DO I HAVE TO KNEEL?

Kneeling is the usual position for prayer, along with bowing the head. Is this the "Bible-approved" position? Yes and no. Yes, some people in the Bible got on their knees to pray. But we also read about people praying while standing (Jer. 18:20), sitting (2 Sam. 7:18), even lying facedown (Matt. 26:39). Some people prayed with hands lifted up, which is now becoming common again (1 Kings 8:22; 1 Tim. 2:8). People prayed silently (1 Sam. 1:13) and out loud (Ezek. 11:13). They prayed alone (Matt. 6:6) and in groups (Acts 4:31). They prayed at scheduled times (Ps. 55:17) or at any time (Luke 18:1). They prayed in an open field (Gen. 24:11-12), in the temple (2 Kings 19:14), by a riverside (Acts 16:13), on a seashore (Acts 21:5), in bed (Ps. 63:6), and on a battlefield (1 Sam. 7:5).

Curiously, only one verse in the Bible even hints that people bowed their heads while they prayed: "King Hezekiah and his officials ordered the Levites to praise the LORD with the words of David and of Asaph the seer. So they sang praises with gladness and bowed their heads and worshiped" (2 Chron. 29:30). Even in this verse, we aren't sure that bowing the head was actually connected with praying.

What about closing the eyes while praying? The Bible never mentions it. It doesn't mention placing the hands together, either.

The place, time, and posture are not important in the Bible. The right attitude is. For the person who comes to God to praise Him, to thank Him, to ask for aid, or to confess sin, any posture is fine.

BUT CAN WE BE JUST A LITTLE SELFISH?

Is it selfish to ask for healing of a disease? Selfish to ask for an end to financial trouble? For a less stressful job? Are these prayers as selfish as praying for a new Jaguar?

No, they aren't. The people of the Bible poured out their requests and their anguish to God in a big way. The classic example is Psalm 22, which begins: "My God, my God, why have you forsaken me? Why are you so far from saving me, so far from the words of my groaning?" Whatever was afflicting this poor soul, he didn't hesitate to put it into words. Interestingly, when Jesus was hanging from the cross, He uttered these words. We should feel good that He did. It meant He was truly human, even if He was the Son of God. It meant that we, in the midst of pain, are not wrong to ask "Why, God?" (It is better than the alternative—assuming there is no God to hear us.)

This is an extreme example. In most cases, the people who prayed to God were in less anguish than the author of Psalm 22. One who had some sort of trouble was the Apostle Paul: "There was given me a thorn in my flesh, a messenger of Satan, to torment me. Three times I pleaded with the Lord to take it away from me. But he said to me, 'My grace is sufficient for you, for My power is made perfect in weakness'" (2 Cor. 12:7-9). We don't know just what Paul's "thorn" was—something serious, obviously. He prayed that it be removed—and there is no indication this was an improper thing to pray for. God's answer was not, in this case, to grant the request. But elsewhere in the Bible, many people do get what they pray for. Jesus and the apostles healed many people who came to them for help. There is never a hint that it is selfish to want to be healthy and whole. So praying for mental and physical health—our own, or anyone else's—is fine. We ought to want everyone in the world to be mentally and physically healthy.

What about death? Most people won't pray that a dead person be brought back to life (even though this occurred a few times in the Bible). But many people do pray that they, or someone they love, be spared death. This happened many times in the Bible. In fact, Jesus Himself asked to be spared. But He ended His prayer by saying to God, "yet not as I will, but as You will."

(Remember that part of the Lord's Prayer is "Your will be done.") Sometimes people are spared, sometimes not. But to pray for it is not wrong.

ON OTHER PEOPLE'S BEHALF

You'll find some prayers in the Old Testament that seem amazingly nasty and spiteful—mean-spirited, to use today's popular term. Some of the Psalms call for God's vengeance on evildoers. But the New Testament takes a very different approach. We shouldn't curse our enemies—we should pray for them. Hanging from a cross, Jesus said, "Father, forgive them"—a hard thing for Him to say, no doubt. We are supposed to do the same. Did anyone say this was easy? It isn't. Nothing in the Bible goes against our grain like asking God's favor on people we dislike. But the Bible never tells us we have to like these people or enjoy their company—that may not even be possible. It tells us to show them mercy, even in our prayers. Someone that we secretly dislike is also someone we should secretly pray for.

Jesus prayed for other people, not just Himself. The New Testament tells us to do the same. It even tells us to pray for government officials. One classic statement of this is in 1 Timothy 2:1-4:

I urge, then, first of all, that requests, prayers, intercession and thanksgiving be made for everyone—for kings and all those in authority, that we may live peaceful and quiet lives in all godliness and holiness. This is good, and pleases God our Savior, who wants all men to be saved and to come to a knowledge of the truth.

Note that this passage doesn't tell us to admire or like officials. But we are told to pray for them—and rightly so, since their actions affect so many people. It makes sense. If you think the President is bad, then, while he is in office, it is logical to pray that he will do as little harm as possible. The same applies to others who may abuse their authority—employers, for example.

Praying for someone else, even a long-time enemy, has a very positive effect on us—it temporarily takes our minds off our wants and our petty grievances. The Bible is anti-selfishness on every page. It presents a God who is pleased when we take a genuine interest in other people's welfare.

THANK YOU VERY KINDLY

The Bible doesn't have much use for the self-centered "gimme, gimme" prayer. It does tell us to say "thank you" for the things we receive. Of the prayers in the Bible, there are many, many more thanksgiving prayers than request prayers.

Thanksgiving—gratitude—isn't quite the same as praise. Praising God is like praising an admirable person we like: "Wow, you're wonderful! I just have to tell you!" Thanksgiving is more specific. God has done something for us, so we feel compelled to express our gratitude. Paul, in his letters, uses the phrase "thanks be to God" again and again. His classic statement on gratitude is in 1 Thessalonians 5:18: "Give thanks in all circumstances, for this is God's will for you in Christ Jesus." This does not come naturally to most people. We might give thanks for something good, but "give thanks in all circumstances"? According to the Bible, yes, be thankful in good times or bad. It is easy to ridicule the eternal optimist who says, "Well, I didn't get that promotion I wanted, but I'll at least have more time to spend with my family." But in the Bible's view this is

UNDER THE INFLUENCE?

Praying silently is a standard procedure today. But in Bible times, most people prayed aloud, even when they were alone. Notice in the following passage what happened to poor Hannah when she didn't pray aloud.

Now Eli the priest was sitting on a chair by the doorpost of the LORD's temple. In bitterness of soul Hannah wept much and prayed to the LORD. . . . As she kept on praying to the LORD, Eli observed her mouth. Hannah was praying in her heart, and her lips were moving but her voice was not heard. Eli thought she was drunk and said to her, "How long will you keep on getting drunk? Get rid of your wine."

"Not so, my lord," Hannah replied, "I am a woman who is deeply troubled. I have not been drinking wine or beer; I was pouring out my soul to the LORD" (1 Sam. 1:9-15).

a healthy attitude—finding the good in situations that seem bad. (This doesn't mean we can't be *more* thankful for some things than for others.)

BARING OUR SOULS

One of the great joys in life is that God forgives—again and again, in fact. But the divine forgiveness hinges on our willingness to admit we did wrong. This is the formula: Repentance, forgiveness. No repentance, no forgiveness. No confession, no fellowship with God. You never see a hint in the Bible that we can evade responsibility for what we've done. "Well, the reason I left my wife was . . ." "I had a very unhappy childhood, so . . ." "I've been abused, so it's no wonder I . . ." These contemporary excuses get people off the hook in the human court, but not (according to the Bible) in God's court.

Psalm 32 shows how an anguished soul found a release: "I acknowledged my sin to you and did not cover up my iniquity. I said, 'I will confess my transgressions to the Lord'—and you forgave the guilt of my sin."

The New Testament presents the same idea: "If we confess our sins, He is faithful and just and will forgive us our sins and purify us from all unrighteousness" (1 John 1:9).

As the Bible sees it, we owe this to God. We follow the same idea in human relations. If we injure or offend someone, we make an apology and promise to do better. Then, to prove we're sincere, we do better. The person should, if he is fair-minded and merciful, forgive us. This doesn't

GRACE BEFORE DINNER?

The old practice of saying a prayer before a meal is dying out—maybe because so many people eat on the run nowadays. But the practice isn't completely dead. For many people, the only memory they have of praying is the memory of someone saying the "grace" or "blessing" before a meal.

Is this practice in the Bible? Indeed it is. The person most noted for practicing it was Jesus Himself. Several places in the Gospels mention Him giving thanks before eating. The Gospels even mention that He "looked up to heaven" when He gave thanks. But Jesus' behavior wasn't unusual at the time. He was doing what any devout Jew did in that era. When He said, in the Lord's Prayer, "give us today our daily bread," He was including more than just bread. But He, and any faithful Jew at that time, would have made sure that He did thank God for "daily bread."

always happen. But according to the Bible, it always happens with God. He never fails to forgive the person who is truly sorry.

Can we get people today to accept the Bible's view of the seriousness of sin? That's a tough one. Maybe the word *sin* itself seems outdated. But ten minutes of channel-surfing on the TV will convince you that people *do* feel a sense of something being wrong—"I know I need help" or "I know I need to grow in the area of. . . ." In other words, people are very aware that they've "missed the mark" in some part of their lives—and this is exactly what sin means in the Bible—missing the mark, failing to be what we should be. The Bible offers an "out" for us: Instead of flitting like a butterfly from one self-help plan or diet or guru to another, we begin (and end) with God, saying, "I'm not all I should be. I've failed in many ways. I'm eager to start fresh, make a new beginning." The Bible presents us with a God who says, "I can accept that. Now, let's get to work on you. . . ."

KEY BIBLE PASSAGES CONCERNING PRAYER

If you want to learn to pray, the Bible offers two kinds of passages: those concerned with prayer, and model prayers (such as the Lord's Prayer discussed earlier).

> Proverbs 15:8; 28:9
> Isaiah 1:15
> Matthew 5:44
> Matthew 6:9-13
> Mark 11:24-25
> Luke 11:1-4
> Luke 18:1-14
> John 16:23-24
> Romans 8:15-16, 26, 34
> Romans 12:12
> Ephesians 3:16-17
> Ephesians 6:18
> Philippians 4:6
> Colossians 4:2
> 2 Thessalonians 3:1-2
> 1 Timothy 2:1, 8
> Hebrews 5:7
> James 5:13-18
> 1 Peter 3:12
> 1 John 1:9

MODEL PRAYERS

PRAYING FOR OTHERS
Genesis 18:16-33
Genesis 25:21
Exodus 32:11-13
1 Samuel 12:23
1 Kings 8:22-53
2 Kings 19:14-19
John 17

FOR HELP
Genesis 32:9-11
1 Samuel 1:9-18
Psalms 3–7; 12–13; 17; 28; 35; 69; 88; 130
Matthew 26:39-44

FOR GUIDANCE
Psalm 25

FOR JUSTICE
Psalms 10; 54

PRAISING GOD
1 Samuel 2:1-10
1 Chronicles 29:10-13
Psalms 8–9;16; 18–19; 24; 27; 100; 103
Luke 1:46-55, 68-79

THANKING GOD
Psalms 30; 40; 65; 92; 116
Jonah 2

CONFESSING SINS
Psalms 32; 51

CONFIDENCE IN GOD
Psalm 139

PAIN AND ANGUISH
1 Kings 19:1-9
Psalms 22; 38–39; 41; 109; 130
Isaiah 38

Jonah 2:2-9

LONGING FOR GOD
Psalms 63; 84

chapter 8

Thanks for the Memory:
Why We Should Memorize the Bible and How We Can

When I was in high school, my church's pastor introduced something new into our Sunday evening worship: memory time. Shortly before his sermon, the congregation would stand and recite (if they could) a Bible verse that he had given them the previous week. He didn't select the verse at random; he chose a verse that related to his sermon on that Sunday.

Most of us liked doing this. We had an entire week to roll the verse around in our minds, and there was a good feeling of doing something as a congregation. Sometimes peer pressure can be a good thing.

Do I now remember what all those verses were? No. I doubt if even the pastor remembers them all. Yet I don't think they've left my mind completely. I'm sure they're in my brain somewhere, probably more accessible than hundreds of things I learned in college (but have had no reason to recall since then).

A BIBLE MEMORY BANK

Memorizing passages from the Bible is an old practice. For centuries, any educated person in Europe and America was

> *No one ever did himself harm from reading the Book.*
> —BENJAMIN FRANKLIN

expected to know the Bible very well. Even if you weren't a college graduate, it was assumed you would know certain verses, or at least phrases, from the Bible (which, until recently, always meant the *King James Version* of 1611). This was something that united people of all social classes and backgrounds. The bank president, the college professor, the housewife, and the farmhand would all share a basic knowledge of the Bible. Until the last fifty years or so, we were a "people of the Book."

There was more to this than just learning the materials you were taught in church and at home. Most people assumed that the Bible was a moral guide for life. You remembered it, not just to be smart, but to help yourself and others in all seasons of life.

For example, it was not unusual to call to mind, when someone close to you died, a verse like John 11:25, "I am the resurrection and the life." These words of Jesus brought a lot of comfort to grieving people over the years, and still do. But of course, most of us don't walk around with a Bible in our hands all the time. In times of stress or anxiety, we may not have a Bible nearby, and even if we do, we may not feel like reading it, searching through it for some word of comfort. This is the advantage of having a Bible memory bank.

My grandmother frequently repeats a verse that was a favorite of her own mother's, Hebrews 10:25: "Not forsaking the assembling of ourselves together." In context, the verse refers to the need Christians have to meet together for worship. In fact, Hebrews presents this as a command, and so my grandmother (and her mother) interpreted it. Whenever I get the urge to skip church, I can practically hear my grandmother's voice saying those words. (Amazing what repetition can do, isn't it?) She did her work well, and apparently so did her own mother. Good. That verse from Hebrews is important. I'm happy to say it isn't the only Bible verse that has been part of my grandmother's "memory bank."

Two friends of mine, a married couple, went through some marital strife a few years ago. They're on the mend now, and the husband mentioned to me that one thing that pulled them through was the verse that says that love "beareth all things, believeth all things, hopeth all things, endureth all things." He couldn't remember exactly where that verse is (it's 1 Cor. 13:7), but he said the "love endureth all things" part stuck in his mind through twelve years of marriage.

In case you were wondering, this practice of tucking away Bible verses in our minds is urged by the Bible itself. Consider a few of these verses:

But in your hearts set apart Christ as Lord. Always be prepared to give an answer to everyone who asks you to give the reason for the hope that you have (1 Peter 3:15).

Your commands make me wiser than my enemies, for they are ever with me. I have more insight than all my teachers, for I meditate on Your statutes. I have more understanding than the elders, for I obey Your precepts (Ps. 119:98-100).

I have hidden Your word in my heart that I might not sin against You (Ps. 119:11).

Let the word of Christ dwell in you richly as you teach and admonish one another with all wisdom, and as you sing psalms, hymns and spiritual songs with gratitude in your hearts to God (Col. 3:16).

These are just a few of the Bible's words concerning memorizing and meditating on God's Word. Keep in mind that for hundreds of years most people did not have their own private copy of the Bible. Bibles were rare and fairly expensive, so people had to share. A person's exposure to the

Bible may have happened only in church or around the family Bible. In such a situation, if people wanted access to the Bible (and many people did), they had to store it in their minds.

The situation has changed, obviously. Most people can afford a Bible, and if you can't, organizations like the American Bible Society and the Gideons give them away. But our need to "hide the word in our heart" hasn't changed. Having the words in the printed book is fine, but there's nothing quite like having them engraved on the mind.

PACKAGING A MEMORY

Religious publishers work on the same principle as all publishers: find a need and fill it. So at least one, NavPress, has found a need (a system for Bible memorization) and filled it with their *Topical Memory System*. The system is wonderful. It uses cards (about the size of a business card) that you take with you in a plastic pocket pack. Carrying them wherever you go, you can look at the verses when you have spare moments, brush up on ones you memorized previously, etc. The system uses verses on key topics of the Bible (temptation, for example), so you usually memorize several verses on the same topic. The verses are usually the most important verses on a particular topic, and also the easiest to memorize. The system also comes with the memory verses printed in several different Bible versions—that is, you can buy the system in the *King James Version*, the *New International Version*, etc.

But of course, a homemade version of this system is easy to make. Using small file cards (which are more durable than slips of paper), you can write a favorite verse on one side, then the reference (book, chapter, and verse) on the other side. You could write on one side of a card "God was reconciling the world to Himself in Christ." On the other side of the card you could write "2 Corinthians 5:19" and maybe the topic ("Salvation" or "Jesus Christ"). As you begin to memorize verses, you can test your memory by looking at the back side

Old Version vs. New Version: Singing Turtles or Cooing Doves?

Can turtles speak . . . or sing? According to the *King James Version* of the Bible, they can: "The time of the singing of birds is come, and the voice of the turtle is heard in our land" (Song 2:12).

Consider the contemporary translation in the *New International Version*: "The season of singing has come, the cooing of doves is heard in our land."

Puzzled? The "turtles" in the old version are turtledoves, as in the two turtledoves of the "Twelve Days of Christmas." (By the way, the picturesque phrase "the voice of the turtle" became the title of a Broadway play. The movie version of the play starred an actor named Ronald Reagan.)

(with the reference) and trying to recite the verse. And, by the way, writing out a verse is a helpful part of memorizing. (And it's a lot more fun and rewarding than in your younger days when you had to write "I will not talk in class" 500 times.)

As with the *Topical Memory System*, you can carry your cards with you to work, to the gym, anywhere. Modern life is full of frustrating spare moments—often waiting in line, waiting on the phone while you're on hold, etc. Instead of doing what most people do—fume—you can put these wasted minutes to good use, rereading your memory verses. Or give your brain something to do while you're working your muscles on a Stairmaster or a treadmill.

If you're new at this, try one verse, a short one. Try 1 John 4:8: "Whoever does not love does not know God, because God is love." (If you feel intimidated by this, try the short form, "God is love.") Read the verse, then write it on a slip of paper or a card. Read it aloud. Then put the paper facedown and see if you can say the verse from memory. Check the paper. If you missed a word or two, don't be frustrated.

When you've chosen a verse you want to memorize, try *paraphrasing* it—that is, restating it in your own words, then writing those down. Understand that "restating it in your own words" doesn't mean "rewording it in a way that suits you." Take one of the Ten Commandments: "You shall not commit adultery" (Ex. 20:14). Although that's a straightforward verse, and easy to remember, you could write it down this way: "I must not be unfaithful to my spouse." That's an accurate paraphrase. It would

not be accurate to paraphrase it "I should not be unfaithful to my wife, except that the last few weeks she's really getting on my nerves and we don't love each other like we used to anyway, so . . ." Putting your own spin on the Bible is something all human beings do—but in doing so, we're missing out on what the Bible really says.

Anyway, you'll find paraphrasing a great aid in memorizing a verse. But make up your mind to *memorize the verse as it is in the Bible* (whatever translation you're using). Your own paraphrase is just an aid, helping you connect the words on the page to your own mind.

Besides paraphrasing, you can aid your memorizing by *visualizing* whenever possible. In our video-saturated age, we are probably more visual than people ever were. We've already said that it helps your memory by writing a verse down, actually seeing it on the page. But even words in ink and paper are less stimulating to us than actual pictures. Take a favorite verse, a saying of Jesus: "Come to me, all you who are weary and burdened, and I will give you rest" (Matt. 11:28). This isn't a very "visual" verse, except notice the word *burden*. Can you visualize a person—yourself, maybe?—carrying a huge load on your back? Maybe you are bending low, sweating, your face pained. Up ahead on the path is someone—Jesus, however you actually picture Him—saying "I will give you rest." Perhaps He has His arms extended, indicating He is ready to take the burden you're carrying (or maybe catch you just before you fall down from fatigue). Does visualizing the verse this way help you? It seems to aid most people. Even if you are no Rembrandt, you might want to make a quick sketch of how you visualize the verse, using just stick figures. (If you have a copy of the *Good News Bible* version, also called *Today's English Version*, it has some excellent drawings showing how Bible verses can be illustrated very simply but dramatically.)

Consider Jesus' words on worry: "Who of you by worrying can add a single hour to his life?" (Matt. 6:27) You could sketch a stick figure of a person, a worried expression on his face, staring at a large clock. Or try this verse: "All a man's ways seem right to him, but the LORD weighs the heart" (Prov. 21:2). Here the most visual words are *heart* and *weighs*. Try sketching a heart (in the usual shape, that is) sitting on scales (maybe the old-fashioned balance-type scales, not your bathroom scales).

A little mental effort is required to do this sort of thing, of course. MTV producers are happy to put the latest song in visual images, and advertisers package their newest ad slogans with dynamic images, but you will have to do this work yourself. Don't let it be said that you're completely lacking in imagination. And remember, you don't have to show your artwork to anybody.

Incidentally, make a habit of memorizing the location of the verse you've memorized. The actual words of the verse are most important, of course, but it helps you to memorize its location as well. You may want to turn back to the Bible to refer to it again, show it to a friend, etc. Remember grade-school spelling bees where you were supposed to say the word, spell it, then say it again? Do that with your chapter and verse references. Let's say you've memorized Psalm 19:1, an easy verse to remember. Repeat it to yourself in this way: "Psalm nineteen, one: 'The heavens declare the glory of God; the skies proclaim the work of His hands.' Psalm nineteen, one."

Most of us are "soft" in the memory, just as a couch potato feels during a first workout at a gym. But with determination a

HANDEL-ING THE BIBLE

IF YOU WANT TO HEAR THE BIBLE'S STORY OF HUMAN SIN, JESUS THE SAVIOR, AND THE FINAL TRIUMPH OF GOOD OVER EVIL, JUST LISTEN TO GEORGE FREDERICK HANDEL'S *MESSIAH*. THIS GREAT CHORAL WORK IS ACTUALLY A COLLECTION OF BIBLE VERSES, SET TO BEAUTIFUL MUSIC. THE VERSES ARE ON THE THEME OF HUMAN SIN AND THE SALVATION THAT CHRIST (THE MESSIAH) OFFERS.

IF YOU'RE INTERESTED IN MEMORIZING SOME BIBLE VERSES, LISTENING TO HANDEL'S *MESSIAH* IS A GOOD METHOD. NOTHING FIXES A VERSE IN THE MIND LIKE HEARING IT SUNG OVER AND OVER.

couch potato can change as muscles gradually come into use again. So with the human memory. The capability for incredible memorization is there—if we put it to use.

FIRST STEP: DECIDING WHAT TO MEMORIZE

There is no "official list" of Bible verses worth memorizing. Still, over the centuries, certain verses have become favorites of many people. Probably one of the most loved and most quoted passages in the Bible is Matthew 5:3-12, a part of Jesus' teaching known as the Beatitudes. (The word is from the Latin *beatus*, meaning "blessed.") The Beatitudes are a list of "blessed are," with Jesus describing the sorts of people who are "the people of God's kingdom." If you're feeling ambitious someday, try memorizing the whole passage of the Beatitudes. (It's shorter than the lyrics to your average pop song—but without the rhymes, unfortunately.)

The list of verses in the next section is arbitrary—which means, any author of a book like this is bound to pick some of his own personal favorites. However, I selected these on the basis of:

- brevity
- popularity with several generations of Bible-readers
- coverage of several basic themes of the Bible

The verses as they are quoted below are from the *New International Version* of the Bible, published in 1978, a popular contemporary translation. Many people (including this author) grew up with the *King James Version* of 1611, a version that was old-fashioned in its language but also (perhaps for that reason) very "quotable." Some people still find the older version easier to memorize—maybe because its language seems "dignified" and different from everyday speech. If you're interested in memorizing some Bible verses, memorize from the version(s) that you're most comfortable with. You might find the *King James Version* very memorizable, or you might prefer a newer translation like the *New International Version* (NIV). One advantage of the NIV is that in many cases it retains the wording of the *King James,* or uses very similar wording. The *New King James Version* does the same.

When you are memorizing verses, don't just pick a verse (including the verses below) without reading it in context. That is, read the paragraph or chapter surrounding the verse so you'll understand it in relation to what precedes and follows it. (Consider: In Shakespeare's *Hamlet*, Prince Hamlet makes his famous "To be or not to be" speech in which he considers committing suicide. The speech is famous and readable all by itself. But it helps your understanding of the speech if you've read the rest of the play and understand *why* this young man is considering suicide.)

As you study the Bible and become more familiar with it, you'll probably become an underliner, marking verses that you find especially meaningful. Thanks to the human mind's underused capacities, you may find yourself memorizing these special verses without even trying (just as you probably memorize pop song lyrics without meaning to). This is fine—memorizing without trying to. But it's also kind of fun, and challenging, to push yourself a little bit to memorize verses on the Bible's key teachings. That is what the verses in the next section are all about.

About the Bible itself:

"All Scripture is God-breathed and is useful for teaching, rebuking, correcting and training in righteousness" (2 Tim. 3:16).

"Your word is a lamp to my feet and a light for my path" (Ps. 119:105).

About nature:

"The heavens declare the glory of God; the skies proclaim the work of His hands" (Ps. 19:1).

About God's love:

"God so loved the world that He gave His one and only Son, that whoever believes in Him shall not perish but have eternal life" (John 3:16).

"Whoever does not love does not know God, because God is love" (1 John 4:8).

"God does not judge by external appearance" (Gal. 2:6).

"God demonstrates His own love for us in this: While we were still sinners, Christ died for us" (Rom. 5:8).

"We know that in all things God works for the good of those who love Him, who have been called according to His purpose" (Rom. 8:28).

About God's guidance:

"Trust in the LORD with all your heart and lean not on your own understanding" (Prov. 3:5).

"The ways of the LORD are right; the righteous walk in them, but the rebellious stumble in them" (Hosea 14:9).

"It is better to take refuge in the LORD than to trust in man" (Ps. 118:8).

"The LORD disciplines those He loves" (Prov. 3:12).

About our love for God:

"'Love the Lord your God with all your heart and with all your soul and with all your strength and with all your mind'; and, 'Love your neighbor as yourself'" (Luke 10:27).

"Whom have I in heaven but you? And earth has nothing I desire besides you" (Ps. 73:25).

"The fear of the LORD is the beginning of knowledge" (Prov. 1:7).

"This is love for God: to obey His commands" (1 John 5:3).

"May the words of my mouth and the meditation of my heart be pleasing in your sight, O LORD, my Rock and my Redeemer" (Ps. 19:14).

About love for other human beings:

"These three remain: faith, hope and love. But the greatest of these is love" (1 Cor. 13:13).

"Do to others what you would have them do to you, for this sums up the Law and the Prophets" (Matt. 7:12).

"Love your enemies and pray for those who persecute you, that you may be sons of your Father in heaven" (Matt. 5:44-45).

"The only thing that counts is faith expressing itself through love" (Gal. 5:6).

"He has showed you, O man, what is good. And what does the Lord require of you? To act justly and to love mercy and to walk humbly with your God" (Micah 6:8).

"He who refreshes others will himself be refreshed" (Prov. 11:25).

"Rejoice with those who rejoice; mourn with those who mourn" (Rom. 12:15).

About human failings:

"He who conceals his sins does not prosper, but whoever confesses and renounces them finds mercy" (Prov. 28:13).

"All have sinned and fall short of the glory of God" (Rom. 3:23).

"All a man's ways seem right to him, but the LORD weighs the heart" (Prov. 21:2).

"There is a way that seems right to a man, but in the end it leads to death" (Prov. 16:25).

"The wages of sin is death, but the gift of God is eternal life in Christ Jesus our Lord" (Rom. 6:23).

"Blessed is he whose transgressions are forgiven, whose sins are covered" (Ps. 32:1).

"The heart is deceitful above all things and beyond cure. Who can understand it?" (Jer. 17:9)

"Man looks at the outward appearance, but the LORD looks at the heart" (1 Sam. 16:7).

About weariness in living:

"Come to Me, all you who are weary and burdened, and I will give you rest" (Matt. 11:28).

"In this world you will have trouble. But take heart! I have overcome the world" (John 16:33).

"I can do everything through Him who gives me strength" (Phil. 4:13).

"If God is for us, who can be against us?" (Rom. 8:31)

"Blessed is the man who perseveres under trial" (James 1:12).

"The eyes of the LORD are on those who fear Him, on those whose hope is in His unfailing love" (Ps. 33:18).

About priorities and worldly success:

"What good will it be for a man if he gains the whole world, yet forfeits his soul?" (Matt. 16:26)

"Whoever wants to become great among you must be your servant" (Mark 10:43).

"Where your treasure is, there your heart will be also" (Luke 12:34).

"Everyone who exalts himself will be humbled, and he who humbles himself will be exalted" (Luke 14:11).

"The love of money is a root of all kinds of evil" (1 Tim. 6:10).

About salvation:

"God was reconciling the world to Himself in Christ" (2 Cor. 5:19).

"God did not send His Son into the world to condemn the world, but to save the world through Him" (John 3:17).

"Jesus answered, 'I am the way and the truth and the life. No one comes to the Father except through Me'" (John 14:6).

"Here is a trustworthy saying that deserves full acceptance: Christ Jesus came into the world to save sinners" (1 Tim. 1:15).

"In repentance and rest is your salvation, in quietness and trust is your strength" (Isa. 30:15).

About eternal life:

"Surely goodness and love will follow me all the days of my life, and I will dwell in the house of the LORD forever" (Ps. 23:6).

"Jesus said to her, 'I am the resurrection and the life. He who believes in Me will live, even though he dies'" (John 11:25).

"As in Adam all die, so in Christ all will be made alive" (1 Cor. 15:22).

"Our citizenship is in heaven" (Phil. 3:20).

"The world and its desires pass away, but the man who does the will of God lives forever" (1 John 2:17).

"Blessed are the dead who die in the Lord" (Rev. 14:13).

About personal renewal:

"If anyone is in Christ, he is a new creation; the old has gone, the new has come!" (2 Cor. 5:17)

"Do not conform any longer to the pattern of this world, but be transformed by the renewing of your mind" (Rom. 12:2).

"Whatever you do, whether in word or deed, do it all in the name of the Lord Jesus" (Col. 3:17).

"A broken and contrite heart, O God, You will not despise" (Ps. 51:17).

"Those who hope in the LORD will renew their strength. They will soar on wings like eagles" (Isa. 40:31).

"Blessed are those who hunger and thirst for righteousness, for they will be filled" (Matt. 5:6).

About freedom:

"Where the Spirit of the Lord is, there is freedom" (2 Cor. 3:17).

"If the Son [Jesus] sets you free, you will be free indeed" (John 8:36).

About temptation:

"Resist the devil, and he will flee from you" (James 4:7).

"God is faithful; He will not let you be tempted beyond what you can bear" (1 Cor. 10:13).

About loving people we don't like:

"Do not be overcome by evil, but overcome evil with good" (Rom. 12:21).

"Above all, love each other deeply, because love covers over a multitude of sins" (1 Peter 4:8).

"Let us not love with words or tongue but with actions and in truth" (1 John 3:18).

"Blessed are the merciful, for they will be shown mercy" (Matt. 5:7).

About forgiveness:

"Do not judge, and you will not be judged. Do not condemn, and you will not be condemned. Forgive, and you will be forgiven" (Luke 6:37).

"Be kind and compassionate to one another, forgiving each other, just as in Christ God forgave you" (Eph. 4:32).

"Forgive as the Lord forgave you" (Col. 3:13).

About joy in living:

"The cheerful heart has a continual feast" (Prov. 15:15).

"[Jesus:] 'I have come that they may have life, and have it to the full'" (John 10:10).

"Light is shed upon the righteous and joy on the upright in heart" (Ps. 97:11).

"The peace of God, which transcends all understanding, will guard your hearts and your minds in Christ Jesus" (Phil. 4:7).

THE BIBLE AS WALL DECORATION

WHEN THE CHURCH OF ENGLAND BROKE AWAY FROM THE CATHOLIC CHURCH IN THE 1500S, CHURCHES SAW A MAJOR CHANGE IN DECOR. INSTEAD OF STATUES AND STAINED GLASS, CHURCHES BEGAN TO PAINT OR ENGRAVE BIBLE VERSES ON CHURCH WALLS. AFTER CENTURIES OF NOT BEING ALLOWED TO READ THE BIBLE IN ENGLISH, PEOPLE WERE THRILLED TO SEE THE SACRED WORDS ON THEIR CHURCH WALLS. THE TEN COMMANDMENTS WERE A FAVORITE. WHEN QUEEN MARY, A CATHOLIC, BEGAN TO RULE IN 1553, SHE MADE THIS ILLEGAL. AFTER HER DEATH, IT BECAME LEGAL AGAIN, AND EVEN TODAY MANY CHURCH OF ENGLAND CHURCHES (WHICH INCLUDES COLONIAL EPISCOPAL CHURCHES IN THE U.S.) HAVE THE TEN COMMANDMENTS ON THE WALLS.

WHEN YOU VISIT SOMEONE'S HOME AND SEE A BIBLE VERSE ON A PLAQUE OR POSTER OR STITCHED IN NEEDLEPOINT, TAKE NOTE: 400 YEARS AGO SUCH THINGS WERE AMAZING NOVELTIES—THE REAL WORDS OF GOD IN THE PEOPLE'S OWN LANGUAGE.

chapter 9

Putting Your Heads ◄···
Together:
Organizing a Bible Study Group

The Old and New Testaments present a community faith, not a private faith. You can, and should, study the Bible on your own. But you can gain a lot—and so can other people—by studying the Bible in a group setting. There is safety in numbers. An individual can (and often has) come up with some pretty kooky interpretations of the Bible. A group could do this also, but it's more likely that someone in the group will say (tactfully, of course), "That's a kooky idea." On the positive side, in the group setting you can share insights. Someone in the group will perceive some aspect of a Bible passage that you didn't see.

HOW TO START A BIBLE STUDY

A. Get in touch with people you think would be interested

You might do this through your church, but you can also study the Bible with fellow workers, neighbors, etc. You might even post a notice on your supermarket's bulletin board, stating your name, phone number, and what you're trying to organize. Churches should, of course, have regular Bible study groups. But there is something to be gained from groups outside the church. For one thing, such a group could be interdenominational—which makes for an interesting mix of viewpoints. It enourages members to shoot for the "meat" of the Bible, not for things that only confirm people's denominational biases. It also allows you to include "seekers" who are (for the present) more interested in the Bible than in attaching themselves to a church.

B. Aim for a group of six to twelve people

As Jesus was aware, twelve was a good number for a group. (It's a commonly used number in the Bible.) Anything more than twelve allows quieter members to fade into the wallpaper. A group smaller than six or seven has the danger of too much agreement, not enough creative discussion.

C. Set up the study as a real study hour, not a social hour

People have come to expect food and drink in any kind of human encounter, and eating does seem to mellow people. But if you want your group to focus on the Bible, keep the munching to a minimum. Coffee and tea are standard, but see if you can do without edibles. (People don't eat during church services, a system that seems to work well.) If food is to be a normal part of the group meeting, count on adding a half hour to the time you actually expect to spend in study.

D. Set up the meetings for a definite time

A weekly meeting usually works best. Generally, an hour is too limiting, but two hours is more than some people want to commit. So compromise with ninety minutes, and try to begin and end the meetings on time. This is particularly important for people who have had to get baby-sitters.

E. Pick a place

Private homes are cozy and relaxing, but there's the danger of group members getting too interested in the host's home and furnishings. There may be a problem with adequate parking in some residential areas. Some other possibilities include a room in a church (not necessarily your own church), a public room available for use in a library or community center or the club room in your apartment complex (only make sure you can shut the door and have quiet). Rooms like these can seem chilly compared to someone's den, but public rooms do seem more "serious" than private homes.

For many reasons, men's study groups often choose to meet over breakfast. If a local restaurant is open to this, why not schedule a weekly meeting over a breakfast? The only flaw with breakfast meetings is that if a lively discussion gets started, it can't continue too long because most people have to leave. Then again, this limitation could be a blessing.

Note: If you expect your group to include people very unfamiliar with the Bible—maybe even people who don't consider themselves believers yet—you should definitely not hold the meetings in a church. Many people have, alas, had unpleasant experiences with churches. It's possible for people to be "interested in the Bible" but not (for the time being, anyway) the least bit interested in attending a church. Holding a meeting in a church suggests to many people that you intend to get them involved in church—that church and its denomination, to be specific. So if you're "casting a wide net," hoping to include seekers who may not yet be prochurch, choose your place carefully.

F. Choose the book or passage or topic the group will study

Go for one of the four Gospels, one of Paul's great letters (Romans, Galatians, Ephesians), Acts, Psalms, Proverbs, Isaiah. In the case of a long book like Psalms or Isaiah, you might opt for only part of the book, not the whole. If this is your first venture with your group, avoid any book that is surrounded by controversy—like

Revelation, Daniel, or Genesis.

In chapter 5 of this book we looked at several approaches to studying the Bible—studying a single book, a key passage, a topic. Any of these methods is suitable for either groups or individuals. But during your first group meeting, it might be wise not to throw out *too* many options, or you may never decide on anything.

G. During your first meeting, decide on the format the meetings will follow

One logical method is to ask members to read a portion of the book and come prepared to discuss it at the next meeting. For example, if you decide to study John's Gospel, assign chapter 1 at your first meeting. Group members will (you hope) read that chapter before the next meeting and be prepared to discuss it then. Discussing the passage involves members telling what they've gotten from the reading, what problems they encountered, how they might apply the text to their lives.

The section Help at Your Elbow, chapter 15, lists some Bible study guides suitable for groups. All the ones listed are ones I recommend highly. They have to be bought, of course, so find out if your group is willing to invest a small amount of money to purchase study guides. Some religious bookstores and mail-order houses offer volume discounts.

H. Designate a leader

This doesn't necessarily mean a lecturer or teacher. It means an organizer, a monitor, one who will arrange the meetings, keep in touch with members, and guide the discussion. The leader will always come to the group prepared, having read the text (even if no one else did) and jotted down some discussion questions, suggestions on how the text applies to life, etc. One necessary role of the group leader is to keep very talkative members from dominating the discussion. The flip side of this is drawing out comments and questions from the quieter members. The leader needs to be (obviously) a "people person." But the leader should not be an egomaniac who likes to be the center of attention constantly. The leader does not need to be a certified Bible scholar or someone with a degree in religion. Christianity is most healthy when laypeople, not scholars and clergy, are willing to interact with the Bible. We don't have to be spoonfed by religious professionals. But the leader of a Bible study does need to come to class prepared. This means not just reading through the assigned passage but consulting at least one good commentary or Bible dictionary to help explain problem areas. Some good,

• • • • • • • • • • •

DIVIDE AND CONQUER, THEN STUDY

Before the Bible was divided into chapters (in the Middle Ages) and verses (in the 1500s), people could not refer to a passage easily. They would use words such as, "As it is written in Isaiah the prophet. . . ." Obviously this raised problems. Someone might ask, "OK, just where in the Book of Isaiah would you find that?" We should be singing the praises of the men who created the chapter and verse divisions.

• • • • • • • • • • •

reliable commentaries and other reference tools are listed in the Help at Your Elbow section, chapter 15.

I. Keep group members focused on what they're studying

This involves two things. First, keep them from going off on tangents concerning events in the news or in their own lives. True, applying the Bible to our lives and to world events is fine. It should be a goal of all Bible study, in fact. But if you have only an hour or so for study, try to stay focused on the Bible itself. Anyone who has worked with a Bible study group knows how easily the members can get "derailed" from actually discussing the Bible. If you sense that a particular group member wants to discuss a personal problem (which may or may not relate to the Bible passage you're studying), you might just want to call that person at home at another time. The group might not be the ideal setting.

Second, keep members from focusing too much on minute details so that they miss the big picture of what they're studying. In every group you'll find an "academic" type who likes to discuss little historical or theological details. This person can be helpful—or a real hindrance if he or she dominates the group discussions. You may also get a person who simply likes to argue. (Consider this example: The group is studying John's Gospel, and you're focusing on chapter 20, the story of the resurrected Jesus. You may have a group member who likes to quibble over Jesus' resurrected body. How could it have wounds in it? How was Jesus able to walk through doors? Legitimate questions, actually, but not if they

dominate the entire meeting. The big picture you should focus on is the fact that Jesus was clearly raised from the dead bodily, and that His resurrected body was like—but also different from—His original body.) The group leader needs tact and a gentle (but firm) hand in steering the group back to the material.

Remember that before the 1400s and for a long time afterward, Bible reading and study was usually a group thing, not a private thing. It was possible for an individual to read the book (or scrolls, in the preprinting press era), but most people were exposed to the Bible in a group setting—in worship, in a family study, in church classes. Much of people's exposure to the Bible came from hearing it read aloud, then discussed or preached on.

So group study of the Bible is an old and respectable custom. When your group meets together, it is carrying on a tradition as old as the Bible itself. The Apostle Paul wrote to one of his assistants, "Until I come, devote yourself to the public reading of Scripture, to preaching and to teaching" (1 Tim. 4:13).

WHY YOU DON'T NEED AN EXPERT TO STUDY THE BIBLE

Throughout this book I've mentioned ways you can get help from Bible scholars, the experts. You probably can't meet them personally, but you'll find their work available in Bible dictionaries, commentaries, and thousands of other books on the market. This is comforting—knowing you aren't "getting in over your head" when you start to read the Bible. The scholars have studied the Bible closely. Some of them make their living this way. They are pleased to make their knowledge available to you (and it helps them sell books, incidentally).

But you don't need to become "expert-dependent." Millions of people over the centuries have read the Bible—and *understood* it—with little or no aid from experts. I have to believe that God is present when a commentary or Bible dictionary helps to enlighten a Bible reader. But I believe that God can work without such books.

One problem with the scholars is that they "swim" in the world of the Bible as easily as a fish swims in water. It is their element. But for most readers, this isn't so. The fish says to the man, "Just jump on in, use your gills, and you can breathe underwater." Easier said than done! Most of us are trying to live our lives, making a living in jobs that have little or nothing to do with the world of the Bible. At the end of a workday, we approach the Bible, not as if we "belong" in it, but hoping to get some good out of it. We want to use it. This isn't selfishness—just being practical. Unlike the Bible scholars, we can't spend an entire day speculating about Assyrian emperors and the exact date that one of them invaded Israel. "That's nice for them," we say, "but please, let's get back to reality. I have a job, a family, hobbies, a retirement plan. I also have problems. What I *don't* have is a huge amount of time to decipher the Bible."

Well, happily, we don't need huge amounts of time. We do need the dedication to read the Bible with some sense of purpose. It does take some commitment. And why not? Dieting does, and so does exercise—and people gladly fling themselves into weight loss and workout programs.

But again, you can do this with little help from the "Bible pros." You do need some help. For many people, what they need is a study partner—a fellow seeker. Think of times in your school days when you benefited from studying with a group. Maybe your teacher was excellent, but when you asked him for help, he (a) explained things you understood already, (b) gave you a lot of information you didn't need, or (c) failed to address the thing that really puzzled you. Teachers can often forget what it was like to be a

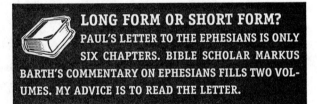

LONG FORM OR SHORT FORM?
PAUL'S LETTER TO THE EPHESIANS IS ONLY SIX CHAPTERS. BIBLE SCHOLAR MARKUS BARTH'S COMMENTARY ON EPHESIANS FILLS TWO VOLUMES. MY ADVICE IS TO READ THE LETTER.

learner, a beginner. A fellow student knows less than the teacher—but maybe he understands your needs and questions better than the teacher does. He has gotten snagged at the same places you have. He may have untangled some of those—and you may have untangled some that he is still struggling with.

So don't underestimate the power of a fellow seeker. Two people beginning from the same point can aid each other. Someone who is, say, just a few steps ahead of you in what he has learned can also help you. Think of it as the high school junior telling the sophomore, "What, you're hung up on geometry? Hey, I had that just last year. Here, let me help you out . . ."

Martin Luther, the great Christian leader in the 1500s, wrote and preached a great deal about the Bible. Yet he went on record as saying, "O that God would grant that my commentaries and those of all other teachers were destroyed. For every Christian should take the Bible in his own hands and read God's word for himself. He would then see that there is a vast difference between the word of God and the words of man."

WHY YOU SHOULDN'T FLY SOLO

The Bible has no conception of a solitary faith. In the Old Testament, the faith community is Israel. In the New Testament, it is the Christian community. An individual can interact with God, and an individual can read and grasp the Bible—sometimes. But not always. An individual can experience the revelation of God. But the Bible pictures people experiencing that revelation as a community.

When you read the Bible, you are reading the words of more than forty authors. In the course of time, their words have been studied and interpreted by thousands of people. Some of these interpretations have been weird, misguided, and maybe just plain wrong. But with the passage of time, some agreement has

• • • • • • • • • • • •

FAMILY TIES

In the 1500s, the religious movement called the Protestant Reformation caused a major change in people's Bible-reading habits. The Bible began to be translated from Latin into the actual living languages people spoke. It is hard to overstate how new and shocking this was: being able to possess and read a Bible in one's own language. Bibles (and all books, in fact) were fairly expensive in those days, so chances were good that there might be only one Bible per household. So the first Bible study groups were family groups, gathered around the hearth, listening to someone read aloud from this book that had always been in Latin, a language they knew nothing of. And "family groups" meant more than Dad, Mom, and two kids. Chances are each household contained grandparents, in-laws, uncles and aunts, etc.

• • • • • • • • • • • •

developed too. Readers, century after century, find some of the same meanings in the words of the Bible—not in every verse, but in many, especially the most important ones.

If you read the Bible on your own, never bothering to find out how other people have interpreted it, you can gain a lot of insight. But you would be depriving yourself of a lot of other people's insights. For 2,000 years people have been making some intelligent observations on the Bible. Doesn't it make sense to know what they thought?

You may find that your own insights into the Bible were the same as theirs. If so, wonderful. You can feel some satisfaction that your own mind (and heart, also) are part of the mainstream. You'll find many times that your own fresh discovery may be 2,000 years old. But it's still valid. It just means your own mind works in ways similar to other readers' minds.

And occasionally you'll find that your own interpretations are radically different from what the commentators thought. Does that mean they were right and you're wrong? Not necessarily. But it doesn't mean they're wrong and you're right, either. Over the years a lot of weird religious groups have begun because someone had a "new insight" into the Bible. For example, the Adamites read Genesis 2:25 and had a "new insight." The verse reads, "The man and his wife were both naked, and they felt no shame." The Adamites concluded that if God made Adam and Eve naked, then that was the normal human state, so let's be naked. So, a group calling itself "Christian" concluded from the Bible that nudity was the norm. Needless to say, most readers have *not* drawn that conclusion.

As part of the human family, we owe it to each other to share insights and ideas. (Sharing is not the same as forcing ideas down people's throats, by the way.) If you find that reading the Bible gives you insights into how to handle stress, find purpose in life, deal with problems, etc., others can benefit from your sharing those insights. Other people might not agree with all of them—just as you might not agree with their insights. But there's a lot to be gained by sharing. This is why Christians have, for 2,000 years, chosen to worship and study together, not just in isolation.

chapter 10

The Bare Minimum to Know:
Just What Is "Bible Literacy"?

Not long ago I interviewed several Christian leaders, asking them about Bible literacy. What, I asked them, were the key things—the basics—that a person should know about the Bible?

THE TEN COMMANDMENTS

This (Ex. 20) is the core of the Old Testament moral law, given by God to Israel. Survey after survey shows Americans' ignorance of this crucial Old Testament passage. There are only ten, and could they be that difficult to memorize? (*Living Bible* author Kenneth Taylor, father of ten and author of several books for children, mentions that children, properly taught at an early age, have no trouble memorizing the Ten.)

No, most of us don't like to memorize things—especially rules. On the other hand, we do so when we feel the need. We're glad to learn rules of the road so we can get our driver's license. Rather than viewing the Ten Commandments as an outdated series of rules irrelevant to a high-tech world, we can look at them as the basic rules God intends for us to follow—for our own best interests.

THE NAMES OF BOOKS OF THE BIBLE AND THEIR SEQUENCE

Bible drills in which children were taught to locate particular verses as quickly as possible have fallen into disuse. Gone also is the standard memorization (again, by children) of the books of the Bible, in order. Still, we do need to know where to find the passage referred to in the pastor's sermon or in the book we are reading.

AN OVERVIEW OF SALVATION HISTORY

No one has to know the names of all the kings of Israel, but all the Christian leaders I interviewed mentioned the necessity of knowing the high points of salvation history—Creation and man's fall; Noah and the Flood; Abraham, Isaac, and Jacob; Moses and Israel's Exodus from Egypt; the kingdom under Samuel, Saul, David, and Solomon; Israel's spiritual decline and exile; the messages of the prophets (particularly Elijah, Isaiah, Jeremiah, and Ezekiel); Jesus' life, death, resurrection, and teachings; the growth of the church in Acts and the Letters, especially the work of Paul; the Final Judgment.

THE SERMON ON THE MOUNT

Matthew 5–7 contains the essence of Christian ethical teaching. Memorization of such a long passage may be too much to hope for, but every Christian should have at least a familiarity with the Beatitudes, the Lord's Prayer, the words on salt and light, etc.

KEY ETHICAL PASSAGES

Besides the Ten Commandments and the Sermon on the Mount, a familiarity with Proverbs is useful. Matthew 19 (on divorce) is perhaps crucial in the modern church, as are Paul's teachings on marriage and family (particularly Eph. 5–6; Col. 3–4).

THE APOSTLES' CREED

A creed is a basic summary of Christian beliefs. Not all churches use a creed, but many do, and knowing (better, *understanding*) the points of this ancient formula are essential. Kenneth Taylor adds one disclaimer: "The Creed is sparse in regard to the Holy Spirit, and this needs expansion regarding the gifts and fruit of the Spirit. We need to know that help is available from the Spirit in crippling the sin nature and helping us in good works and thoughts."

Pastors have preached sermon series on the Apostles' Creed. It could be called a "Bible creed," since all parts of it are drawn from the Bible. And in case you're not familiar with the creed, here it is.

I believe in God the Father Almighty, maker of heaven and earth; And in Jesus Christ His only Son our Lord; who was conceived by the Holy Spirit, born of the virgin Mary, suffered under Pontius Pilate, was crucified, dead, and buried; the third day He rose from the dead; He ascended into heaven, and sits at the right hand of God the Father Almighty; from thence He shall come to judge the living and the dead.

I believe in the Holy Spirit, the holy universal Church, the communion of saints, the forgiveness of sins, the resurrection of the body, and the life everlasting.

You may know this creed already, or it may surprise you to know that for many years people recited it (by heart, not by reading) in churches all over the world. It's a good summary of the Bible's teaching about God and Christ.

BASIC DOCTRINES

The Apostles' Creed is a good summary of doctrine, but it leaves out some critical points (sin and our need of redemption, for example). Pastor Brett Griffith, whose congregation studies the Westminster Confession of Faith, gave a more complete summary of the basic doctrines we should know: "Creation, the nature of God, the Trinity, Christ as true man and true God, the nature of sin (Genesis 3 and Romans 5), the atonement, salvation through faith, sanctification ('made holy by union with Christ'), the last things (particularly the implications of Judgment for our walk with God)."

WHAT'S A FAMILY TO DO?

Charity begins at home, and so does Bible literacy. Attending Sunday School and weekly worship is essential to a knowledge of the Scriptures, but can we really expect two or three hours of church activity each week to give us enough Bible? Relying on those few hours communicates a message to children: the Bible is just "a church thing," something reserved for Sunday mornings, largely separate from the rest of the week, and from real life. Here are some modest proposals for families wanting to become more biblically literate.

A. Study the Bible together, and use a plan

Yes, the contemporary family is supremely busy, but every family ought to set aside a time daily for systematic study of the Bible. Many parents have found that immediately after dinner (assuming all members can be assembled together for one meal a day) is a good time. For a systematic (as opposed to haphazard) study of the Bible, please see chapter 5, which offers several different (and effective) approaches to studying the Bible.

B. Read

The decline of Bible literacy is connected with the general decline in literacy. For many people, books—especially older books—do not seem user-friendly. How much easier to turn on the TV or stereo! Yet consider how many centuries passed without video or audio, which meant that families entertained themselves by reading, playing games together, making their own music, etc. If you are out of the habit of reading, it may take some nudging to force yourself. Consider it a worthwhile personal investment—like dieting or exercising. Communicate the message to your children that reading is a pleasant way to pass the time. More importantly, make it clear that private reading of the Bible is a normal part of everyday life.

C. Play with the Bible

There is no reason parents can't combine education with play, and all Christian bookstores (and many secular stores as well) sell Bible board games and quiz books for all age levels. While we should never lose sight of the fact that we are to take the Bible's teachings with the utmost seriousness, Bible trivia games can be a delightful way for a family to spend time together.

D. Encourage memorization

Memorizing is a good thing. Why should Sunday School be the only place where memorization takes place? As a modest beginning, have the entire family aim to memorize one short Bible verse per month—an important verse (John 3:16, for example, or any one of the Beatitudes in Matt. 5). Then you might increase to one verse every two weeks, and so on. Use such a plan as a way of memorizing longer passages—for example, memorizing two of the Ten Commandments per month, so that in five months the family can recite all ten.

Do you think the human memory is limited? Listen closely to the man who can rattle off sports statistics from the last fifty years. Listen to the aging baby boomer who knows the words to a limitless number of rock-and-roll oldies. Most educational experts agree that human beings underuse their memories even more than they underuse their bodies' muscles.

See chapter 8 for tips on memorizing the Bible.

E. Discuss the day's events in the light of the Bible

This can occur during the family's daily Bible study, or at any time parent and child are interacting. Where a healthy parent-child situation exists, the child will probably feel comfortable discussing events of the school day. On a broader level, if the family watches the evening TV news together, discuss world, national, and local news in light of the Bible's view of God's will for mankind. You can also discuss any TV show—a sitcom, talk show, drama, even a sports event—in light of what the Bible teaches about God and human beings.

The Bible, like anything written hundreds of years ago, helps us put things in perspective by reminding us that human nature never really changes. The evening news will assure you that human beings are often greedy, immoral, militaristic, cruel, hypocritical—in short, just plain selfish. The Bible will assure you that none of this is new. There were saints and heroes in Bible times, as there are today. There were also lying politicians, unjust laws, religious persecution, oppression of the weak, wars, broken homes, alcohol dependence. Does the world really change much?

chapter 11

Taking Those First Steps: ◄···

A Pathway through the Bible

You begin reading a Tom Clancy novel on page 1. You could do that with the Bible too, beginning on page 1 with the first chapter of Genesis, the creation of the world. It seems like a logical place to begin—the birth of the universe. But you may get bogged down in some parts of Genesis (the genealogies in chapter 10, for example). Even if you don't, if you finish Genesis and move on to Exodus, you will definitely get bogged down in the Israelite law codes. Is this, you ask, supposed to inspire me?

But if you don't begin at the beginning, where do you start? Can you just dive in anywhere, hoping you'll open the pages to a really inspiring passage? You might—or might not. What to do?

Most people need some guidance here—a path through the Bible. The Gideons, the men's organization that places free Bibles in hotel rooms, understand this. If you ever look at a Gideons' Bible, you will notice that

it supplies some brief study aids. The endpapers (the pages you touch when you open the book's cover) ask you some pointed questions:

- Are you discouraged?
- Have you suffered loss?
- Are you confused?

The endpapers refer you to a Bible passage that responds to these questions. (As lonesome and impersonal as hotel rooms are, the Gideons are right in assuming that

> *I have spent a lot of time searching through the Bible for loopholes.*
> —FILM COMIC W.C. FIELDS

travelers may be asking questions like these.) The Gideon Bibles include something else: an outline of the major themes in the Bible, such as: the creation of the world, man's fall from grace, and redemption in Christ. The Gideons have provided a map through the Bible.

We need such a map because the Bible seems so unorganized. It throws together different types of writing that seem unrelated—sermons, poetry and songs, letters, histories, parables, even family trees.

Like the endpapers in the Gideon Bibles, this chapter will help you find a path through the Bible. First, you will find a list of "Great Passages in the Bible." You might call these Bible Highlights.

Next you will see a list of Great Bible Stories. The key word here is *Stories*—actual narratives, which readers agree are some of the best (that is, most interesting) stories in the Bible.

Following this are "Old Testament Highlights," "Psalm Highlights," and "New Testament Highlights." (Psalms is part of the Old Testament, but I treat it separately since this book of poetry is so big and so varied.) If you read through all the passages listed in these highlight sections (which will take some time), you will have exposed yourself to the main people and teachings in the Bible.

Following these lists of highlights, are three related thematic sections: "What the Bible Says about God," "What the Bible Says about Sin and Salvation," and "What the Bible Says about the Community of Believers."

Finally, I've included a section on "Facing Life's Crises, Challenges, and Changes." This section points you toward key Bible passages on the large and small problem areas of life—money, marriage, forgiveness, sickness, etc.

GREAT PASSAGES IN THE BIBLE

Creation
　The world's dramatic beginning
　Genesis 1–3

The Ten Commandments
　The heart of the moral law
　Exodus 20

Challenge for Joshua
　Moving words of strength and encouragement
　Joshua 1

David's Great Prayer of Praise
　1 Chronicles 29:10–19

The Shepherd's Psalm
　Assurance of God's care and guidance
　Psalm 23

Psalm of Nature
　Praising God's creation
　Psalm 19

Psalm of Praise
　Answer of the sheep to the Shepherd
　Psalm 100

Psalm of Salvation
　Thankful memories
　Psalm 107

Proverbs of Wisdom
　Good advice for the young men
　Proverbs 3

The Suffering Servant
　Isaiah's prophecy of the Messiah
　Isaiah 53

Ezekiel's Peculiar Vision
　Wind, fire, winged creatures
　Ezekiel 1

The Greatest Thing in the World
　Paul's moving chapter on love
　1 Corinthians 13

The Secrets of Happiness
　The source of true contentment in this life
　Philippians 4

Great Heroes of Faith
The "Faith Hall of Fame"
Hebrews 11
The City of God
New heaven, new earth
Revelation 21–22

GREAT STORIES IN THE BIBLE

Noah and the worldwide flood
God's rescue of a moral man
Genesis 6–8
Abraham and Isaac
Abraham's trust in God tested
Genesis 22:1-19
Jacob and Esau
Sibling rivalry, in a well–told story
Genesis 27:1-46
Joseph: the dreams, the coat,
the brothers
Joseph's rags to riches story
Genesis 37–49
The rescue of the infant Moses
God's provision for Israel's deliverer
Exodus 1:7–2:10
The exodus from Egypt
Liberating a tribe of slaves from a
world power
Exodus 7–14
The fall of Jericho
Espionage and a miraculous victory
Joshua 5:10–6:27
Jael and Deborah to the rescue
A tale of two women
Judges 4
Gideon's army
Some ingenious underdogs
Judges 6–7

Samson's story
The great Hebrew muscle man
Judges 14–16
Ruth, Naomi, and Boaz
A faithful woman's story
Ruth
God's calling of the boy Samuel
A midnight caller
1 Samuel 3
David's call to be king
God's surprising choice
1 Samuel 16:1-13
David and Goliath
Five smooth stones, a sling, and faith
1 Samuel 17
David and Jonathan
The world's most famous story of
friendship
1 Samuel 20
David and King Saul
Loyalty to one's king
1 Samuel 23–24
King David and Bathsheba
God's man falls into sin
2 Samuel 11–12
David and Absalom's rebellion
A favorite son's treason
2 Samuel 15–18
Solomon's sword
The king shows his God-given wisdom
1 Kings 3
Elijah and the false prophets of Baal
Israel's God displays His power
1 Kings 18
Chariot of fire
The Prophet Elijah taken to heaven
2 Kings 2:1-12
Josiah and the Book of the Law
The king's reform movement
2 Kings 22

Poor Job
The suffering of a good man
Job 1–3; 9–10

Daniel and Nebuchadnezzar's dream
God's interpreter
Daniel 2

The fiery furnace
Daniel's friends come out unharmed
Daniel 3

Daniel in the lions' den
God's protection of his man
Daniel 6

Jonah, the runaway prophet
The problem of saying no to God
Jonah

Philip and the Ethiopian
African becomes a follower of Christ
Acts 8

Conversion of Saul
Dynamic Jewish leader stopped in his tracks
Acts 9

The Philippian jailer
Earthquake almost leads to jailbreak
Acts 16

Paul's shipwreck
One danger after another
Acts 27–28

OLD TESTAMENT HIGHLIGHTS

The beginning of everything
Genesis 1

Man's fall into sin
Genesis 3

The great Flood
Genesis 6–8

Abraham's faith tested
Genesis 22

Jacob's dream at Bethel
Genesis 28

The birth of the liberator Moses
Exodus 2

Moses' encounter at the burning bush
Exodus 3

The miraculous crossing of the Red Sea
Exodus 14

Manna and quail from heaven
Exodus 16

Moses and the glory of the Lord
Exodus 33

The death of Moses
Deuteronomy 34

God's command to Joshua
Joshua 1

Israel's crossing over the Jordan
Joshua 3

The fall of Jericho
Joshua 5–6

Gideon and the Midianites
Judges 7

Samson and his exploits
Judges 13–16

The Lord calls Samuel
1 Samuel 3

David and Goliath
1 Samuel 17

Elijah's showdown on Mount Carmel
1 Kings 18

Benefits of wisdom
Proverbs 3

Sayings of the wise
Proverbs 22

The wife of noble character
Proverbs 31

Remember your Creator while young
Ecclesiastes 11–12

The Prophet Isaiah's commissioning
Isaiah 6

Predicting a Messiah
Isaiah 9
Consolation for God's people
Isaiah 40
The suffering of God's Servant
Isaiah 52–53
The king burns Jeremiah's scroll
Jeremiah 36
The mysterious handwriting
Daniel 5
Daniel in the lions' den
Daniel 6

PSALM HIGHLIGHTS

The Psalms are the Bible's "hymnal" and were (and still are) set to music. They are poems and songs, usually addressed to God or speaking about God. The Psalms run the gamut of feeling—joy, depression, doubt, anger, despair, guilt, gratitude, you name it. Some are almost shocking in their display of raw emotion. But Psalms is a great book, a book for whatever emotional state you are in.

True happiness through a moral life
Psalm 1
A cry for help and mercy
Psalm 6
God's glory and His love for man
Psalm 8
God's glory in creation
Psalm 19
A song of anguish and praise
Psalm 22
"The Lord is my shepherd"
Psalm 23
God the great King
Psalm 24
Praise for the saving Lord
Psalm 27

Confession and cleansing
Psalm 32
The fate of the evil and the good
Psalm 37
David's prayer of repentance
Psalm 51
Confidence in God's protection
Psalm 62
A cry for help
Psalm 69
Comfort in distress
Psalm 77
Longing for God's house
Psalm 84
God the supreme Ruler
Psalm 97
The amazing love of God
Psalm 103
The cry of a troubled soul
Psalm 116
Happiness in following God's commands
Psalm 119
The Lord our protector
Psalm 121
Trusting in God's constant love
Psalm 130
"His love is eternal"
Psalm 136
God's complete knowledge and care
Psalm 139
Not human aid, but God's
Psalm 146

NEW TESTAMENT HIGHLIGHTS

God's eternal Word becomes man
John 1:1-18
Jesus Christ is born
Matthew 1:18–2:16; Luke 2:1-20

Jesus introduced by John the Baptist
Matthew 3:1-17

Jesus' temptation
Matthew 4:1-11

Jesus' ministry begins
Luke 4:1-21

Jesus' Sermon on the Mount
Matthew 5-7

Jesus feeds 5,000 people
Mark 6:30-56

Jesus heals the sick and calms the storm
Matthew 8:1-34

The Parable of the Sower
Matthew 13:1-23

Parables of the Kingdom of Heaven
Matthew 13:24-52

The Parable of the Lost Son
Luke 15:11-32

The conversion of Zacchaeus
Luke 19:1-10

The Parable of the Talents
Luke 19:11-27

Jesus rides into Jerusalem
Luke 19:28-48

The Last Supper
Mark 14:12-26

A parting message to the disciples
John 14:1-21

Jesus arrested
Mark 14:32-56

The trial of Jesus
Mark 15:1-20

Jesus crucified
Matthew 27:32-44

Jesus' resurrection
Matthew 28:1-20

Jesus' ascension into heaven
Acts 1:1-14

The Holy Spirit comes to the believers
Acts 2:1-39

Stephen, the first martyr
Acts 6:6–7:60

An Ethiopian converted
Acts 8:26-40

Paul's change from persecutor to apostle
Acts 9:1-25

Peter and Cornelius
Acts 10

The meeting at Jerusalem
Acts 15

Paul preaches to the men of Athens
Acts 17:16-34

Paul's defense before King Agrippa
Acts 26:1-32

God and sin
Romans 1

Life in the Spirit
Romans 8

Life in God's service
Romans 12

Gifts of the Spirit, and the greatest gift
1 Corinthians 12–13

The resurrection of believers
1 Corinthians 15

The Spirit and human nature
Galatians 5:16-26

God's armor for believers
Ephesians 6:10-20

The old life and the new
Colossians 3:5-17

Great people of faith
Hebrews 11

God's loving discipline
Hebrews 12:1-11

Faith, wisdom, and perseverance
James 1:1-18

The last days
2 Peter 3:1-18

What we should love
1 John 2:7-17

New heaven and new earth
Revelation 21

Jesus is coming soon
Revelation 22

WHAT THE BIBLE SAYS ABOUT GOD

God the Creator
Genesis 1

Man in God's image
Genesis 2

God's dazzling holiness
Isaiah 6

God as the Ruler of all
Job 38–41

God without equal
Isaiah 40

The song of amazement
Psalm 8

God's awareness of the individual person
Psalm 139

His promise of healing
Isaiah 57:14-21

WHAT THE BIBLE SAYS ABOUT SIN AND SALVATION

The beginning of human sin
Genesis 3

A song of confession
Psalm 51

Our sin and God's Suffering Servant
Isaiah 53

Jesus, Nicodemus, and the new birth
John 3

The answer to universal sin
Romans 3:10-26

From death to life
Ephesians 2:1-10

A city without sin
Revelation 21–2

WHAT THE BIBLE SAYS ABOUT THE COMMUNITY OF BELIEVERS

God's new covenant on human hearts
Jeremiah 31:31-34

The sending of the Spirit
John 14:15-31

The birth of the church at Pentecost
Acts 2

Adoption into God's family
Galatians 4:1-7

The first Christians' fellowship
Acts 2:41-47

The believers' charity
Acts 4:32-35

The different gifts of believers
1 Corinthians 12–13

Warning against outside influences
2 Corinthians 6:14–7:1

Gathering together for worship
Hebrews 10:19-25

Baptism and witnessing
Matthew 28:16-20

Baptism as identifying with Jesus
Romans 6:1-5

The Last Supper
Matthew 26:20-29

The practice of Communion
1 Corinthians 11:17-34

FACING LIFE'S CRISES, CHALLENGES, AND CHANGES

The God revealed in the Bible isn't just a fair-weather friend. He is a loving Father, pleased that people reach out to Him in both good and bad times. It's true that (as with our earthly parents) we are more inclined to run to them in times of need than in times of joy. But God doesn't mind this. He desires our fellowship, even if we are "bad-weather believers."

The following list directs you to key Bible passages that cover a wide range of problems and challenges. I have not listed every verse on the topics, just some important ones. If you'd like a book that gives more comprehensive lists, you might consider investing in a topical Bible or in *The Complete Book of Bible Promises* (Tyndale House, 1997).

People who have read the Bible for years have the advantage of knowing where to turn in the Bible when they encounter life's difficulties. In fact, they may not even need to turn to the Bible. They may have memorized key verses—if not the exact words, at least the basic ideas. Longtime Bible readers have in their heads a "Bible memory bank," something valuable in any predicament in life. (If you read history, American history in particular, you'll be amazed at how often notable speakers and authors quote from or refer to the Bible—as if they knew its words and ideas by heart. Many of them did, even if they weren't particularly "religious" people.)

Aging
Psalm 90:1-6, 10-12
Psalm 92:12-14
Proverbs 16:31
Proverbs 20:29

Anger
Proverbs 15:1
Romans 12:19-21
Ephesians 4:31-32
James 1:19-20

Bad company
Romans 12:1-2
Ephesians 5:6-9
1 Peter 4:1-5

Career choices
Proverbs 31:10-30
Matthew 19:4-6
Ephesians 5:22-33
Jude 24–25

Children
Psalm 127:3-5
Proverbs 13:24
Proverbs 22:6

Citizenship
Matthew 22:15-21
Romans 13:1-7
Philippians 3:20-21
1 Peter 2:13-15, 17

Comfort
Psalm 73:25-26, 28
Psalm 23
Matthew 10:29-31
John 14:27
2 Corinthians 1:3-7

Confessing sin
Psalm 32:1-6
Proverbs 28:13
Romans 14:11-12
1 John 1:9

Conflict
Proverbs 10:12
Proverbs 20:3
1 Corinthians 3:3
James 4:1-6

Contentment
Proverbs 15:15
Proverbs 23:17
Philippians 4:11-13
1 Timothy 6:6-7

Death
Isaiah 25:8
Matthew 22:30
1 Corinthians 15:51-55
Hebrews 2:14-15

Depression or discouragement
Romans 8:28-29
2 Corinthians 4:8-18
Hebrews 12:1-3
1 Peter 4:12-13

The Devil
2 Corinthians 11:14-15
Ephesians 6:11-17
1 Peter 5:8-9
1 John 3:8-10

The Earth
Genesis 9:1-3
Psalm 8:3-9
Luke 12:27
1 John 2:15-17

Enemies
Psalm 118:6-9
Proverbs 24:17-18
Matthew 5:43-48
Luke 18:7-8

Eternal life
Luke 20:37-38
John 11:25-26
1 Corinthians 15:19-22
1 John 5:11-14

Faith
Matthew 17:20
Romans 5:1-3
Colossians 2:6
1 John 5:4

Fear
Psalm 27:1-3
Isaiah 43:1-3
Matthew 10:28
John 14:27

Feeling far from God
Psalm 42:5-11
Psalm 139:1-18
Acts 17:22-30

Feeling inadequate
1 Corinthians 1:20-31
2 Corinthians 12:9, 10
Philippians 4:12, 13

Forgiveness
Matthew 5:7, 39-48
Matthew 6:14-15
Ephesians 4:31-32
Colossians 3:13

Friends
1 Samuel 18:1-4
Proverbs 17:9
Proverbs 20:6
John 15:12-17

God's guidance
Psalm 23
Psalm 73:22-26
Isaiah 42:16
John 14:16-17, 26

Guilt
Psalm 103:12-14
Ezekiel 18:21-22
Romans 3:23-24
2 Corinthians 5:17-19

Hatred
Proverbs 10:12

Matthew 5:43-44
1 John 3:10-15
1 John 4:20-21
Heaven
Job 19:25
Matthew 6:19-21
John 14:2-3
Colossians 3:1-4
Hell
Ezekiel 33:11
Matthew 13:41-43
Matthew 13:47-50
1 Thessalonians 1:7-10
The Holy Spirit
Ezekiel 36:26-28
John 3:5-6
John 16:13-15
1 Corinthians 2:12, 14-16
Hope
Psalm 31:23-24
Lamentations 3:22-26
Ephesians 2:12-13
Hebrews 6:18-19
Jealousy
Luke 15:25-32
Galatians 5:19-26
James 3:13-18
Joy
Psalm 30:5, 11
Isaiah 61:10-11
John 15:9-11
Philippians 4:4-7
Judging people
1 Samuel 16:7
Matthew 7:1-5
James 2:12-13
James 4:11-12
Loneliness
Psalm 25:16, 21
Psalm 40:17

Psalm 68:4-6
2 Corinthians 6:18
Loving people
Proverbs 17:17
Luke 6:31-36
Luke 10:25-28
Romans 13:8-10
Marriage
Proverbs 5:15-19
1 Corinthians 7:2-3, 7-9
Ephesians 5:21-33
Hebrews 13:4
Money
Psalm 37:16
Psalm 49:10-13, 20
Ecclesiastes 5:10-15
1 Timothy 6:10, 17-19
Obeying God
Psalm 103:17-21
Matthew 7:24-27
John 15:10-16
Romans 6:16-18
Oppression
Psalm 9:9
Psalm 12:5
Amos 5:7-15
Micah 2:1-3
Parents
Exodus 20:12
Proverbs 22:6
Proverbs 22:15
Patience
Psalm 37:7-9
Proverbs 16:32
1 Corinthians 13:4-5
2 Corinthians 6:3-7
Peace, inner
Isaiah 26:3
Matthew 5:9

Romans 8:6
Philippians 4:7

Personal growth
John 15:5-9
Ephesians 4:14-24
Philippians 1:6, 9-11
1 Thessalonians 4:1-8

Politics and government
Psalm 2:1-4
Psalm 33:10-16
Psalm 146:3-8
Isaiah 40:15-23

Prayer
Psalm 145:18-19
Matthew 7:7-11
James 1:5-7
1 John 5:14

Repentance
2 Chronicles 7:14
Psalm 51
Luke 5:31-32
Luke 15:4-10

Revenge
Leviticus 19:18
Proverbs 26:27
Matthew 5:38-47
Romans 12:17-19

Salvation
Ezekiel 36:25-28
Matthew 7:13-14
Matthew 16:25
John 3:3-7

Self-control
Proverbs 5:22-23
Matthew 16:24-27
Romans 8:12-13
2 Peter 1:6

Self-esteem
Ecclesiastes 5:13
Proverbs 3:5-8

Matthew 6:33-34
Matthew 16:26

Sex
1 Corinthians 6:9-11, 15-18
Galatians 5:18-21
Ephesians 5:3-14
Colossians 3:5-10

Sickness
2 Corinthians 4:16
2 Corinthians 5:1-4
2 Corinthians 12:8-10
James 5:13-15

Sin
Psalm 14:3
Romans 1:18-25
Romans 3:22-25
2 Corinthians 5:19, 21

Success
Matthew 16:26
Romans 12:2
1 Corinthians 1:20
1 Corinthians 7:31

Temptation
Proverbs 2:10-12
Romans 6:14
1 Corinthians 10:12-13
James 1:13-17

The tongue
Psalm 34:12-15
Matthew 12:33-37
Matthew 15:18-20
James 3:2-10

Trusting God
Psalm 37:3-5
Psalm 46:1-2
Habakkuk 2:4
Matthew 6:28-33

Work
Genesis 1:27-28
Genesis 2:15

Ecclesiastes 5:12
Ephesians 6:6-7
2 Thessalonians 3:6-13
Worry and anxiety
Psalm 112:1-8
Matthew 6:25-34
Philippians 4:6-8
1 Peter 5:6-7

TEN COMMANDMENTS FOR MAKING YOUR WAY THROUGH THE BIBLE

Rule 1: Don't start at the beginning as you would any other book, working your way through to the end. The Bible has a basic plot, but you will have trouble discerning it if you just plunge in. You will find yourself diverted here and there down side roads as you proceed from book to book and may have trouble finding your way back to the main highway.

Rule 2: Don't start at the end to see how the story comes out. The last book of the Bible, Revelation, is the hardest of all to understand, and it may also scare the wits out of you. Who wants to be both scared and confused? (If you wanted that, you could just read the daily newspaper.)

Rule 3: Don't study the Bible as though it held impenetrable secrets or is infinitely subtle. There is plenty in the Bible that is unclear, but many things may have been unclear to the authors as well. Besides, the Bible doesn't try to answer all questions that interest you. The Bible is right for the ages, but each book was written for specific purposes in the past and deals immediately with that time and audience, not ours. Don't instantly demand of a passage "What is God telling me here?" Determine first what He was telling the people at the time, then see how your situation may be similar.

Rule 4: Don't expect science or literalism or perfect consistency. The Bible contains revelation, not laboratory research. We know more about the physical world than the Bible's authors did, but that does not make us right and them wrong. Look for the moral truth. It is good for all time, for the wise and simple alike. Complex truths are, of themselves, no better than simple truths. In fact, simple truths tend to humble us and clear our minds and will. (Remember the title of the best-selling book, *Everything I Need to Know I Learned in Kindergarten*.)

Rule 5: Don't be put off by the chapter and verse numbers. These road signs were imposed on the ancient texts in modern times to help people locate passages. That is their only function.

Rule 6: Don't expect to be inspired by the characters in the Bible. Sunday School tends to make heroes of key characters, but even these protagonists lapse into jealousy, cruelty, greed, cowardice, and worse. Think of Abraham who passed off his wife as his sister and Peter who denied that he even knew Jesus. One of the reasons the Bible is so persuasive is that its cast of characters is so true to life, which is to say, full of contradiction. But these flawed characters become heroic when, presented with hard decisions, they choose to obey God's command.

Rule 7: Don't be put off by the miraculous. See wonders as signs of God's interest and intervention. You may prefer natural explanations of the Flood, the parting of the Red Sea, and Jesus' healing the sick. What is important is to see God's hand in miracles. The miraculous is a sign that God cares, not that God is a Mister Fix-It, stepping in to patch up every problem. Yet God has the freedom to perform miracles when the time is right.

Rule 8: If you think of the Bible as a vast supermarket, you are not far wrong. But you can shop for the wrong things in it and come up with a bad diet. The devil can quote Scripture to his benefit. Generations of Jews and Christians have cited portions of the Bible as justification for outrageous behavior. Deny the temptation to cite the Bible to support your own prejudices and rationalizations, thereby enrolling God in your righteousness. Instead, seek God's wisdom and God's will.

Rule 9: Reading and quoting the Bible is no substitute for acting on what God reveals there. The two great commandments are to love God and to love one's neighbor. All the rest is footnote. There are Bible scholars who are "moral idiots" because they have head knowledge of the Bible but don't apply it to their lives. (In the Bible, the word "fool" refers to a person who is morally deficient, not mentally deficient.)

Rule 10: Read with others who will protect you from eccentricity. Remember that the church created the Bible, and it is in the church that we gain perspective on God's revelation, which speaks to us corporately, not individually. C.S. Lewis observed that group study "takes us out of our solitary conceit."

chapter 12

In a Nutshell: ◄···

The Books of the Old Testament, What They're About, Problems They Have, Parts You Might Want to Skip

A s I already mentioned, I believe the Bible—the whole thing—is inspired by God. As a whole, it teaches human beings all we need to know about God, our relationship with Him, our destiny in this world and afterward.

This doesn't mean that you can open the Bible at random and get "inspired." You might open to the wonderful Beatitudes of Jesus in Matthew 5. These beautiful teachings seem relevant for all times and all peoples. But then, you might open the Bible to the gory details about animal sacrifice in Leviticus. These details may be inspired, but most readers today don't find them very inspiring to read. So, to state the obvious, it might help readers to know which of the books (and portions of books) in the Bible are most rewarding to read . . . and which ones aren't.

This chapter and the next contain capsule summaries of each of the Bible's sixty-six books. Following each summary is a list of problems—"snags" you may encounter in reading the book. Listing these is not intended to cast doubt on the book's worth. Knowing about the snags before you encounter them can be a helpful thing. For each book I've also listed "skippable" passages for those who skip. These lists aren't intended to steer you away from any part of the Bible. Read the whole thing if you can. But if you can't (and most people don't, frankly), these skippable parts are ones that most readers agree are not extremely rewarding.

One warning: The books are presented here in their sequence in the Bible. I don't recommend you read them in that order. For more information on a logical plan for Bible reading, see chapter 11.

THE FIRST FIVE BOOKS

Known as the Torah, the Law, the Books of Moses, and the Pentateuch, the first five books are concerned with the world's beginnings and the beginnings of God's chosen nation, Israel. Tradition says the books were written, or compiled, by Moses, who is the chief character in all but the first (Genesis). For the Jewish religion, the first five books are *the* sacred books, more important than all other books, including the other books in the Old Testament. They are most often referred to by the Hebrew word *Torah*, which means "law"—more accurately, "instruction." (Instruction seems more appealing, since most of us dislike laws.) For Christians the importance of these books is that they show God as Creator and as One who provides people with a moral law to guide them in this life. These books also show God making a covenant—a binding agreement—with Abraham and his descendants (the Hebrews). The agreement, basically, is "If you will obey Me and be My law-abiding people, I will be your Guide and Protector in the world. When you abandon Me and My Law, and when you worship false gods, you will run into trouble."

Moses is the key figure here, and when the New Testament refers to the Bible's first five books, it uses phrases like "Moses said" and "Moses wrote" and "Moses commanded." No other person in the Old Testament has the authority Moses has. He is the great law-giver and deliverer from Egypt—although in fact he is only the *human* leader, since it is God Himself who reveals the Law and leads the people from Egypt.

Much of the first five books is fascinating—the creation of the world, Abraham and his family, Jacob and his sons (the basis for a popular Broadway musical), the inspiring tale of Moses, and the miraculous deliverance from the Egyptians (re-created in a great movie with Charlton Heston). But much of these five books leaves people cold—notably the page after page of rules, rules, rules. Most of these rules no longer apply to human life—the rules regarding animal sacrifices, for example. But many of the rules about ethical dealings with each other still have value. The Ten Commandments (found in Ex. 20 and Deut. 5) are considered to be the high point of divine law in the Old Testament. If you remember nothing else from these five books, try to memorize the Ten Commandments.

Genesis

Summary: Genesis, in fifty chapters, deals with the world's beginnings. God creates the world, including man and woman. Man and woman fall into sin, but God promises salvation. The plan of salvation comes to focus on the tribe of Israel, descended from the patriarch Jacob and his twelve sons.

Genesis includes some of the best-known and most interesting characters and events in the Bible: Adam and Eve, Cain and Abel, Noah and the Flood, the tower of Babel, Abraham, Isaac, and Jacob and sons, particularly the son Joseph. It is interesting reading throughout, and a knowledge of the book is essential for understanding the rest of the Bible. The book's title is the Greek word for "beginnings" or "origins."

Problems: One of the most fascinating documents in the world is, alas, the center of controversy, mostly because of questions about the nature of Creation. Scoffers, armed with the data of science, snicker at the Genesis account of the world's and mankind's creation. These age-old controversies should have no effect on appreciating this remarkable book. (In fact, the Big Bang theory of the world's creation isn't radically different from Genesis' story of God creating the universe out of nothing.) Rather than getting caught up in the scientific controversies, readers should focus on the key teachings in the early chapters: God created the world from nothing; man was made in God's image and was originally good; man fell (and still falls) into sin because of his desire to be independent of God. These teachings in no way contradict science.

For those who skip . . . Hardly anything. However, the "family tree" chapters (10, most of 11, 36, most of 46) can be breezed through quickly.

Exodus

Summary: The tribe of Israel, enslaved in the Egyptian empire, is led to freedom by the power of God, whose spokesman is the great figure Moses. An Israelite raised in the Egyptian court, Moses faces off with the formidable Pharaoh. God sends plagues on Egypt, and Pharaoh frees the Israelites, only to pursue them later. The Egyptian forces are drowned in the Red Sea. Once out of Egypt, Moses receives the Ten Commandments and other decrees from God. The freed Israelites prove to be a cantankerous and thankless mob as they progress toward their promised homeland in Canaan. The book's title is a Greek word meaning "going out."

Problems: "Did the plagues really happen?" some would ask. An open-minded person, aware of the wonders regularly being discovered by scientists, would answer, "Why not?" Even if they can be explained as natural phenomena, the faith question remains: "Couldn't God have acted through natural means?" The Israelites at that period in history would not have drawn a hard line (as we do today) between "natural" and "supernatural" because they believed God controlled all natural processes. One passage that puzzles almost everyone is Exodus 4:21-26. This is one of the Bible's most notorious fish bones. (See chap. 4 for an explanation of fish bones in the Bible, this one bone in particular.)

For those who skip . . . Chapters 21–40 are mostly regulations for worship. These are less interesting than the fascinating narrative of the earlier chapters. However, they do contain some enlightening examples of moral instruction.

Leviticus

Summary: The book consists mostly of rules—for worshiping God, for making sacrifices, for handling everyday problems concerning cleanliness. The laws of kosher are contained here. The book's title refers to the Levites, Israel's tribe of priests. The leader Moses was from this tribe.

Problems: The book's detailed description of animal sacrifices will repel some readers, particularly since the sacrificial system is no longer part of either Jewish or Christian worship. Readers need to understand, though, that animal sacrifice has played a role in most major world religions, and in some areas it still does. You also need to have some understanding of the basic concept of sacrificing something in order to restore the right relationship with God.

For those who skip . . . While the book

"Eye for an Eye" . . . Progressive Morals?

Yes, the idea of "eye for an eye, tooth for a tooth" really is in the Bible:

"If anyone injures his neighbor, whatever he has done must be done to him: fracture for fracture, eye for eye, tooth for tooth. As he has injured the other, so he is to be injured" (Lev. 24:19-20).

This law from the Old Testament strikes us as spiteful and vindictive (or "mean-spirited," to use the now-popular phrase). In the New Testament, Jesus taught a higher ethic:

"You have heard that it was said, 'Eye for eye, and tooth for tooth.' But I tell you, Do not resist an evil person. If someone strikes you on the right cheek, turn to him the other also" (Matt. 5:38-39).

Doesn't that sound better—more "Christian"?

For the record, the Old Testament law was compassionate and progressive. "Eye for eye, tooth for tooth" was a limit. It meant "tit for tat"—but no more. The common custom (human nature never changes!) was (and is) to get more than even. But the enlightened law in Leviticus said, "No, if you're injured you can't take two teeth because you lost one tooth." It was actually a progressive law. Jesus took it a step further.

We wonder: How would the Bible authors view personal injury lawsuits today?

---

ought to be read through at least once in one's lifetime, most of it is skippable. Chapter 19, however, contains some interesting laws about social ethics. Chapter 11 is somewhat interesting because it is the basis of the Jewish kosher foods laws. Chapter 16 lays down the rules for the Day of Atonement, which Jews still observe. This chapter is the origin of the concept of the "scapegoat." Likewise, chapter 23 lays down the rules for the other Jewish holy days. This is important, since Jews still observe these today, and the days play an important role later in the New Testament.

Numbers

Summary: Having left Egypt, the nation of Israel is still on its way through the wilderness to its homeland. The book is largely concerned with the people's rebellions against their God-appointed leaders, and with God's miraculous provisions for the people's needs. Numbers also has several chapters of worship regulations. The book's title refers to the censuses of Israel (chaps.

1 and 26). (In fact, "Censuses" would be a more accurate title, although a lot more happens in the book besides census-taking.)

Problems: Many people would question the miracles in the book—for example, the miraculous provision of manna and quail for the Israelites. These are not "problems" for any who accept the possibility of miracles. Perhaps a greater problem is the book's attitude toward non-Israelites—hostile, to say the least. Keep in mind that, in Jewish and Christian tradition, God's salvation plan involved settling the Israelites in their ancestral homeland. Any individuals or nations who opposed this were, in effect, opposing God's will.

For those who skip . . . As with Leviticus, the "rule" chapters can be skipped (7–10; 15; 18–19; 28–30). So can the many chapters accounting the Israel censuses and other lists (chaps. 1–5; 26; 33–36). The story of Balaam and his talking donkey in chapter 22 is one that most people enjoy. By all means, read the famous "priestly blessing" in 6:22-27. And read about the miraculous flocks of quail and the rebellion against Moses in chapters 11–12.

Deuteronomy

Summary: On the threshold of the Promised Land, Moses addresses the Israelites and reiterates much of the Law (including the Ten Commandments) from the earlier books. He encourages Israel to follow God's Law faithfully. Moses dies and is buried by God. The book's title means "second law," since it repeats many earlier rules.

Problems: As with Numbers, Deuteronomy takes a hostile view toward non-Israelites. This is not in keeping with the Christian view of love for one's enemies. It does reflect the Hebrews' belief in keeping their religion pure, which meant not accepting the ways of the heathen nations they encountered. Some of the practices of the other nations—such as child sacrifice and ritual prostitution—were truly horrible.

For those who skip . . . Many of the rule chapters are skippable (12–29), as is Moses' blessing of the twelve tribes. However, considering how often Deuteronomy is quoted in the New Testament (Jesus Himself quoted it more than once), this important book deserves at least one good read-through in a lifetime. Be sure to read the consequences of obeying and disobeying (chap. 28) and the story of Moses' death (chap. 34). Most people are touched by this depiction of the great leader who led his people to their new homeland but died before he could live there. The chapter explains the Hebrews' deep reverence for Moses.

THE HISTORICAL BOOKS

There is history in the first five books but, being so full of regulations, those books are often called "the Law." The books that follow are more directly concerned with historical events. Oddly, the Jews consider the books from Joshua through 2 Kings to be "the Former Prophets"—"prophets" not meaning "those who predict" but "those who reveal God's will to humankind." Several of these prophets—notably Samuel in 1 Samuel and Elijah in 1 Kings—are important figures in the Old Testament.

These books continue the story begun in the Law. Led out of Egypt by Moses, the Israelites now settle in their promised homeland, Canaan. Doing so involves driving out the heathen inhabitants, not coexisting peacefully with them. This violent process takes a long time, and the Israelites are constantly tempted to follow these people in their idolatrous worship. Even after the military leaders (called "judges") secure peace for the Israelites, the people still go astray, forgetting that God gave them the land after leading them from slavery in Egypt.

Following the lead of the neighbor nations, Israel asks God for a single leader, a king. The first king, the great military leader Saul, begins well but ends as a failure. The second, David, becomes one of the great heroes of Hebrew history, second only to Moses in reputation. David's story and personal life are told in more detail than any-one else's. He is succeeded by his wise and wealthy son Solomon.

After Solomon's death, the kingdom of Israel splits into two nations—the Southern Kingdom, known as Judah, and the Northern Kingdom, still known as Israel. Both nations and their kings constantly lapse into idol worship and forget God. Both nations find themselves as pawns in the international power games of empires like Egypt, Assyria, and Babylon. Israel is, generally, even more heathenized than Judah, and Israel is the first to fall to a heathen power (Assyria). Judah lingers on a bit longer but is finally conquered by Babylon. The leading people of Judah are taken into exile in Babylon. The authors of the historical books assure the reader that all this occurred because the people would not keep the agreement to worship God alone. They neglected Him, worshiped other gods, and depended on foreign power instead of God's power, and they paid the price.

Many people and events in the Law, the first five books, seem to us almost legendary. But with the historical books we are on pretty firm historical ground, as the archaeologists continually find. No one today seriously doubts that the kings Saul, David, and Solomon (and those who followed them) were real, historical human beings.

The small Book of Ruth is set in the period of the Judges, and in our Bible it follows the Book of Judges. In the Hebrew Bible, though, Ruth is actually part of the group of books known as the Writings. (I discuss this group of writings later in this chapter.)

When you read the historical books, try not to focus on the minute details. The authors weren't giving information to prepare you for a quiz on names and dates. They were interested in God and His relation to people, particularly the nation of Israel. Focus on the forest, not the individual trees. The forest is God's shaping rebellious people into a people of faith.

Joshua

Summary: Joshua, Moses' successor as leader of the Israelites, leads the settlement of Canaan, the land God gave to Israel. Key events are the conquests of Jericho (with the tumbling walls) and Ai. The book (named, obviously, for its main human character) is essentially a story of conquest, a process that would have been impossible without God's help.

Problems: As with earlier books in the Old Testament, Joshua paints a harsh (and non-Christian) picture of non-Israelites. But the picture is in keeping with the divine plan for establishing the true faith. Israel had no choice but to reject the beliefs and worship (often grossly immoral) of the pagan inhabitants of Canaan.

For those who skip . . . Some of the "list" chapters are skippable (12–21), since much of the book is concerned with how the twelve tribes of Israel divided the land of Canaan among themselves. In fact, the whole book could be skipped, except that it contains some wonderful and dramatic stories, such as the fall of Jericho in chapter 6 (the source of the old spiritual, "Joshua Fit de Battle of Jericho").

Judges

Summary: After Israel's settlement in Canaan, the people are periodically harassed by the neighboring nations. A series of judges arise to help conquer the enemies. ("Deliverers" or "champions" would be more accurate terms, since they aren't judges in our modern legal sense. They are judges in the sense that they bring justice to the people by getting their enemies off their backs.) Settled in Canaan, the Israelites often fall into worship of false gods, which inevitably leads to disaster. Three of the Bible's most colorful characters, Samson the strongman, Jephthah, and Gideon, are key actors in the story. The woman judge Deborah is also an important figure.

Problems: The book paints a painfully realistic picture of these violent and immoral times. Blood flows freely in the book, and even some of the heroes, such as Samson, engage in some morally questionable acts (consorting with a prostitute, for example). These can be overlooked if the reader remembers that the main issue here is God's concern that His people, Israel, will forget their deliverance from Egypt and fall into the worship of false gods.

For those who skip . . . Chapters 17–21, the book's closing section, are skippable (and downright gruesome to boot). The stories of the key judges are contained in the earlier chapters. Don't skip Gideon (6–8) or Samson (13–16). The book's last verse painfully summarizes the key theme.

Ruth

Summary: Ruth, a woman of the neighbor nation of Moab, marries an Israelite man. Widowed, she leaves Moab with her Israelite mother-in-law, settles in Israel, and marries an Israelite. She becomes an ancestor of the famous King David.

Problems: None, since the book is a lovely story of a woman's devotion to her mother-in-law and her embracing of the faith of Israel.

For those who skip . . . With only four chapters, this sweet tale can be read in ten minutes. Considering it is set in the same violent period as the Book of Judges, it is blissfully calm and bloodless—a nice relief if you've finished reading Judges.

1 Samuel

Summary: The boy Samuel is called to God's service. Becoming an adult, he serves as leader and judge of Israel. Oppressed by the Philistines, Israel cries out for a warrior leader, and Samuel anoints Israel's first king, the handsome and militaristic Saul. But Saul proves to have some personal weaknesses, and God chooses a better man, David. Much of the book concerns the rivalry between Saul and David. The book ends with Saul's death after

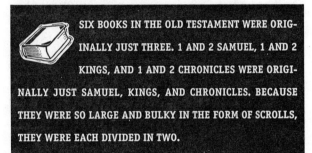

SIX BOOKS IN THE OLD TESTAMENT WERE ORIGINALLY JUST THREE. 1 AND 2 SAMUEL, 1 AND 2 KINGS, AND 1 AND 2 CHRONICLES WERE ORIGINALLY JUST SAMUEL, KINGS, AND CHRONICLES. BECAUSE THEY WERE SO LARGE AND BULKY IN THE FORM OF SCROLLS, THEY WERE EACH DIVIDED IN TWO.

a battle with the Philistines.

Problems: In telling the story of the fascinating character David, the book seems to present two versions of how he came into the service of King Saul (chaps. 16 and 17). However, the two accounts can be easily reconciled.

For those who skip . . . The entire book is great reading, containing such stories as God calling the boy Samuel, David slaying Goliath, David's close friendship with Jonathan, Saul using the witch of Endor to summon Samuel's ghost. Some readers may want to "fast-forward" through the accounts of battles with the Philistines.

2 Samuel

Summary: David laments Saul's death. After a brief war between his followers and those of Saul, David becomes king over all Israel. He makes Jerusalem the capital city. (This choice of Jerusalem as the Jewish capital still has an impact on affairs in the Middle East today.) Although devoted to God, David commits adultery and his various children (by several wives) engage in incest, murder, and rebellion against the king. David reigns a long time but endures many setbacks.

Problems: The book is blunt in its descriptions of adultery, incest, court intrigue, and bloodshed. While David is an admirable character in many ways, his failings are described in painful detail. The book is an object lesson in the problems associated with the ancient practice of polygamy. It is clear that "blended families" had problems even in Bible times!

For those who skip . . . Most of the book is interesting, particularly the parts covering David's family affairs. Some of the battle and rebellion accounts (chaps. 10; 20–21; 23–24) can be read through quickly.

1 Kings

Summary: King David dies, and some of his sons compete for the throne. His chosen successor, Solomon, eventually triumphs, and he establishes a reputation for wisdom. He also becomes the great builder of Israel, constructing the magnificent temple and other public buildings in Jerusalem. However, his many pagan wives (most of whom he marries for political alliances) lead him into idolatry. After his death, ten of Israel's twelve tribes rebel against his son Rehoboam, and afterward there are two separate kingdoms: Israel (ten tribes) and Judah (two tribes, ruled by David's descendants). The later chapters alternate between

the two kingdoms. The fiery Prophet Elijah is a major player, working to lead Israel back to worship of the true God. His adversaries, nasty King Ahab and the equally vile Queen Jezebel, are also key players.

Note: 1 and 2 Kings claim to draw on some long-vanished court histories—such as "the book of the annals of Solomon" and "the book of the annals of the kings of Israel."

Problems: Many of the events in 1–2 Samuel and 1–2 Kings are retold in 1–2 Chronicles. There are some disagreements in the parallel accounts, but none of any great importance.

For those who skip . . . The accounts of the building of the temple and other buildings (chaps. 5–8) can be read through very quickly (but read closely the temple prayer, 8:22-61). Beginning with chapter 14, the alternating accounts of the kings of Judah and Israel can be read quickly. But give full attention to the Elijah stories, beginning at chapter 17. He is one of the key figures in the Old Testament, one who is mentioned several times in the New Testament. For the people of Israel, Elijah became the symbol of the true prophets of God.

2 Kings

Summary: As in the later chapters of 1 Kings, the book alternates between accounts of the two kingdoms of Judah and Israel. The Prophet Elijah is miraculously taken to heaven, and his successor is the Prophet Elisha, who works many miracles. Most of the kings of Israel, and some kings of Judah, prove to be idol-worshipers, but a few try to lead the people back to worshiping the true God. The kingdom of

Israel is conquered by the Assyrian empire. The kingdom of Judah is threatened by the Assyrians but is delivered by God. However, Judah eventually is conquered by the Babylonian empire, and the country's ruling class is taken to exile in Babylon. Both Israel and Judah are punished for neglecting their duties to God.

Problems: As with 1 Kings, some of the stories in 2 Kings do not totally agree with the stories told in 1 and 2 Chronicles. None of the points of disagreement are terribly important. Some of the miracles of the Prophet Elisha may seem farfetched to the modern reader. (Some even seem cruel— as the one in which he sics bears on children who poke fun at his baldness.) It is interesting that in 1 and 2 Kings the stories of Elijah and Elisha are almost the only stories containing miraculous elements.

For those who skip . . . Many of the accounts of the various kings can be read quickly, but do attempt to read the entire book through at least once. Focus particularly on the reformer kings, Jehu (chaps. 9–10), Hezekiah (18–20), and Josiah (22–23). The concluding chapter, giving the whole book's "moral," is important to read.

THE WRITINGS

The Books Joshua through 2 Kings tell history. So do 1 Chronicles through Esther. But the Jews have always put Chronicles, Ezra, Nehemiah, and Esther in a separate category, the Writings—which also includes Job, Psalms, Proverbs, Ecclesiastes, the Song of Songs, Ruth, Daniel, and Lamentations. In Jewish tradition, these writings are considered sacred, but not studied or honored like the Law, the Bible's first five books.

First, consider the Writings that are historical in nature. First and 2 Chronicles, Ezra, Nehemiah, and Esther tell the story of Israel from the reign of David to the time whensome Jews were still living in exile in Persia (as in Esther) while some had returned to resettle the land of Israel (as in Ezra and Nehemiah). Joshua, Judges, 1 and 2 Samuel, 1 and 2 Kings tell Israel's story, interpreted by authors who see the events as the working out of God's purposes in history. (By the way, the small Book of Ruth, though it follows Judges in our Bibles, is considered part of the Writings.)

Second, consider the other books in the Writings: Job, Psalms, Proverbs, Ecclesiastes, and Song of Songs. These are more literary than historical. And these are some of the most-loved and most-read books in the Bible (except for Song, which isn't read that much, and which never mentions the name of God). These are not historical (although Job tells, in poetic form, the history of the poor suffering Job). They are poems (Pss.), advice (Prov.), speculation about the meaning of life (Ecc.), and a celebration of the pleasures of man and woman together (Song).

The Writings were the last group of books that the Jews accepted as being holy and authoritative. However, Jews and Christians have always loved and honored the Book of Psalms, considering it to be a high point of the Old Testament.

1 Chronicles
Summary: The book begins by listing the genealogy from Adam to King David.

Beginning at chapter 10, it covers much of the ground of 1 and 2 Samuel, beginning with the death of Saul and focusing on David's reign. Many of the more sordid details of David's life are excluded from 1 Chronicles. In some ways, 1 Chronicles is the cleaned-up, G-rated version of David's story that is told (with more painful details) in 1 and 2 Samuel.

Note something new in 1 and 2 Chronicles: the first case of a book of the Bible using other books as sources. It is obvious that the author(s) of Chronicles freely used materials from 1 and 2 Samuel and 1 and 2 Kings.

Problems: The David we encounter here is a more idealized figure than the all-too-human David of 1 and 2 Samuel. It is the same man, but some of his failings are glossed over. First Chronicles also differs in some other historical details, but nothing of importance.

For those who skip . . . This is one of the most skippable books of the Old Testament! So many chapters of lists and genealogies! (1–9; 12; 15; 18; 23–27) And generally speaking, all the stories of David's life are told better in 1 and 2 Samuel.

2 Chronicles

Summary: David's son Solomon reigns and builds the Lord's temple in Jerusalem. Ten of the twelve tribes rebel, forming the new kingdom of Israel (the two remaining tribes being called Judah). Unlike 1 and 2 Kings, 2 Chronicles gives almost no attention to the kingdom of Israel. Most of the later chapters cover the same ground as the Judah accounts in 1 and 2 Kings. Judah is conquered by the Babylonians. The book ends with the promise of Cyrus, the Persian emperor, to return the people of Judah to their homeland.

Problems: As with 1 Chronicles, the book does not agree in all its historical details with the accounts in 1 and 2 Kings (which are probably older and, perhaps, more accurate). However, none of the disagreements are terribly important. The book seems to take a great interest in details of worship in the Jerusalem temple, details that probably interest few readers today.

For those who skip . . . Since most of this material is covered in 1 and 2 Kings, much of the book is skippable. However, the earlier chapters dealing with Solomon are interesting.

Ezra

Summary: The Jews (meaning, people of Judah) are allowed to return from their exile in Babylon. Cyrus (whose empire, Persia, conquered the Babylonians) allows this return. Cyrus' successor takes an interest in the Jews' rebuilding of the temple and other buildings. A new temple is dedicated. Ezra, a priest, comes with a second wave of exiles and helps the people focus on true worship of God, which includes rejecting the religious practices of neighbor nations. Ezra specifically forbids marriage of Jews with non-Jews—an interesting development, since the early king Solomon had allowed his non-Jewish wives to lead him away from worshiping the one true God.

Problems: Bible scholars have problems pinning accurate dates on the events in the Books of Ezra and Nehemiah. None of these historical issues is of real concern to the non-scholar who may be more interested in the book's attitude toward non-Jews. This attitude is understandable, considering that the nation of Judah had been conquered as a punishment for abandoning the worship of the one true God. Ezra was concerned that the people never again lapse into worshiping the false gods of the surrounding nations.

For those who skip . . . With so many lists and genealogies, some of the book is very skippable (chaps. 2, most of 8, most of 10). However, Ezra is an important character in the Old Testament, a good example of a moral reformer.

Nehemiah

Summary: Nehemiah, a Jew, gives up his comfortable job as steward to the Persian king. He goes to Jerusalem and becomes governor of the Jews who have returned from exile in Babylon. He leads them in repairing the city walls, opposed by nearby tribesmen. The priest Ezra is a key player in the story.

Problems: Historians and Bible scholars have difficulty fixing dates on all the events in Ezra and Nehemiah. None of these problems is of any real concern to most Bible readers. One minor problem is that Nehemiah seems to have a high opinion of himself, as he says more than once in the book, "Remember me with favor, O my God, for all I have done for these people."

For those who skip . . . Like 1 and 2 Chronicles and Ezra, Nehemiah has many "list" chapters that are skippable (7; 10–11; most of 12).

Esther

Summary: The Persian king Ahasuerus (Xerxes in some translations) gets rid of his impudent wife and replaces her with Esther, a Jewish girl. Keeping her ethnic background a secret, Esther helps thwart the anti-Jewish plots of Haman, a Persian official who has a deep grudge against the Jews. Esther is aided by her relative, Mordecai. The Jews end up slaughtering the Persian henchmen who were pledged to kill them.

Problems: The book never once mentions God or even prayer. It seems much more pro-Jewish than pro-God, and many historians have suggested it may just be a Jewish folk tale that serves to explain the Jewish feast of Purim. Though much treasured by Jews today (especially during their holiday of Purim), the book is never quoted or even mentioned in the New Testament. However, the traditional Christian view is that the book shows how the Jews' God is in control of the nation's destiny—even if He is never mentioned by name. He works to preserve His people in the midst of great danger.

For those who skip . . . With only ten chapters, the book is easily read in one sitting. Most people find it entertaining but not terribly inspiring.

Job

Summary: Job, a rich and very righteous man, loses his wealth, his children, and his health because Satan attempts to prove to God that religious people love God only because they profit from it. Job's three wise friends arrive to comfort him, but they end up hinting that for someone who suffers as much as Job has suffered, he must have sinned in some way. Job protests that this is not so, that he truly is innocent. God Himself speaks to Job out of a storm, asking what right Job has to question the working of the Almighty. The book ends with God restoring Job's health and fortune.

Problems: The speeches of Job's fourth friend, Elihu (found in chaps. 32–37) add nothing new to what the other three friends have already stated. Some scholars think the Elihu chapters were a later addition to the book. (If you skip from the end of chapter 31 to the beginning of 38, you'll notice that it reads quite smoothly.)

For those who skip . . . The Elihu chapters can be skipped, but not a word of the rest of the book should be skipped. Job is one of the most beautiful books in the entire Bible, dealing with one of life's most painful questions: Why do good people suffer? The answer hits home forcefully: We don't know why. We must trust that God, who controls everything, will be just. Job's speeches, and those of his three friends, express important ideas about justice in God's world. The book gives a hint (in 19:25) that perhaps justice has to occur in the next world, not in this one.

Psalms

Summary: The longest book in the Bible is not divided into chapters as is the rest of the Bible. Rather, it is 150 individual psalms, which are poems (or songs) expressing praise, worship, gratitude, anguish, or repentance. Written by many different authors over hundreds of years, they are the "hymnal" of the Old Testament, displaying a wide variety of emotions and attitudes. Of the 150, 73 are attributed to King David, famous in Israel as a "sweet singer." Of the "David Psalms," some of the most famous are 23 (the "Shepherd" Psalm) and 51 (the great song of sin and repentance).

Problems: Many of the psalms seem to have an un-Christian (maybe we should say *pre*-Christian) attitude toward one's enemies. "Love your enemies," a key teaching in the New Testament, does not seem to be a guiding factor in the Psalms. Several call for God's wrath to fall upon the enemy. However, take these psalms at their face value, not as a description of the attitude we *ought* to have, but as a description of the authors' states of mind. The "vengeance psalms" reflect the situation of a deeply oppressed soul crying out to God. They are feelings we have all felt.

For those who skip . . . All the Psalms should be read—but not at one sitting, since this is a long book. Since most of the psalms are no longer than a page, the practice of reading one per day is not a bad idea. The longest psalm (119) is also the longest chapter in the entire Bible—and not one that many people find inspiring, since it seems to continually repeat itself.

Some highlights: Psalms 9, 19, 23, 24, 37, 42, 46, 49, 51, 86, 90, 100, 103, 130, 139, 145.

* * * * * * * * * * *

Charismatic churches often "lift up hands to the Lord" in their worship services. They base this practice on Psalm 134:2: "Lift up your hands in the sanctuary and praise the LORD."

* * * * * * * * * * *

Proverbs

Summary: This is a collection of wise sayings, good advice about conducting one's life. The various sayings focus on money, friendship, family, marriage, justice, wisdom and folly, social behavior. While the Psalms focus on the relationship of God and man, the Proverbs focus on relationships between people. However, God is never far from the author's mind, for "The fear of the LORD is the beginning of knowledge" (1:7). The Proverbs are attributed to several authors, notably the wise king of Israel, Solomon. It is the most "practical" book in the entire Bible, and even unbelievers have admired the book's wisdom.

Problems: The book gives some readers the impression that life will always go well for the wise and religious man—something that the Book of Job obviously contradicts. Much of the book has a "this-worldly" orientation which bothers some people. It shouldn't, since there is no reason a spiritual person can't also be a practical person.

The description of the ideal wife (31:1-25) may strike some feminists as being outdated. Many women (and almost all men!) find it appealing.

For those who skip . . . Like Psalms, Proverbs isn't meant to be read straight through at one sitting. And like Psalms, the whole book is important. Skip nothing. This is great stuff, as even unbelievers have admitted over the centuries. An atheist could still pick up some wise tips from Proverbs.

Ecclesiastes

Summary: The Teacher (or "Preacher" in some translations) reflects on the emptiness and meaninglessness of the things people believe bring happiness—pleasure, wisdom, wealth, fame. All these things have value only if God is at the center of man's existence. Man's duty is to obey God's commands. The book's title means "things said before the assembly." Tradition says the author was the wise King Solomon—a man who had wisdom, wealth, and power, but who learned that they do not bring complete satisfaction in life.

Problems: Ecclesiastes has a much more pessimistic tone than the rest of the Bible, but the tone is in keeping with the book's theme: most of the goals people pursue in life are a total waste of time. The book's structure puzzles many people because it doesn't seem to follow a logical line of thought, but skips around from one topic to another. But the whole book points to the main conclusion that honoring God and keeping His commandments is the only way to a meaningful life.

For those who skip . . . Skip nothing. The twelve chapters are all fascinating, if occasionally puzzling.

Song of Songs

Summary: A man and woman in love sing of their deep feelings for each other. They praise each other's physical charms in extravagant poetry.

Problems: Like the Book of Esther, this book never once mentions God or anything even remotely spiritual. For this reason, both Jews and Christians have tended to interpret the book as symbolic—that is, the two lovers represent God and His people, bound together in deep love. The obvious truth is that the book, attributed to the wise King Solomon, is a collection of love poetry. (Since Solomon had hundreds of wives and concubines, it is a subject he should have known quite well.) The Song

178 THE BIBLE: WHAT'S IN IT FOR ME?

provides a nice antidote to the idea that religious people are antisex and anti-body.

For those who skip . . . The entire book is skippable, since it will not increase many readers' faith. However, it is short and quite interesting. It does remind us that God has no problem with genuine human love and physical attraction. It can easily be read in ten minutes.

THE MAJOR PROPHETS

In our Christian Bibles, the Major Prophets category includes Isaiah, Jeremiah, Lamentations, Ezekiel, and Daniel. (The Jews lump Lam. and Dan. in the group known as the Writings.) We agree that Isaiah, Jeremiah, and Ezekiel are "Major" because their books are very long and (in terms of spiritual impact) very influential. Isaiah is one of the most-quoted books of the Bible, and Jeremiah and Ezekiel are not far behind. Christians are especially fond of the Major Prophets because many of their proclamations were fulfilled in the life of Jesus.

The prophets provide some balance in the Old Testament. The five books of the Law (Genesis through Deuteronomy) almost give the impression that being a good person means following a lot of ceremonial rules. The prophets made it clear that people could be technically "Law-abiding" but still be unjust, oppressive—and spiritually corrupt. The prophets were "exposers"— men who showed that beneath an outward respectability, people could still be far from God. They were a sort of combination of preacher and journalist—uncovering immorality and proclaiming it far and wide so that people would (they hoped) see their errors and reform. They were, in a deep sense, alarmists, carrying the message, "Warning! There's a moral and spiritual crisis! Do something, quick!"

Isaiah

Summary: The prophet Isaiah, ministering in the kingdom of Judah, warns the people that they will be judged because of their wickedness. Beginning in chapter 40, he offers comfort and predicts that the exiles in Babylon will return home. He also p redicts a "Suffering Servant" of God, a Savior who will bring deliverance. He predicts that God will set up a new and righteous kingdom.

Problems: The Bible scholars like to squabble over the obvious change that occurs between chapters 39 and 40. The tone and language of the book change dramatically, and some scholars believe there was a prophet named Isaiah (the source of chaps. 1–39) and also a "Second Isaiah" who authored chapters 40–66. (The first section is mostly warning about coming disaster, while the second section is a more gentle word of consolation.) Most Bible readers have nothing to gain from getting caught up in this controversy. The entire book has inspired people for centuries.

For those who skip . . . Isaiah is one of the most loved books in the Bible. It is quoted or referred to frequently in the New Testament. While it is long (sixty-six chapters), and much of the material deals with ancient empires, the whole book focuses on the need to rely on God alone. The book is especially interesting because many of Isaiah's words seem to be fulfilled in the life and work of Jesus. At least once in a lifetime every Bible reader should give Isaiah a slow, thorough read. Definitely do *not* skip Isaiah's commission (chap. 6), the predictions of a Messiah (9; 11; 42; 49), words of comfort (40; 43). The warnings against ancient empires can be read through quickly or skipped (15–23).

Jeremiah

Summary: Jeremiah, called to be a prophet while a young man in the kingdom of Judah, preaches during the reign of good King Josiah. Later kings despised Jeremiah for his dire words of warning, and much of the book concerns Jeremiah's sufferings at the hands of his political enemies. Jeremiah predicts a "new covenant" between God and man, something that Christians believe was fulfilled with the coming of Jesus. After Jerusalem's destruction by the Babylonians, Jeremiah stayed with the group that remained in the land. Eventually he flees with a group that goes into Egypt.

Problems: Jeremiah's prophecies in this book are not in chronological sequence, so it is hard to read the book without a familiarity with Judah's history (found in 2 Kings and 2 Chron.).

For those who skip ... As with Jeremiah, this much-loved, much-quoted (and long) book deserves a slow steady read-through. Jeremiah was a sensitive soul, painfully aware that his country had turned its back on God and was about to pay the price for its sins. The prophecies against ancient nations (chaps. 46–51) can be skipped.

Lamentations

Summary: The author (who may have been the Prophet Jeremiah) grieves over the

BOOK BURNING?
CHRISTIANS—AND SOME PEOPLE WHO OPPOSE CHRISTIANS—HAVE BEEN ACCUSED OF BEING "BOOK BURNERS." THE FIRST BOOK-BURNER WAS WICKED KING JEHOIAKIM. WARMING HIMSELF BY THE PALACE FIRE IN JERUSALEM, JEHOIAKIM RECEIVED A SCROLL FROM THE PROPHET JEREMIAH. WHILE AN AIDE READ FROM THE SCROLL (WHICH HAD NOTHING GOOD TO SAY TO THE NASTY MONARCH), JEHOIAKIM SLICED OFF THE PORTION JUST READ AND TOSSED IT INTO THE FIRE. HE CONTINUED UNTIL THE ENTIRE SCROLL HAD BEEN BURNED (JEREMIAH 36:21-23).

Babylonians' destruction of the holy city, Jerusalem. He recognizes that the country brought the calamity on itself, and God's love still endures for His people.

Problems: None, except that the tradition that Jeremiah wrote the book is sometimes doubted. The book itself does not name its author. It is probably an accurate reflection of Jeremiah's feelings at seeing the city in ruins.

For those who skip ... With only five chapters, this brief book of sad poetry is hardly skippable. It is sad, but comforting, because it conveys the message that God is still in control, in spite of hardships.

Ezekiel

Summary: The author, a Jew living in exile in Babylonia, sees visions of God in His majesty. Ezekiel explains to the exiled people that they suffered the destruction and deportation by the Babylonians because they brought it on themselves by their own sin. But Ezekiel promises that God will regather the Israelites from the ends of the earth and restore them to a new kingdom. The countries who oppose this will be defeated. One of Ezekiel's key messages is that God is the divine Judge of all people, but that He takes no pleasure in punishing the wicked. God, who is loving and forgiving, is eager to pardon the repentant person. This theme, which occurs at many places in the Bible, sees its fulfillment in the New Testament in the life and teachings of Jesus.

Problems: Ezekiel strikes some readers as a weird book, with so many strange visions. Some so-called scholars have even suggested that Ezekiel was a psychotic, not a prophet from God. While it's true that Ezekiel's visions (as in chap. 1) are sometimes strange, their weirdness *does* have the desired impact: it catches and holds the reader's attention. God, communicating to and through Ezekiel, was revealing His "otherness," His supernatural separateness from human beings—while at the same time drawing near to them to communicate. The vision of the "dry bones" (remember the old song, "Dem bones, dem bones, dem dry bones"?) is the most famous of the visions (chap. 37).

For those who skip . . . Do *not* skip the key "vision" passages (chaps. 1–5; 17; 37), nor the chapter on individual responsibility (18), on God's care (34), on having a "new heart" (36). Some of the warnings against the nations are skippable (25–32; 35; 38–39). The closing chapters (40–48) describe God's restoring of the city of Jerusalem, with much more detail than most readers care for. The book's last verse, though, packs a wallop.

Daniel

Summary: The book is in two sections. The first (chaps. 1–6) tells the story of the young Israelite Daniel, exiled in Babylon, later in Persia. Living under pagan kings who persecute true believers, the golden boy Daniel remains steadfast and true. The second section (chaps. 7–12) consists of visions of the "end times," visions similar to those in the New Testament's Book of Revelation.

Problems: Historians and scholars have cast some doubts on the truth of Daniel's story. The book mentions the Babylonian King Nebuchadnezzar going insane and living in the wilderness. While the king definitely was historical, no other history of the times mentions Nebuchadnezzar's madness—a notable oversight. On the other hand, we wouldn't necessarily expect the official Babylonian records to mention this embarrassing incident, would we?

King Belshazzar was doubted as being a real person—until, around 1854, archaeologists found him named in some Babylonian histories. The historians say he wasn't actually king, nor was he the son of Nebuchadnezzar, as the Book of Daniel says. But the book may be using "son of" in a wider sense—that is, "descendant of." And "king" may be used in the broader sense of "ruler" or "official," not just "the one and only king."

The "experts" have been arguing for years over the visions (chaps. 7–12). Do the symbols in them refer to ancient empires or to events at the end of the world? We can't answer that here. Like the visions in the Book of Revelation, they do carry the message that God, not the world's rulers, is in control of history and will bring justice, finally.

For those who skip . . . Definitely read chapters 1 through 6—interesting (and familiar) stories of Nebuchadnezzar's dream of the statue, Daniel's friends in the fiery furnace, the ghostly hand writing on the wall at Belshazzar's feast, and (of course) Daniel in the lions' den. The visions in chapters 7 through 12 puzzle even the wisest of readers, so skip them if you like. But do note that 12:1-3 contains one of the few Old Testament statements about life after death, with heaven for some people and hell for others.

THE MINOR PROPHETS

"Minor" doesn't mean "unimportant," but only distinguishes these writers from the Major Prophets, whose books are much longer. Some of the Minor Prophets do seem minor to us, since their messages seem to apply only to the distant past (literally, ancient history). But some of them are still highly readable because of their teachings on the need for justice (notably Amos), God's willingness to forgive (notably Hosea), and the need for us to "keep the faith" even when injustice seems to rule in the world (Habakkuk). Some passages in the Minor Prophets are treasured by Christians because they predict certain events in the life of Jesus (Micah's prophecy of the Messiah being born in Bethlehem, for example).

The twelve books of the Minor Prophets were originally one book (scroll, that is) in the Hebrew Bible. It was usually referred to as "the Twelve."

Hosea
Summary: Hosea is a prophet living in the kingdom of Israel (the Northern Kingdom, which had split from the Southern Kingdom, Judah, after King Solomon's death). The book often refers to the nation as "Ephraim," after its largest lump of territory. The book uses Hosea's own experience with his unfaithful wife Gomer to illustrate God's love for the unfaithful kingdom of Israel. As Hosea forgives Gomer for chasing other men, so God will forgive Israel for worshiping other gods. Note that idolatry in the Old Testament involves more than bowing down before statues. It means neglecting the true God, which inevitably results in mistreating other people as well.

Problems: None, really. Some experts doubt that the chapters are always in the right sequence, but this is not important to the reader.

For those who skip . . . Don't. Hosea is only fourteen chapters, so read it all. It is a beautiful book about God's forgiveness. If Hosea could forgive the sluttish Gomer, God can forgive people too.

Joel
Summary: The Prophet Joel describes a plague of locusts—crop-devouring grasshoppers. It is a symbol of judgment and destruction for those who neglect God. But Joel also predicts the coming of God's Holy Spirit on His people and warns disaster for the nations that oppress Israel.

Problems: Unlike some of the prophetic books, Joel does not open with any indication of date. Most of the books indicate their date by mentioning the reign of some particular king. Joel doesn't. This isn't important, except to the scholars who like to date everything.

For those who skip . . . With only three chapters, don't skip. Note especially the prophecy of the Spirit in 2:28-32.

Amos

Summary: Here is a prophet for our times, the great advocate of justice. Amos, a simple shepherd in the Northern Kingdom of Israel, warned the Israelites that the injustice heaped on people (especially the poor) would bring doom on the nation. For those who live rightly, God will restore the kingdom. Among the twelve Minor Prophets, Amos is often considered the most important. His words about oppressing the poor make the book easy for modern readers to relate to.

Problems: None. Amos is one of the best-preserved books in ancient manuscripts.

For those who skip... Oddly, chapters 1 and 2 are skippable, since they are warnings against the sins of neighboring nations. Do not skip the rest of the book, where Amos warns the Israelites against "trampling the poor" and other social sins. Note especially the warning (5:18-27) against people who appear religious on the outside but take advantage of other people.

Obadiah

Summary: One chapter! Obadiah prophesies doom for Israel's neighbor nation, Edom. It had invaded and plundered Jerusalem four times, and Obadiah predicted its comeuppance. (His prophecy was fulfilled. The Edomites are heard of no more after A.D. 70.)

Problems: Although there are literally dozens of Obadiahs in the Bible, we don't know which one wrote this book. We also can't date the book with precision. These are unimportant problems.

For those who skip... Skip a book with only twenty-one verses? No, read it through at least once. Most people don't find it especially inspiring.

Jonah

Summary: The Hebrew Prophet Jonah is told by God to go to Nineveh, capital of the Assyrian empire, and preach against its wickedness. Jonah runs away by ship, is tossed overboard, and lands in a huge fish's belly. He is coughed up on land, goes to Nineveh to preach, and then is disgusted when the heathen people actually do repent. The message here has nothing to do with whales or fish but with God's purpose for the world: He wants all people to repent, even those we perceive as heathen outsiders.

Problems: No part of the Bible (except maybe the opening chapters of Genesis) causes more snickers among unbelievers than the Book of Jonah. "Swallowed by a whale? Yeah, right." Well, scientifically speaking, people *have* survived after being swallowed by whales (and no doubt thought their survival was miraculous). The whale problem is a minor difficulty. The fact is, many people find that the book reads like a folk tale, not history. Why, for example, when the Bible takes such pains to record the names of foreign kings (Nebuchadnezzar, Sennacherib, etc.) does Jonah fail to mention the name of the king of Nineveh—even though that king repents and turns to God? Why do the archaeologists find no mention of such a nationwide repentance? We can't answer these questions, except to say that acceptance of faith involves accepting God's miraculous intervention in human affairs. Rather than concentrating on the historical and scientific problems, consider the more important message that God does not just love His "chosen people" (the Hebrews, in this case), but all people. Jonah represents a "chosen one" who does not wish to share the message of divine love for all people. God shows him—vividly—that he shouldn't run away from preaching this message.

Curiously, of the twelve Minor Prophets, Jonah is the only one mentioned by Jesus. Jesus even refers specifically to Jonah's time in the sea creature's belly. So don't pass off Jonah too quickly.

For those who skip ... Don't. It's four chapters, and easy to read. Pay attention to the message, not the historical details (or lack of them).

Micah

Summary: Living in Judah (the Southern Kingdom), Micah preaches God's judgment for His people's sins. They will be judged for oppressing the poor and living unholy lives. But the kingdom will be restored by God, and a ruler born in Bethlehem will build a kingdom that will last forever.

Problems: None, really.

For those who skip ... Don't. Micah is only seven chapters and easy to read. Pay special attention to the prophecy of a king from Bethlehem (5:2), which was supposed to prophesy Jesus' birth in Bethlehem and the famous statement on walking humbly with God (6:8).

Nahum

Summary: The cruel nation Assyria will get its comeuppance, says Nahum. The nation and its capital, Nineveh, have oppressed many nations. But like all evil empires, it will fall, doomed to ruin. God decrees this, and His people can rejoice that justice is done.

Problems: None, except that most readers don't find the book very inspiring. We ought to read it with the understanding that human oppressors, no matter how powerful they seem, are doomed. God did not intend that oppressive powers would endure forever.

For those who skip ... With its message of doom for a long-past nation, the book can be skipped. However, with only three chapters, it should be read through at least once.

Habakkuk

Summary: In a dialogue with God, Habakkuk (pronounced rather like *tobacco*) raises an eternal question: "Why do wicked people seem to prosper?" God replies that another nation, the Babylonians, will come as a punishment on the wicked people of Judah. Habakkuk then asks, "Why send a cruel oppressive nation to punish us?" God answers that good people live by faith, and God will always do what is right. The book ends with a song of praise to God, very like some of the Psalms. This book with the funny name is one of the most inspiring books in the Old Testament.

Problems: The prophet gives no information about the date of his writing, so we have no idea when the book was written. This is unimportant, since the book's eternally valid message is the important thing.

For those who skip ... Don't. It's only three chapters, and very readable.

Zephaniah

Summary: Like other prophets, Zephaniah warns people against pride and oppression. He predicts a "day of the Lord," a day of judgment. He also predicts that the oppressive neighboring nations will be destroyed.

Problems: None.

For those who skip . . . The warnings against the neighboring nations (2:4-15) can be skipped, but the entire book is only three chapters long.

Haggai

Summary: The Persian King Darius allows the exiled Jews to return to their country. The Prophet Haggai, part of the returned group, encourages Zerubbabel, the Jewish governor, in rebuilding the Jerusalem temple, which the Babylonians had wrecked many years before.

Problems: None. The scholars like this neat little book, since it is very clear about its date (520 B.C., precisely) and purpose.

For those who skip . . . You can skip all of Haggai, since it concerns a long-past event, rebuilding the Jews' temple. But with only two chapters, why not read it through once?

Zechariah

Summary: Working at the same time as Haggai, Zechariah encouraged the rebuilders of Jerusalem at a time when they were ready to give up. His sermons include various visions—four horns, a flying scroll, etc. The book's second section (chaps. 9–14) prophesies a coming Messiah, the final judgment, and a long-term kingdom.

Problems: As in the Book of Daniel, this one has two sections radically different from each other (chaps.1–8; 9–14). None of this really concerns the average reader.

For those who skip . . . Chapters 1–8, concerning events in Zechariah's own time, can be skipped. The other chapters, prophesying events that seem to be fulfilled in the life of Jesus, should be read.

Malachi

Summary: Malachi, who prophesied after the time of Haggai and Zechariah, warned the Jews who had returned from exile: "Your religious life is not what it should be. You have married foreign (that is, unbelieving) wives and have neglected God. Judgment will come, but for good people there is nothing to fear. Before the day of the Lord comes, God will send a great prophet."

Problems: We don't know who Malachi was, and it is possible his name (it means "messenger") may be just a title ("The Messenger"), not his actual name.

For those who skip . . . Some of the warnings about the temple and tithing (1:6–2:9; 3:6-12) seem unimportant to modern readers. However, the book is only four chapters, and some of Malachi's prophecies (especially chap. 4) seem to be fulfilled in the New Testament. Note that the prediction of Elijah coming (4:5) was thought to be fulfilled with the career of Jesus' relative, John the Baptist.

THE YEARS BETWEEN THE TESTAMENTS

You can turn the page in your Bible and go immediately from the end of the Book of Malachi to the first words of the Gospel of Matthew. But in spite of this proximity, several hundred years elapsed between the end of the Old Testament period and the beginning of the New Testament. In this period many things were happening in the Jews' religion, morals, and politics. Much of it was recorded in the books we call the Apocrypha. Some Bibles include these books; most do not. Why?

A WORD ABOUT THE APOCRYPHA

The Jews inherited the sacred writings of their Hebrew-Israelite ancestors. By the time Jesus was born, the Jews had accepted all the books that we now call the Old Testament. They had not officially accepted the books written during the period between the two Testaments. These books were read by the Jews, but they weren't as old as the Old Testament books and not as widely respected. Some of the apocryphal books had been written in Hebrew, but even these had never been included in the Hebrew version of the sacred books.

The first Christians accepted the Jewish sacred writings as their own. This included the books we call the Apocrypha. However, some Christians noted that none of the books of the Apocrypha is ever quoted by Jesus or anyone else in the New Testament. They doubted that the Apocrypha was inspired and authoritative in the way the Old Testament was.

When the great translator Jerome translated the Old and New Testaments into Latin, he was living in Palestine, the Jews' old homeland. Conversations with the Jewish teachers there convinced him that the apocryphal books did not belong in the Bible. But his superiors pressured him to translate them anyway. He did, but reluctantly. They became part of the Vulgate, Jerome's Latin translation, Christianity's "official" Bible for hundreds of years. So for centuries after Jerome, the Apocrypha was part of all Bibles throughout Europe.

A change came with the Protestant Reformation in the 1500s. Some of the Protestant leaders remembered Jerome's hesitancy about having the Apocrypha in the Bible. Didn't the Jews exclude the Apocrypha from their Hebrew Bibles? "Well," said the Protestants, "so should we." The Catholic authorities reacted to the Protestants by issuing a decree saying that, yes, officially and finally, the apocryphal books really are sacred Scripture. So the great divide came: Protestant Bibles dropped the Apocrypha, but Catholic Bibles included it. This is still the case. Some companies today publish Bibles with the Apocrypha, marketing it to both Catholics and Protestants. (To make things even more complicated, the Eastern Orthodox churches accept *part* of the Apocrypha, but not all of it.)

The books of the Apocrypha are Tobit, Judith, the Wisdom of Solomon, Ecclesiasticus (don't

• • • • • • • • • • •

Martin Luther, the great German leader of the Protestant Reformation in the 1500s, translated the entire Bible into German. He included the Apocrypha, but had some doubts. He placed it in a section between the Old and New Testaments and made a note: "These books are not equal to the holy Scriptures, but they are useful and good for reading."

• • • • • • • • • • •

confuse this with Ecclesiastes, a book in the Old Testament), Baruch, the Letter of Jeremiah, 1 and 2 Maccabees, and additions to the Old Testament books of Esther and Daniel. All Catholic Bibles include these books. Some of these, particularly Wisdom of Solomon (which is not by Solomon) and Ecclesiasticus, are full of wise sayings, much like the Old Testament Proverbs.

If you are new to the Bible, it's probably wise to stick with the sixty-six books in the Old and New Testaments. All Christians agree that these are sacred writing, whereas there are (and probably always will be) some doubts about the Apocrypha. If your denomination encourages reading the Apocrypha, fine. If not, you'll find that the sixty-six books are quite enough to manage.

One curious item about the Apocrypha: Its version of the Book of Esther does mention God and prayer. The shorter Book of Esther in our Old Testament does not.

chapter 13

In a Nutshell: ◄···

The Books of the New Testament, What They're About, Problems They Have, Parts You Might Want to Skip

You don't have to read far to realize that the two Testaments are very different. Personal names, for example, are quite different—a lot of names ending in *-iah* in the Old Testament, a lot ending in *-us* in the New. The action of the New Testament takes place in the Roman Empire, which used a form of Greek (called *Koine*, "common") as its empire-wide language of trade and mass communication. (In a similar way, India today uses English as an official language in a nation speaking hundreds of native Indian languages.) Being under Rome's political thumb, the Jews in the New Testament can see their old dominance of their land is history. Rome is powerful and seems destined to stay. The Jews look back to Old Testament prophecies of a king, a Messiah (meaning "anointed one") who will lead the people politically, militarily—and spiritually.

The authors of the writings that became the New Testament believed that this Messiah was Jesus Christ (Christ has the same meaning as Messiah). Jesus was not a political leader but a spiritual leader. More than that, He became the Mediator between God (loving, but angry at human sin) and man (sinful, unable to approach a holy God and have a relationship with Him). This was what Jesus' followers, the Christians, believed. Their opponents were Jews and pagans who accused them of preaching nonsense—or preaching a heretical form of Judaism that had no right to exist. But the Christians persisted, claiming that Jesus the Messiah had put them in a right relationship with God forever. Jesus, who had been executed by crucifixion, had actually been raised up from death and was living in a new spiritual body. Someday all His followers would be raised up in the same way. And at the end of history Jesus would bring this present world to a close and begin a new world with no sorrow or pain.

THE GOSPELS

Gospel means "good news." (It's from the Anglo-Saxon word *Godspell*—same as the popular musical play.) The early Christians thought it was "good news" that Jesus was the Messiah who enabled people to live in a right relationship with God, a relationship that would endure beyond death.

In the early days of Christianity there were dozens of Gospels. So how come only four made it into the Bible? The ones that didn't make it were often so fantastic and ridiculous that we now wonder how anyone could have believed them. (For example, one gospel shows the boy Jesus making birds out of clay, clapping His hands, and bringing them to life.) Many of these "fake" gospels were written by teachers pushing their own brands of strange philosophy or occult teaching, hoping to make it seem respectable by putting their words in the mouth of Jesus. These pseudo-gospels were often circulated under the name of one of Jesus' apostles—the Gospel of Thomas, for example.

The fact is, the early Christians, over the course of time, came to agree that Matthew, Mark, Luke, and John were somehow *right*— that the Jesus they presented was the real Jesus, the one remembered by His followers.

Matthew

Summary: Through his legal father Joseph, Jesus is descended from the faithful patriarch Abraham, the father of the Hebrew people. Jesus is born of the Virgin Mary through the power of God's Holy Spirit.

Outline Before Writing

Oddly, these summaries of all sixty-six books of the Bible were hard to write. Why? Because so many books of the Bible aren't easily summarized in a few sentences. Many of the books can't be outlined in the same way you could outline a magazine article or nonfiction book today. The books of the Bible seem to "jump around," moving from one topic to another, not always with a sense of logic or a sense that the author had carefully *planned* the writing. In very few cases does it appear that the writer thought things through before writing.

But then, the Bible authors weren't "pros." They lived before the days of journalism schools and creative writing programs. They had no notion of topic sentences, outlines, smooth transitions from one paragraph to the next. Thus, the great Book of Proverbs jumps willy-nilly from one topic to another—instead of (as a modern author is taught to do) lumping all the proverbs on marriage in one section, the proverbs on drunkenness in another, etc. The Book of Proverbs is so helter-skelter in its organization that a few of the Proverbs are actually repeated word for word within the book.

This doesn't mean the Bible authors weren't intelligent or that they weren't good with words. They were. People have been reading their words for centuries, and they are still being read. But don't approach the Bible text expecting the organization that you would find in, say, a home repair how-to book or a marriage manual.

Some books are more organized than others. In the New Testament, Matthew's Gospel is organized so that big lumps of Jesus' teachings are found in special sections, alternating with other sections that focus on His miracles. Paul's Letter to the Romans comes close to being a well-organized summary of Christian beliefs. But Paul's other letters bounce around from one topic to another, the way we bounce around in conversations with old friends, changing the subject, then saying, "Let's get back to what we were talking about earlier."

When He reaches adulthood, His relative John the Baptist is leading a spiritual revival, telling people to repent and turn to God. John baptizes Jesus, beginning Jesus' public life. The devil tempts Jesus to become a political Messiah and wonder-worker, but Jesus resists. Jesus calls a group of twelve disciples, and He goes throughout the country, healing people of diseases and demon-possessions. He teaches people that the Law in the Old Testament was good, but God is also concerned about people's inward attitude toward other people and toward God. A key teaching is the "kingdom of heaven," meaning God's reign among human beings. He tells many parables—illustrations of what this kingdom of heaven is like. Around the time of the Passover, the Jews' main religious festival, Jesus goes to Jerusalem. On the way He is hailed as the Jews' Messiah by many of the common folk. The Jewish religious authorities see Him as a rebel and a threat to their positions. One of Jesus' disciples, Judas Iscariot, arranges to hand Jesus over to the Jewish authorities. Jesus has a fellowship meal with His disciples (the Last Supper), then Judas arranges for His arrest. Jesus is tried before the Jewish religious court, then by the Roman governor, Pilate. Pilate finds Jesus guilty of no crime, but under pressure from the Jews, he allows Jesus to be executed by crucifixion. Jesus dies on the cross and is buried. Afterward His tomb is found empty. He appears to His disciples and tells them to make new disciples throughout the world. He promises He will always be with them.

Problems: Matthew has no problems—

except that his story of Jesus' life and teachings doesn't always agree in every detail with the stories in the other three Gospels (Mark, Luke, and John). Most of these details are very, very minor. If you have ever had to give testimony in court, you know that several eyewitnesses (even if they're all intelligent and sensible people) can differ slightly on the details of something they all saw.

The ever-popular musical play Godspell *bills itself as "based on the Gospel According to St. Matthew."*

For those who skip . . . Matthew is one of the most quoted books in the Bible—one of the most quoted books in the world, in fact. Matthew is especially known as the "teaching" Gospel, full of Jesus' teaching on ethics and the real spiritual life. Especially quotable are the Sermon on the Mount (chaps. 5–7), parables of the kingdom of heaven (13; 20), the "woes" against hypocrites (23), and the parables of being ready for God (25).

But . . . you might skip the genealogy in 1:1-17.

Mark

Summary: Mark is like a short version of Matthew. It omits Jesus' family tree and the story of His birth and goes right to His adult career. It also omits many (not all) of the parables and other teachings found in Matthew. Mark is a Gospel of action, with Jesus moving about frequently, healing the sick and demon-possessed. As in Matthew, Jesus is crucified and raised from the dead, but . . .

Problems: Mark lacks an ending—or,

looked at another way, we don't know where the *real* ending is. Chapter 16, telling of Jesus' empty tomb, breaks off suddenly. Some of Jesus' followers see that His tomb is empty, then—a break in the ancient manuscripts. The break occurs at 16:8. Your Bible will include the passage 16:9-19, which shows Jesus appearing to His disciples. The break puzzles the Bible scholars because the oldest manuscripts don't have 16:9-19. So is 16:9-19 the "real" ending, or was the original ending lost? We don't know. (Perhaps this is a reason to be glad we have four Gospels instead of one. What if we only had Mark?) Mark, by the way, is supposed to have been a friend of Peter, Jesus' disciple. So Mark's Gospel is based on the reports of a reliable eyewitness, Peter.

For those who skip ... Everyone ought to read every word of all four Gospels. It's true, however, that Mark (which may be the first of the Gospels written down) does not give us as much teaching as Matthew and Luke. If there is one Gospel to give scant attention to, it is Mark.

Luke

Summary: In most ways Luke's Gospel agrees with Matthew's, though he arranges the material in different sequences. But Luke also includes some material that no

• • • • • • • • • • •

The New Testament was written in Greek, but the language spoken by Jesus and His disciples was Aramaic, a common language of the Middle East in those days. Occasionally you'll find places in the New Testament where one of the writers translates an Aramaic word. In Mark 5:41, Jesus says the Aramaic words Talitha, koum, and Mark translates it as "Little girl, get up."

• • • • • • • • • • •

other Gospel does—notably the "Christmas" sections dealing with Jesus' mother Mary, Jesus' relative John the Baptist, and the birth of Jesus (including the angels and the shepherds), found in chapters 1 and 2. Chapter 2 also includes the only story of the boy Jesus, who at age twelve amazes the religious authorities with His wisdom. Luke's Gospel, unlike Matthew's and Mark's, ends with Jesus being taken into heaven (known as the Ascension).

Problems: Again, Matthew, Mark, and Luke don't agree in every detail. The differences are minor.

For those who skip ... Well, you can skip Jesus' genealogy in 3:23-38. But, like Matthew, Luke is a gem, almost every word. But it also covers much of the same ground as Matthew. If you read Matthew closely (which you should), you could skip much of Luke. But do *not* skip the important material that is found only in Luke's Gospel: the Christmas story (1–2), the miraculous catch of fish (5:1-11), the "woes" (6:24-26), the Good Samaritan parable (10:29-37), Mary and Martha (10:38-42), the Parables of the Rich Fool (12:13-21), the Prodigal Son (15:11-12), the Rich Man and Lazarus (16:19-31), the Unjust Judge (18:1-8), the Pharisee and the Tax Collector (18:9-14), the story of Zacchaeus (19:1-10), Jesus' trial before Herod (23:6-16), the risen Jesus on the road to Emmaus (24:13-35), and Jesus' ascension into heaven (24:36-49).

John

Summary: John's Gospel, supposed to have been written by one of Jesus' disciples (John, naturally), is very different from the other three. While this is the same Jesus, John chooses to emphasize other miracles and other teachings. He begins not with Jesus' birth or public ministry but before the world begins. According to John, the Christ was "the Word," the revelation of God, who existed with God before the world was made. In John's Gospel Jesus is also "the Lamb of God, who takes away the sin of the world." This Jesus engages in some dialogues about being born again (in the heart, that is) in His famous dialogue with Nicodemus (chap. 3) and about His being "living water" (chap. 4). In fact, John's Gospel is full of Jesus' "I am" statements: Jesus refers to Himself as "the bread of life" (6:35), "the light of the world" (9:5), "the gate for the sheep" (10:9), "the good shepherd" (10:11), "the resurrection and the life" (11:25), "the way and the truth and the life" (14:6), "the true vine" (15:1), etc. Obviously, John does not present Jesus as a ranting egomaniac. Jesus says these things about Himself because they are true. He is the Son of God, the Savior, and all these other things as well.

John's Gospel has been called a "painted portrait" instead of a "photograph" like the other three Gospels. This is a good analogy. While it is the same Jesus in all four Gospels, John's picture of Jesus is like an oil portrait that took a long time to paint, a lot of time to reflect on the real character of the person. Matthew's, Mark's, and Luke's are more like photographs—a kind of "you are there at the moment" kind of picture. This does not mean those three Gospels are truer than John's. A good portrait captures the real person in a way different from a photo. Not *better than*, but *different from*. This is just an analogy. The fact is, all four Gospels present a lot of details about geography and customs of Jesus' day, enough to convince historians that all four are based on solid fact.

As in the other Gospels, Jesus is crucified and buried, then raised from the dead. John's Gospel includes some additional post-Resurrection stories, including the famous one about "doubting Thomas," the apostle who had to touch the resurrected Jesus' wounds before he would believe it was really Jesus and not a specter.

Problems: John has no problems, except that it is different from (but doesn't really contradict) the other three Gospels. For a long time scholars believed that John's Jesus, being somewhat different from the one in Matthew, Mark, and Luke, must be

* * * * * * * * * * *

The popular rock opera **Jesus Christ Superstar** *is based on the Bible, but it offers an alternative view of Jesus' end.* **Superstar** *ends with a musical number called "John 19:41," which is this verse: "At the place where Jesus was crucified, there was a garden, and in the garden a new tomb, in which no one had ever been laid." The Jesus in* **Superstar** *is buried, but not raised from the dead. This is one reason the play aroused so much controversy among Christians.*

* * * * * * * * * * *

a fiction. Scholars no longer believe this, and neither should the general reader. In John's Gospel Jesus makes a lot of "I am" statements—"I am the vine," "I am the resurrection and the life," etc. Coming from an ordinary human being, these statements would be viewed as raw ego. But the authors of the Gospels believed Jesus was not just fully human, but also the Son of God—the one person who could make these amazing "I am" statements and really mean them.

For those who skip . . . Don't skip a word. John's Gospel is so rich that, like a hearty meal, it ought to be eaten slowly, savoring every bite. Because it includes a lot of material that the other Gospels omit, it is important to study this fascinating document—up close and personal.

Acts

Summary: Luke continues his Gospel with the story of the early Christians, concentrating on some key apostles, notably Paul and Peter. It begins where Luke ends, with Jesus being taken up to heaven. Judas, the disciple who betrayed Jesus, kills himself and is replaced. At the Jewish festival of Pentecost in Jerusalem, the Holy Spirit comes, as Jesus predicted. The Spirit gives new power to the apostles. The believers engage in prayer and fellowship, and the apostles work miracles of healing. Like Jesus, they are jailed and harassed by the Jewish authorities, but the church continues to grow. Stephen, a faithful Jewish Christian, becomes the first Christian to die for his beliefs, stoned to death by an angry Jewish mob. Paul, a Jewish persecutor of Christians, becomes a Christian himself.

Later as the most widely traveled apostle, he preaches the Gospel and starts new Christian communities among the Gentiles (non-Jews), breaking Christianity out of its Jewish mold. Paul, like Jesus, riles the Jewish authorities, who hate the new religion. He is arrested and goes to Rome, awaiting trial and preaching while under house arrest.

Problems: None of any significance. Archaeologists have found that Luke did his homework, since the historical people he mentions (Roman officials like Felix and Festus, for example) were exactly as he presents them.

For those who skip . . . Don't do it! Acts is a wonderful, readable book. While it is

THE NEW TESTAMENT IS A CHRISTIAN BOOK, E THE WORD *CHRISTIAN* APPEARS ONLY THI TIMES. ITS FIRST APPEARANCE IS IN THE BOO ACTS: "THE DISCIPLES WERE CALLED CHRISTIANS FIRST ANTIOCH" (ACTS 11:26).

not as important as the Gospels, it runs a close second. It is a neglected part of the Bible. It is almost the only eyewitness account of the first Christians. With executions, exorcisms, visions, arrests, martyrdoms, sorcerers, and a shipwreck, it is a colorful book. It shows how the faith could spread in a world with a diverse mix of people, religions, and beliefs (not so different from our own world, in fact).

THE EPISTLES

"Epistle" and "letter" are the same, more or less. Actually, "epistle" is more like a "sermon on paper"—the Epistle to the Hebrews is like this, and so is the Epistle of James. The New Testament from Romans to Jude consists of epistles/letters from the early Christian leaders to Christian groups or individual Christians, instructing them in Christian teaching and behavior. Since most of these are addressed to groups, not individuals, they don't have the coziness of a person-to-person letter. However, in many cases Paul does personally know the people he is writing to, so the letters do have a close, personal feeling.

People not familiar with the Bible may well ask, "Why are someone's *letters* so all-fired important?" Well, the fact is they are about all we have left of the life of the first Christians (besides the Book of Acts). While the letters are neither history nor theology, they do show—vividly—what the early Christians believed, how they lived, how they interpreted God's will for their lives. Later Christians accepted the letters as sacred writing, the instructions of the apostles to Christians everywhere. The letters were accepted as the authoritative writings of people who knew Jesus best—an important point, since Jesus Himself wrote nothing.

The main letter-writer

• • • • • • • • • • • •

THREE-IN-ONE AND ONE-IN-THREE

The belief in the Trinity is that God is Three in One—God the Father, God the Son, God the Holy Spirit. But only one Bible verse mentions all three together, Matthew 28:19: "Go and make disciples of all nations, baptizing them in the name of the Father and of the Son and of the Holy Spirit." A related verse is Galatians 4:6: "Because you are sons, God sent the Spirit of His Son into our hearts, the Spirit who calls out, 'Abba, Father.'"

But the idea of the Trinity occurs throughout the New Testament. That is, the authors believed that God the Father, God the Son (Christ), and God the Holy Spirit are all God—One in Three, and Three in One. It puzzles a lot of people, but after 2,000 years, it shows no signs of being forgotten. (Check your local Yellow Pages under "Churches" and inevitably at least one church in your area is named "Trinity.")

• • • • • • • • • • • •

was Paul, the high-energy apostle who dominates the last chapters of the Book of Acts. Paul, a Jewish Christian, became the apostle to the Gentiles (non-Jews). His work among the Gentiles was decisive, since it ensured that Christianity wouldn't be just one form of Judaism, but something entirely new—a global faith that could be "exported" to any land, any group of people, regardless of their religious background. With Paul, Christianity became a universal faith in a way that its parent religion, Judaism, would not. The Epistles have a lot to say about this, and it is of more than historical interest. Paul constantly fought against *legalism*, the attitude (common among Jews of his day) that we can gain our salvation by obeying rules, "racking up points with God." According to Paul's epistles, salvation is a *gift* from God. Our good behavior is done out of *gratitude*, not just out of a sense of duty.

Paul's epistles run from Romans to the one-chapter Philemon. The long epistle Hebrews (whose author is unknown) is addressed to "the new Hebrews"—that is, to all Christians, wherever they are. The other epistles, brief ones, are by James, Peter, John, and Jude. They, and Hebrews, were written as "catholic" (meaning "universal") epistles, addressed to Christians everywhere and circulated widely. But eventually all the epistles became catholic and are still read by Christians the world over.

Romans

Summary: Paul wrote this long letter to the Christians in Rome, a city he had not then visited. The letter looks at human beings in general, showing how all people—Jews and non-Jews—have sinned and fallen short of what God intended for us. All of us are "dead in our sins" but can be made spiritually alive through Jesus Christ, who sets us free from sin and enables us to fellowship with God. God gives us a new life by the Holy Spirit. This occurs not because of our own efforts but because of God's kindness. In His goodness He gives Christians different spiritual gifts, enabling us to work for each other's good.

Problems: None. Some readers may not like Paul's moral teaching (particularly on the troublesome topic of homosexuality), but Christians have considered this teaching to be authoritative for 2,000 years.

For those who skip . . . Don't miss a word. The sixteen chapters here are some of the most important in the New Testament. It is the closest Paul came to writing a concise, organized theology, a well-thought-out statement of basic Christian belief. And—Hallelujah!—it is much briefer than most books of theology are.

1 Corinthians

Summary: Paul wrote to Christians in Corinth, a notoriously immoral city in what is now Greece. Being a faithful believer in this decadent city wasn't easy. The church had signs of strain, Christians arguing over beliefs and morals. Paul warns them against divisions and against allowing flagrant sinners to remain in the fellowship. Paul talks at length about Christian marriage and sexual morals. He talks about the right way to worship together and about the various spiritual gifts Christians have. Chapter 13 is the "love chapter," discussing love as the greatest gift. Chapter 15 is a description of what Christians will be like in the afterlife.

Problems: None. The modern world likes to argue with some of Paul's moral teaching (such as his words on homosexuality, 6:9). Paul's morality seems strict, but in our time, with so many people concerned about moral decay, this strictness should be a plus, not a minus.

For those who skip . . . Not a word! This letter is on a par with Romans. Read the entire letter, and make a point to reread chapters 13 and 15 often.

2 Corinthians

Summary: Writing to the Corinthian Christians again, Paul discusses many issues, including the hardships he has experienced as an apostle. He assures his readers that these burdens are nothing compared to the glory awaiting Christians. Paul defends his position as apostle, warning the readers against the many false apostles around.

Problems: Some Bible scholars claim that 2 Corinthians is composed of more than one letter. Most Christian readers today will ask a logical question: "So what?"

For those who skip . . . This epistle should be read through at least once. It is not as "rich" as Romans and 1 Corinthians, but these passages warrant a rereading on occasion: our home in heaven (5:1-10), reconciling people to God (5:11-21), and Paul's belief that God's power is shown in human weakness (12:1-10).

Galatians

Summary: Paul wrote to Christians in Galatia, a province of the Roman Empire (it's in what is today Turkey). The Galatian Christians were being influenced by a group called Judaizers, who taught that Christians must obey all the Jewish regulations—circumcision, the kosher laws, observing Jewish holidays, etc. Paul says loudly, "No! You're Christians! You're free from all those rules now! Don't let anyone impose this legalistic burden on you!" A key word is *freedom*. Christ sets us free from rules—not so we can run wild and be immoral, but so we can be kind, loving children of God. Instead of living by rules, we live by the Holy Spirit. We live a good life out of gratitude to God, not out of a feeling of duty and obligation and fear of punishment.

Problems: None. Let the Bible scholars argue over just what section of Galatia received this letter. (Yes, they really do like to debate such matters.) Most readers won't care.

For those who skip . . . This six-chapter letter should be read through, every word. It seems to focus on problems that are ancient history, but not so: legalism has always been a problem among Christians, and Galatians is a good antidote for it.

Ephesians

Summary: Paul wrote to Christians in Ephesus, a large coastal city in what is now Turkey. The letter deals with the church—not the building, but the community of Christians. They are "one in Christ," all members of God's household. The Holy Spirit gives unity to all Christians, and the Spirit enables us to live moral lives in an immoral world. Paul comments on how faith ought to affect relations of spouses, parents and children, masters and servants. He ends with a description of the "spiritual armor" that defends Christians against evil.

Problems: Some Bible scholars doubt that Paul wrote Ephesians. They claim that the letter (in the original Greek) is so different from Paul's other letters that it is probably by some other author, writing under Paul's name. But many other scholars have no doubt that Paul is the real author. We know that Paul used secretaries, who wrote down his words as he spoke, and it's likely that different secretaries might "polish" the words a little.

For those who skip . . . Don't skip this. It is six chapters and good reading. Its passages about Christian unity help break us out of the idea that we can be "solitary Christians."

Philippians

Summary: Paul wrote this warm, friendly letter to the Christians at Philippi, a city in Greece. It frequently uses the words joy and rejoice, and Paul was joyful that the Philippians were so loving and kind. (Interestingly, this happy letter was written from prison. Perhaps Paul's spirits were lifted by remembering dear old friends.) Paul claims that his persecutions are unimportant, since the new faith is growing in the world. The Philippians are encouraged to be humble, since Jesus Himself was humble. The Christian goal is heaven, and everything earthly is small compared with that. Paul encourages them to hold to the faith, be joyful, and think on noble things.

Problems: None.

For those who skip . . . Don't. It's short and easy to read. The chapter on humility (2) deserves rereading occasionally. This is a good letter to read when you're in the dumps. It's a reminder to be content, even to rejoice, when things go wrong.

Colossians

Summary: Paul wrote the Christians at Colossae, a town in what is now Turkey. False teachers were leading them away from Christianity, claiming they needed to add to it by following special rules and diets and ceremonies and by worshiping angels. He encourages pure belief and warns against the immorality of the world. He provides guidelines for moral life.

Problems: Some scholars doubt that Paul wrote this (see the same note on Ephesians), but most agree that Paul did.

For those who skip . . . Don't skip this short letter. In our day of New Age teachings and various sects and cults, this letter (chap. 2 in particular) reminds us that Christ is enough, so we don't need to clutter the Christian life with useless man-made rules. (Considering our present-day hang-ups about the foods we eat, maybe we need reminding of this.)

1 Thessalonians

Summary: Paul praises the Christians in Thessalonica (a city in Greece) for being brave during persecution. Paul instructs them on something that had been causing them anxiety: When would Jesus return as He had promised?

Problems: None, except that Paul seems to indicate that Jesus is returning to earth soon, which obviously (2,000 years later) hasn't happened yet. Many parts of the New Testament predict that Jesus will return to earth. This doesn't mean the predictions were wrong (how would we know yet?), but that the authors clearly looked forward to this event. By the way, 1 Thessalonians was probably the first part of the New Testament to be written. Put another way, its words may be the oldest Christian writing in the world.

For those who skip . . . At five chapters, why skip? It isn't as inspiring as Paul's other letters, however.

2 Thessalonians

Summary: Written shortly after 1 Thessalonians, this letter tells the Christians that, contrary to their expectations, Jesus may not come back for a while. Paul warns them not to stop working while they await Jesus' return.

Problems: None. The letter, like 1 Thessalonians, speaks about the return of Jesus to earth, and it sounds as if this will happen soon. It hasn't . . . yet.

For those who skip . . . This is a (relatively) unimportant letter, but with only three chapters it should be read through once. Verse 3:16, almost at the end, is a beautiful blessing.

1 Timothy

Summary: This is a "pastoral letter," so called because it (plus 2 Timothy and Titus) deals with how Christian pastors are to lead their churches. Paul warns the young pastor Timothy against false teachers. He instructs him about worship, about church officers, and lay members of the church. Paul warns against love of money and against rich Christians being cocky.

Problems: The scholars question whether Paul wrote this. In the original Greek, the vocabulary is very different from Paul's other letters. This is natural, since he was addressing different issues. It is clear in the New Testament that Paul took a great interest in the works of his young colleagues, Timothy and Titus. Paul's words on women teaching in the churches (2:9-15) have caused some minor controversy.

For those who skip . . . Read this letter through once. It has some vital insights into how to conduct a church. The section on money (6:6-10; 17-19) is a good summary of the Bible's teaching on this important subject.

2 Timothy

Summary: Again, Paul instructs Timothy, the young pastor. He encourages him to stand fast in the faith he was brought up in. In doing this, he gives a concise overview of some key points of faith. He warns Timothy against people who claim to be Christians but aren't. He also reminds Timothy that all Scripture (he was referring to the Old Testament) is "God-breathed" and is useful for training believers.

Problems: None, except that, like 1 Timothy and Titus, some scholars doubt that Paul wrote this.

For those who skip . . . This epistle, short as it is, should be read through at least once. The encouragement to be faithful in chapter 1 is worth an occasional reread.

Titus

Summary: Paul writes Titus, a pastor on the Greek island of Crete. He comments on the duties of pastors, elders, and deacons in the church.

Problems: As with 1 and 2 Timothy, some (not all) scholars doubt that Paul actually wrote Titus.

For those who skip . . . Titus is not the most important of Paul's letters, but it deserves one read-through. Pastors and other church leaders ought to read it often.

Philemon

Summary: Paul writes Philemon, a Christian friend whose slave, Onesimus, has stolen money from him and run away. Onesimus runs to Paul, then becomes a Christian. Paul sends Onesimus back to Philemon, carrying this letter. He begs Philemon to welcome Onesimus back as a Christian brother.

Problems: None, except that some readers ask an obvious question: Why would Paul send the slave back to his master? Shouldn't a Christian oppose slavery? We can't solve this issue here, except to say that slavery was an accepted fact in the ancient world. Paul does emphasize that the Christian master and the Christian slave are brothers.

For those who skip . . . Why skip a one-chapter letter? It's a good read—quite touching. It shows a rather sweet side of Paul.

Hebrews

Summary: Jesus Christ, God's ultimate revelation to humanity, is superior to any past revelation, including Moses and the Old Testament Law. Christ is the great "High Priest," the One who mediates between God and man. Being both priest and sacrifice, He does away with the old Jewish system of animal sacrifices. The letter's final chapters discuss faith and some great role models of it, the way God disciplines His children, and a reminder that the Christians' true home is in heaven.

Problems: This is the "mystery letter"—we don't know who the author was, nor who exactly received the letter. Unlike the other epistles in the New Testament, this one names no author. Its style (in English or the original Greek) indicates that it is not by any of the other New Testament writers. It is in very "elegant" Greek, which suggests the author was an intellectual. Besides this, we don't know exactly who "the Hebrews" were. By the time this letter was written, "Hebrews" as a national or tribal term was no longer used. Scholars like to argue about this. Did "Hebrew" mean "Christians who had been reared as Jews," or could the term be symbolic—"Hebrews" meaning "God's chosen people," that is, Christians? These questions haven't been answered, even after centuries of debate. But the early Christians saw fit to include this fascinating letter in their list of holy books, and readers throughout the centuries have found the letter inspiring.

For those who skip . . . Don't. Hebrews, a long letter, deserves one good read-through. It is chock-full of quotations from the Old Testament, and some readers find it puzzling. But it contains some beautiful passages about Jesus Christ and the role of faith in Christian life. Worth a reread is the famous "Faith Hall of Fame" in chapter 11. So is the passage on enduring hardship as a Christian (12:1-13).

James

Summary: Here is the first epistle named not for its recipients but for its author. James (who may have been the brother of Jesus) is more of a moral adviser than a the-

---

SOME STATISTICS

(in case you're interested)

····► *The Bible has 66 books,*
39 in the Old Testament,
27 in the New Testament.

····► *There are 1,189 chapters in the Bible,*
929 in the Old Testament,
260 in the New Testament.

····► *There are 31,173 verses in the Bible,*
23,214 in the Old Testament,
7,959 in the New Testament.

····► *The most common word in English Bibles is*
(surprise!) "and."

····► *The longest book of the Bible is Psalms, with*
150 chapters (actually, they're individual psalms,
not chapters). (Note: If you place your finger
midway in the unopened pages of your Bible,
you'll find it at Psalms when you open it.)

····► *The longest chapter in the Bible (by far) is*
Psalm 119, with 176 verses.

····► *The longest verse in the Bible is Esther 8:9—*
about ninety words in most translations.

····► *The shortest verse in the Bible is two words:*
"Jesus wept" (John 11:35).

ologian. He writes Christians everywhere about practical matters—enduring temptations, controlling anger, showing favoritism to the rich, controlling the tongue, praying for healing. Above all, this is the letter emphasizing that faith and good deeds go together—that is, a person with faith will do more than just talk about it.

Problems: None. There are several men named James in the New Testament, but the scholars feel certain that the author of this letter is James the brother of Jesus (mentioned in the Book of Acts, chapters 15 and 21). Some people have claimed there is a conflict between James' teaching on faith ("faith without deeds is useless") and Paul's teaching that Christians are saved by faith alone, not by their good deeds. But there is no conflict. Paul and James agreed that both are essential in the Christian life.

For those who skip . . . Don't. This is a short letter, full of solid, practical advice—a basic how-to book for living the Christian life. The passage on taming the tongue (3:1-12) ought to be required reading—daily.

1 Peter

Summary: Peter, the most notable among Jesus' twelve disciples, writes to Christians everywhere. He asks Christians to live holy lives, remembering that heaven is more enduring than this earthly life. He gives advice on living in a way that will impress unbelievers. He especially looks at how the Christian can endure suffering for his faith. And he gives advice on a loving Christian marriage.

Problems: Some scholars have wondered how the Apostle Peter, a simple fisherman, could have written a letter in such excel-

lent Greek. Since authors often used secretaries in those days, we can assume Peter's aide might have been more skilled with words than Peter himself was. (Many a secretary today is more skilled with words than the boss giving the dictation.)

For those who skip . . . Skip nothing. It's short, full of good advice. Particularly rewarding is the passage on suffering (4:12-19).

2 Peter

Summary: Peter writes Christians who were facing the challenge of false teachers. Peter predicts dire consequences for these teachers. He discusses the "Day of the Lord," the time of Jesus' return to earth, and reminds Christians that they look forward to a new heaven and new earth. This letter is the only place in the Bible that refers to another part of the Bible as being "hard to understand" (Paul's letters).

Problems: None, although the scholars note that the Greek style of 1 Peter and 2 Peter are very different (easily explained, since Peter could have used two different secretaries).

For those who skip . . . Don't. These three chapters deserve reading.

1 John

Summary: John (the same one who wrote the Gospel of John) urges Christians to "walk in the light" of God's truth. He emphasizes love for God and fellow Christians, more important than being attached to this world and our possessions. He gives advice on distinguishing false teaching from true. Above all, he emphasizes love, the true test of our life as Christians.

Problems: None.

For those who skip ... Don't. This short letter is a neglected treasure. It is the "love letter" of the Bible, focusing especially on how believers ought to love each other. It ought to be read more often than it is.

2 John

Summary: John writes to "the chosen lady and her children"—which may refer to a Christian community, not to an actual woman. As in 1 John, he emphasizes the importance of Christians loving each other and obeying God's commands.

Problems: None.

For those who skip ... This tiny letter is skippable, but with only thirteen verses it deserves a read-through.

3 John

Summary: John writes his "dear friend Gaius" about an arrogant Christian brother who is causing problems. He advises Gaius to imitate good instead of evil.

Problems: None.

For those who skip ... Well, why skip fourteen verses? This letter isn't the high point of the New Testament, but it can certainly be read through one time.

Jude

Summary: Jude (who may have been a brother of Jesus) warns against false teachers, who have always been a problem for people of faith. Jude urges Christians to flee these teachings and to be kind to people wavering in their faith.

Problems: None, except we aren't completely sure just who this Jude was. The name (it was actually Judas) is fairly common in the New Testament. The letter is *not*, of course, by the Judas Iscariot who betrayed Jesus. The letter was (obviously) written by one of the *good* men named Judas.

For those who skip ... Don't, since this is a short letter. However, it does cover much the same ground as 2 Peter.

Revelation

Summary: Revelation is partly epistle (chaps. 1–3), partly a vision of the end of time. John, a Christian leader, writes to seven Christian communities in Asia (a Roman province, the area that is now called Turkey). Speaking on behalf of Jesus, he praises their good deeds and warns them against laziness and false teaching. Then, beginning in chapter 4, he describes visions of strange events taking place on earth and in heaven—persecution of Christians, plagues on the earth, evil rulers, corrupt empires, and—finally—a triumphant Jesus, the judgment of all the dead, with a happy

● ● ● ● ● ● ● ● ● ● ●

PEARLY GATES IN HEAVEN?

How many cartoons have you seen of St. Peter standing at the gate of heaven? Is that in the Bible? No. But according to the New Testament, heaven does have gates. And yes, they are pearly gates. "The twelve gates were twelve pearls, each gate made of a single pearl" (Revelation 21:21). And in case you were wondering, the same verse says, "The great street of the city was of pure gold, like transparent glass."

● ● ● ● ● ● ● ● ● ● ●

ending of a new heaven and earth for God's people. The vision chapters are full of symbolic animals, people, and heavenly messengers. The book ends with the triumph of God and His people and the downfall of evil.

Problems: "What does this mean?" is the key problem. John's letters to the churches (chaps. 1–3) are clear enough, but the visions have puzzled readers for centuries. Did the visions forecast events in the lives of John's original readers in the Roman Empire? Events at the end of time, whenever that may be? Or do the visions report things that happen repeatedly—persecution of God's people, with the ending in heaven for every believer who dies? Ask ten Bible scholars—or ten people off the street—and you'll get vastly different responses. But one thing is clear: the book predicts the final triumph of Christ and Christians over Satan and the powers of evil. The Christian's final destination is a heavenly reward, with no pain or sorrow.

For those who skip . . . Don't skip chapters 1–3, since they are straightforward. You might skip the rest of the book, since its symbolism may only leave you bewildered. But do read the final chapters (21–22), since they are an appropriate ending to the Bible (and to the Christian life).

chapter 14

Bridging the Culture Gap: ◄
An Alphabetical Mini-Encyclopedia of Key Bible Words and Ideas

The newest parts of the New Testament were written around, say, A.D. 100. The oldest parts of the Old Testament were written . . . well, a long, *long* time ago. Given that much time between their world and ours, we face a culture gap. Does the contemporary reader—even one with a good education—know enough about the Bible world to read the Bible without pausing at every sentence to ask "What the heck are they talking about here?"

Well, actually, most of the Bible isn't that difficult to read. Some of it—the Book of Proverbs, for example—is as refreshingly straightforward as today's newspaper (assuming you're using a fairly recent Bible translation). However, there *are* things that need explaining. Do you know what a *covenant* is, and what it implied in the Bible? Do you know what relevance circumcision had (other than being a surgical procedure performed on baby boys)? Maybe you do, and maybe you don't. Since the book you are holding is a "square one" manual, we assume no prior knowledge on your part.

In chapter 15 of this book you'll find a discussion of various types of reference books that can help you bridge the culture gaps—books like Bible dictionaries and commentaries that explain religious and historical terms and concepts that were easily grasped by the Bible's original audience, not so easily grasped today. But let's assume you don't have any of these reference books, and maybe you never will. Let's also assume you'd like a guide—maybe an alphabetical one, like the one here—to some key words and ideas in the Bible. This list is, happily, nontechnical and, I hope, user-friendly.

ANGELS

Angels with or without wings?
Browse any bookstore and you'll see that there's been a renewed interest in angels in recent years. Well, the Bible is chock-full of angels—some of them bearing little

resemblance to the beings pictured in art masterpieces (and nothing at all like the infantile cupids that some people find so adorable). Our word *angel* comes from the Greek word *angelos*, simply meaning "messenger." In the Bible, angels play that role: messengers from God. These messengers are often so humanlike that the people they visit notice nothing unusual about them, as with the two who visit Lot in the sinful city of Sodom; Lot doesn't discover their supernatural power until they strike the local perverts with blindness (Gen. 19). Likewise, the warrior Gideon doesn't realize he has been conversing with an angel until the visitor sets a rock on fire by tapping it with a cane (Jud. 6).

But some of the angels in heaven are not so low-key in their appearance. The Prophet Isaiah has a vision of the angels called *seraphim* (that's plural—one seraph, two seraphim): "each with six wings: With two wings they covered their faces, with two they covered their feet, and with two they were flying" (Isa. 6:2). Another prophet, Ezekiel, had a vision of *cherubim*, even more striking in appearance than the seraphim:

> *Their entire bodies, including their backs, their hands and their wings, were completely full of eyes, as were their four wheels. . . . Each of the cherubim had four faces: One face was that of a cherub, the second the face of a man, the third the face of a lion, and the fourth the face of an eagle (Ezek. 10:12, 14).*

Not exactly the cute and pudgy cherubs of Christmas card art!

The Bible's angels are nameless, except for two: Michael (Dan. 10; Rev. 12) and Gabriel (Luke 1). Michael is mentioned in the Revelation passage as being the leader—captain, if you will—of the angels who fight against Satan's armies. Jude 9 refers to Michael as an archangel, which also indicates a position of authority. Gabriel is best known for announcing the birth of Jesus to the Virgin Mary.

Are there *bad* angels? According to the New Testament, yes. The great Christian poet John Milton based his long poem *Paradise Lost* on the belief that Satan and his demons were actually rebellious angels who had been cast out of heaven. You'll find the biblical basis for this in 2 Peter 2:4: "God did not spare angels when they sinned, but sent them to hell, putting them into gloomy dungeons to be held for judgment." Since Satan had been an angel, it is no wonder that "Satan himself masquerades as an angel of light" (2 Cor. 11:14). But these fallen angels face a certain doom at the end of time, vividly described in the Book of Revelation.

(*See also* Satan.)

APOSTLES

(*See* Disciples.)

ARK

Just what was the ark?
The Bible talks of two notable arks. One was the enormous boat that sheltered Noah and his family during the universal Flood (Gen. 7). The more famous ark was called the ark of the covenant—which enjoyed a renewal of interest after the 1980 Harrison Ford movie *Raiders of the Lost Ark*. The ark that appeared in that movie was based on the description in the Old Testament. It

was a chest (ark is from *arca*, the Latin word for "chest") made of wood, covered with gold and carried by two gold-covered poles. On the gold lid were two winged creatures—the *cherubim*—facing each other. Inside the ark were the two tables of the Law (stone tablets) brought down by Moses from Mount Sinai. The ark was carried by the Israelites on their journey through the desert and, notably, was carried seven times around the pagan city of Jericho until the city's walls fell down. The Israelites constructed a sanctuary housing the ark in the town of Shiloh.

The ark was more than just a pretty, shiny box, of course. For the Israelites it symbolized God's presence among them. They could not make any statue or other image representing the invisible God. But the ark, shining in gold and with the cherubim with their outstretched wings, was a stunning (and mysterious) reminder of the majestic (but invisible) God who guided Israel.

As the Harrison Ford movie indicated, the ark, being a sacred object, had great power associated with it. No one was supposed to actually touch it (the reason it was carried by poles), and when it was captured by the heathen Philistines, it brought them such bad luck that they returned it to the Israelites. It caused a statue of their god Dagon to fall on its face—within Dagon's own temple. The invisible God of Israel had beaten the fish-shaped god Dagon on its home turf!

After King Solomon built his beautiful temple in Jerusalem, the ark was placed in the inmost chamber, called the holy of holies, which only the high priest could enter, and only once a year. Solomon placed it there, and it is last mentioned in the much later reign of King Josiah (2 Chron. 35:3). It disappeared from history, perhaps carried off by the Babylonians, who raided Jerusalem in 586 B.C. When the Jerusalem temple was rebuilt many years later, the ark was not there. What became of this important object? As *Raiders of the Lost Ark* pointed out, the amazing chest might still be somewhere on earth—but where? The more likely alternative is that the Babylonians stripped the gold from it and used the wooden chest for firewood. But who knows?

Interestingly, the climactic scene at the movie's end, when the Nazi raiders dare to open the sacred chest, isn't too different from the Bible's last mention of the ark, a vision in the Book of Revelation: "God's temple in heaven was opened, and within His temple was seen the ark of His covenant. And there came flashes of lightning, rumblings, peals of thunder, an earthquake and a great hailstorm" (Rev. 11:19).

(*See also* Covenant.)

BLOODSHED

Too much gore?
The Old Testament Books of Joshua and Judges show the tribes of Israel settling in the land of Canaan—and butchering the original dwellers. Is this Christian behavior? Hardly—but then, this slaughter predates Jesus and His teaching on love and nonviolence. But would God really command His people, the Israelites, to conquer—and slaughter—other people?

Consider what the Israelites faced: Tribes

that worshiped gods of nature and fertility. Worship of these gods—Baal, Ashtaroth, Molech—often consisted of sex with temple prostitutes and even sacrifice of children. The religion of Israel had no place for such horrors. The Israelites were constantly tempted to fall into heathen worship. The only way they saw to keep their religion pure was to exterminate the heathen. They believed that as long as idol-worshipers were at hand, there was the danger of the true religion being corrupted. And it often was.

A word about blood itself: Until fairly recently, most human beings had a fair amount of exposure to blood—usually in the butchering of animals. The Book of Leviticus strikes some people as gross in its bluntness about sacrificing animals. But in fact, our own squeaky clean society, in which we seldom see an animal bleed, is unusual in the world's history. (How long has it been since you've had blood pudding or blood sausage?) In Bible times, and in many parts of the world today, people got a lot of exposure not only to animal blood but to human blood as well. Up until the last hundred or so years, most people did not die in hospitals. They died at home, with their families (children included) exposed to bleeding and other unpleasantness. Horrible, but something that most people accepted as the natural order of things.

(*See also* Idolatry, Israel.)

CANAAN

Where was Canaan?
Many old hymns refer to "Canaan land." Canaan in the Old Testament referred to the general area occupied by the Israelites—

roughly the same area as is occupied today by the nation Israel. The Canaanites referred to the land's original inhabitants, idol-worshipers who were driven out when the Israelites settled in the area.

A familiar, and poetic, name for Canaan was the Promised Land. This refers to the promise—mentioned dozens of times in the Bible—that the patriarch Abraham and his descendants (the Hebrews) would possess the land of Canaan, "the land you have given us as you promised on oath to our forefathers, a land flowing with milk and honey" (Deut. 26:15). The Jews who live today in the modern nation of Israel still believe the promise that Abraham's descendants would possess that piece of land.

(*See also* Holy Land, Israel, Palestine, Patriarchs, Zion.)

CHOSEN PEOPLE

This name applies in the Bible to the nation (or tribe) of Israel. These people are referred to as Israelites, Hebrews, or Jews. The key idea in the Old Testament is that the one true God chose Israel (the descendants of Abraham) to be the recipients of His moral and spiritual guidance. The idea is expressed many times in the Bible, notably in Deuteronomy 7:6: "You are a people holy to the LORD your God. The LORD your God has chosen you out of all the peoples on the face of the earth to be His people, His treasured possession." This is similar to the idea Americans have that we are a "special" nation dedicated to freedom and equality. The Bible makes it clear that the "chosen people" are never to be arrogant or cocky because God has chosen them. In fact, because God revealed Himself and His moral law to Israel, the people of Israel will be severely punished when they break the moral law. So, being chosen is a privilege but also an obligation.

(*See also* Covenant, Israel.)

CHRIST

Messiah and Christ

Was *Christ* the last name of Jesus? Hardly. In Jesus' day most people did not have last names (though they might be referred to as, for example, "John the son of Zechariah"). The New Testament many times uses the phrases *Jesus Christ, Christ Jesus, Jesus the Christ*, and *the Christ*. *Christ* is not a name, but a title. It means "anointed one." Anointing, rubbing the forehead with a small amount of oil, was a ritual that marked a person for some special purpose in life—to be a king or priest, for example. Calling Jesus *the Christ* meant that He was "God's anointed One," the One whom God had chosen for an extraordinary mission on earth.

Christ, a Greek word, has the same meaning as the Old Testament's Hebrew word *Messiah*. (You're familiar with this word from Handel's popular choral work, often performed at Christmas. Handel could have called his work *Christ*, except that *Messiah* does have a nice ring to it.) In the Old Testament the word *Messiah* can refer to almost any person (or even an inanimate object) that is anointed. But as time passed, the Jews began to believe that God would send one special person, *the* Messiah, who would restore the nation of Israel to its political and spiritual glory. Many people saw this figure as a warrior king who

would chase the foreign oppressors from the land. Groups of guerrilla fighters and terrorists banded together occasionally, trying to put the dream into action. One group of these was called the Zealots, and one of Jesus' disciples was a Zealot named Simon. No doubt Simon and some other followers of Jesus wondered if He was the long-awaited Messiah who would chase the Roman armies out of the land.

Jesus certainly failed to meet these expectations. He told the Roman governor Pilate, "My kingdom is not of this world. ... My kingdom is from another place" (John 18:36). Jesus the Messiah was a *spiritual* savior, one who would save people not from foreign armies but from their own sins (which, in the Bible, is more of a problem than war is). Jesus' most outspoken follower, Peter, exclaimed, "You are the Christ, the Son of the living God" (Matt. 16:16).

Ironically, this spiritual Christ ended up being executed by those who believed He was trying to be the political Messiah: "They began to accuse Him, saying, 'We have found this man subverting our nation. He opposes payment of taxes to Caesar and claims to be Christ, a king'" (Luke 23:2).

(*See also* Covenant, Lord, Savior.)

CIRCUMCISION

So much fuss about a surgical procedure. Circumcision today is a quick surgical procedure that some (not all) parents choose for their male babies. In biblical times it was a religious, not medical, matter. For the people of Israel, circumcision, performed on the eighth day after a boy's birth, was a living sign of God's tie to His people, Israel.

Abraham, the patriarch and ancestor of the Israelites, was told to be circumcised (he was already ninety-nine years old!) and to do the same to all men in his household (Gen. 17). This was one of God's first commands to His people, way before the Ten Commandments.

Some of Israel's neighbor nations also performed circumcision—sometimes on babies, but sometimes on adolescents and adults. Archaeologists find that the well-preserved mummies of Egyptian men were sometimes circumcised, sometimes not. The Philistines, a warlike tribe that was a constant thorn in Israel's side, was noted for *not* performing circumcision. The Philistines are sometimes referred to (sneeringly) as "the uncircumcised." When the warrior David killed a hundred Philistines, he brought back foreskins as proof—since a hundred foreskins could have been obtained from no other people but the Philistines.

The prophets of Israel, by the way, insisted that circumcision was more than just a physical ritual. The faithful man was also supposed to be "circumcised in heart"— that is, devoted to God fully. His outward condition was only a reminder of the condition of his heart. The Prophet Jeremiah said, "'The days are coming,' declares the LORD, 'when I will punish all who are circumcised only in the flesh'" (Jer. 9:25).

The Israelites/Jews considered circumcision so important that a male convert to their religion had to undergo it, even if he was an adult. (This was in the days before medical anesthesia—ouch!) Many non-Jews who admired the Jewish religion chose to be "God-fearers"—practicing the Jewish religion but not taking the final step of becoming full Jews by being circumcised. (The Jews' Greek and Roman neighbors generally thought the practice was disgusting. Many modern Europeans have the same attitude, believing that circumcision is cruel and unnatural.)

We read the letters of Paul in the New Testament and wonder why he made such a fuss about circumcision. Paul had to keep insisting that, no, a man did *not* have to be circumcised to become a Christian. Some Christians—known as Judaizers — claimed that a man had to be circumcised before becoming a Christian. Paul believed that this meant that Christianity would always be just a wing of Judaism. He knew that Christianity was destined to be a universal faith. So he drove home the point that non-Jews could become Christians without being circumcised—that is, they could come to Christianity without "jumping through the hoop" of the Jewish religion. Paul insisted that circumcision was "inward"—our tie to God is spiritual, not a matter of cutting away a piece of skin. So Christianity has never insisted on circumcision, though Jews still do.

(*See also* Covenant.)

CONCUBINES

In the New Testament period the rule was "one wife per man"—or one wife at a time, anyway, since it was possible to divorce then remarry.

But the Old Testament shows a bewildering array of marital options. No woman could have more than one husband at a time, but a man (if his assets allowed) could support a number of wives . . . and concubines.

Just what were concubines? We're told that the wealthy King Solomon had " seven hundred wives of royal birth and three hundred concubines" (1 Kings 11:3). The common man could not afford such an extravagant household, naturally. Many of Solomon's marriages were made to forge political alliances (note that the verse says the wives were "of royal birth"). Generally, concubines were sort of secondary wives—often chosen from among slaves, servants, and captives of war. A concubine wasn't a girlfriend or mistress, and certainly not "the other woman" that threatened to break up the marriage. The Israelites seemed to have accepted that a man—particularly a wealthy one—could have certain female servants who provided sexual services in addition to their other duties. When a wife proved to be sterile (considered a horrible fate in those days), a concubine could provide the man with children. The patriarch Abraham, whose beautiful wife Sarah was sterile, fathered a son by his concubine, Sarah's servant Hagar. The patriarch Jacob (also called Israel) fathered his twelve sons by two wives and two concubines. The sons of the concubines were not considered illegitimate.

The Old Testament takes this situation for granted. Presumably a good man would ensure that all his wives and concubines were provided for and would treat all the women well (though probably not as equals, which naturally caused domestic strife). Still, the Old Testament issues some warnings about the dangers: "He [a ruler] must not take many wives, or his heart will be led astray" (Deut. 17:17). This proved true, for Solomon's many women "led him astray" (1 Kings 11:3). Note that the immorality was not having so many wives and concubines, but the fact that they led him astray—that is, caused him to neglect God and/or worship other gods.

COVENANT

A book of covenants and sacrifices
It's hard to understand the Old or New Testament without grasping the idea of *covenant*. A covenant was an agreement—a contract, to use a popular word of today. There were covenants between human beings, but the Bible is particular interested in the covenants between man and God.

A. Rainbow

The first covenant mentioned is the one between God and Noah. After surviving the worldwide Flood with his family, Noah is told by God that this disaster will never again happen. As a reminder of the covenant, God gives Noah the rainbow.

This particular covenant carries no condition on man's part. It is simply God's promise—not just to man, but to all created things—that He will never again blot out all life with a flood (Gen. 9).

B. Circumcision

Abraham, considered the father of the Hebrews (or Israelites) had an agreement with God: all males in his household and all his male descendants would be circumcised (Gen. 17). Circumcision was to be a sign that Abraham and his descendants were God's special people, the "people of the covenant." Failure to circumcise was so serious that the person could be expelled from the faith community: "Any uncircumcised male, who has not been circumcised in the flesh, will be cut off from his people; he has broken my covenant" (Gen. 17:14).

C. The Law

The third covenant was not between God and an individual but between God and the entire community of Israel. The Book of Exodus (which contains the Ten Commandments) depicts the leader Moses guiding the Israelite slaves out of Egypt toward their new homeland in Canaan. At Mount Sinai, in the desert, Moses passes on to the people the laws given to him by God. If the people will obey God's laws, they will settle in the Promised Land and prosper in it. If they disobey, they will bring disaster on themselves. It is a conditional covenant: obey and thrive, disobey and suffer. The Israelites mark the agreement by sacrificing oxen (Ex. 24:8). Interestingly, the covenant was broken almost immediately after it was made. When Moses returned to the mountain to receive more instructions from God, the Israelites set up a golden calf idol. (You might remember this from the movie *The Ten Commandments*.) One of the Ten Commandments strictly forbids setting up idols. But, as often happened, God forgave the people and the covenant continued to be binding. Much of the Old Testament is the story of how Israel continually failed to keep the covenant—only to be forgiven again and again by God. Still, the condition applied. The people didn't keep the covenant, so they suffered—ultimately by being deported by invading empires.

The Sinai covenant never assumed that people could be sinless. The Law provided a system of sacrifices—gifts of animals or grain given to the Hebrew priests. Israel's religion, like many world religions, provided that sinners could make up for their failings (and prove they were sorry) by giving something valuable to God—a sheep or cow, for example. The sacrifice did not "undo" the sin, of course. It did prove the person was aware of the sin and willing to give up something as a sign of repentance. The Old Testament's Book of Leviticus, which is mostly concerned with the various types of sacrifices, makes it clear that there is nothing "magical" about sacrifices. That is, it isn't the slaughtered animal that heals the sin, but the more important fact that the person is aware of his sin and honestly confesses it. Incidentally, Israel's system of sacrifices was certainly more humane than the neighboring nations who sacrificed their own infants to idols.

D. Heart covenant

The Prophet Jeremiah watched tearfully as his sinning countrymen were carried off to exile in Babylon—a result of breaking the Sinai covenant. Jeremiah predicted a new covenant that would amend the Sinai agreement: " 'This is the covenant I will make with the house of Israel after that time,' declares the LORD. 'I will put My law in their minds and write it on their hearts. I will be their God, and they will be My people'" (Jer. 31:33). This new covenant would not replace the old one. Rather, it would add something new: an inward motivation to please God.

E. Jesus' covenant

According to the Letter to the Hebrews, "Christ is the mediator of a new covenant, that those who are called may receive the promised eternal inheritance—now that He has died as a ransom to set them free from the sins committed under the first covenant" (Heb. 9:15). In other words, the old covenant (the laws given to Israel at Sinai) is no longer binding. The new agreement involves Christ who, in effect, "pays a ransom" so we don't have to suffer for the sins we've committed. Jesus Himself made this new covenant clear at the Last Supper with His disciples: "This is My blood of the covenant, which is poured out for many" (Mark 14:24). The wine (probably red) symbolized the blood He was about to shed by being crucified. It is a key belief in the New Testament that Jesus' death was the ultimate sacrifice. It did away with the old system of animal sacrifices. Instead of continually sacrificing lambs and cattle and doves, we point to Christ, whose death cancels out all the sins we committed or ever will commit.

When Christians celebrate the Lord's Supper (or Communion or Eucharist) they remind themselves that Jesus' body and blood (symbolized by bread and wine) are the final sacrifice that cancels out our sins and makes us "right with God."

Most of us have probably never seen an animal being slaughtered, so we're repelled at the whole idea of animal sacrifice. Likewise we don't like the idea of Jesus as a sacrifice—as if God somehow took pleasure in seeing Jesus bleed and die. But if we're going to grasp the Bible, we need to project ourselves back into that world. If we thought seriously about the Lord's Supper, we would realize that, yes, it is unpleasant to think about Jesus dying. It should be! The whole point of the New Testament is that Jesus, who lived a sinless life, willingly presents Himself as a sacrifice on behalf of . . . sinners. That a completely innocent man is willing to die to benefit guilty people should shock and offend us . . . and make us glad.

(*See also* Christ, Circumcision, Israel, Patriarchs, Sin.)

DISCIPLES

Disciples, apostles, and so forth

Jesus selected His "dream team," twelve men who were to be His special followers. He had more than twelve (there is a group referred to as the Seventy), but these twelve were His "inner circle," in a special master-pupil relationship with Him. These are the *disciples*, and the New Testament sometimes refers to them simply as "the Twelve." A disciple is a pupil, one who learns.

After Jesus' death and resurrection, the disciples (minus the traitor Judas Iscariot, who killed himself after betraying Jesus) were always referred to as *apostles*—that is, ambassadors on someone else's behalf (Jesus', that is). While Jesus was on earth He used the title Himself to distinguish the Twelve from His other followers: "He called His disciples to Him and chose twelve of them, whom He also designated apostles" (Luke 6:13). Jesus entrusted these twelve men with representing Him in the world.

The New Testament's Book of Acts, which follows the four Gospels, is sometimes called Acts of the Apostles. But in fact, Acts doesn't tell the doings of all twelve apostles. It focuses on a select few, like Peter, and even on some nonapostles (like the martyr Stephen and the deacon Philip). And the chief player in Acts is not one of the Twelve at all, but the great missionary and teacher Paul. As far as we know, Paul, unlike the Twelve, had never known Jesus personally—at least, not until the risen Jesus appeared to Paul as Paul was headed on a Christian-persecuting mission. In his many letters that make up a huge part of the New Testament, Paul frequently refers to himself as "an apostle." In terms of energy, enthusiasm, travel, and influence, none of the original Twelve held a candle to the great Apostle Paul.

(*See also* Christ.)

GENTILES

In the Old Testament, God chose to reveal Himself to the particular tribe (or nation) known as Israel. The people of that nation were known (at different periods and in different parts of the Bible) as Hebrews, Israelites, or Jews. Any person who was not one of these "chosen people" was called a *Gentile*, a word that occurs many, many times in the Bible. When you see a reference to "the Gentiles," it is referring to all the world's nations except Israel.

In the Old Testament, it is generally assumed that Israel is the only "saved" nation. It is the only tribe that God has a binding covenant with (*see* Covenant, above). But the New Testament takes a radically different view: God's salvation (which is spiritual, not political) is extended to all people who put their faith in Jesus Christ. Jesus Himself was

a Jew, as were His original band of followers. But the Book of Acts shows how the faith in Jesus spread to the Gentiles. Some of the Jews who became Christians resisted this expansion, and they claimed that the new Gentile converts had to become Jews as a part of becoming Christians. The great Apostle Paul (a Jew who became known as "the apostle to the Gentiles") insisted that, no, a Gentile could become a Christian without having to become a Jew. So in the New Testament the message of salvation goes global. God wants everyone, Jew or Gentile, to put his or her faith in Christ and have fellowship with God.

Jews and Gentiles almost always disliked each other. (Sometimes the hostile feeling went way, way beyond disliking.) The New Testament has a lot to say about the problems that arose when both Jews and Gentiles became Christians. Paul's letters, which make up a big chunk of the New Testament, deal with this question that is still relevant: How can the Christian faith find a place for people of diverse backgrounds? How can people who are so different get along?

(*See also* Circumcision, Covenants, Israel.)

HEAVEN AND HELL

The Old Testament says very little about the afterlife. For the people of Israel, the main goal in life was to live on earth and have a good relationship with God and with other human beings. After death . . . what? Most of the Israelites did not speculate about that. They focused their attention on this life.

But the New Testament makes it clear that God designs human beings for an afterlife—a happy, joyous afterlife with Him (heaven) or an unhappy, despairing afterlife apart from Him (hell). Jesus, who is shown as the Son of God, says a lot about God's love and kindness, but also a lot about what happens to us when we reject that love. By our own choice we come running to God, sorry for our failures and wishing to be forgiven and accepted. Or we choose to live strictly for ourselves, ignoring God and neglecting our duties to other people. God doesn't put us in hell. We do so ourselves. In a sense, hell is like locking ourselves up in a closet, shutting out God and other people. The key idea in hell is total selfishness.

Is hell a hot furnace, and is heaven a cloudy place with harps and golden streets? The Bible actually says very little about the physical attributes of either place. The Book of Revelation does paint a picture of heaven as a beautiful city with streets of gold, pearly gates, and constant singing and music praising God. Revelation uses these images to communicate the ideas of beauty, order, and fellowship with God. Revelation also refers to the devil and all evil people being destroyed in a lake of fire. Jesus Himself spoke of the fire of hell—the idea being that the person apart from God is in agony. Is it a "literal" fire? That question misses the point. And the point is that the person who chooses to separate himself from God is in the worst possible circumstance.

HEBREWS

(*See* Israel.)

HOLY LAND

Where is the Holy Land?
You won't find this name on the map, but many tour operators could take you on a "Holy Land tour." Jews, Christians, and Muslims can all point to places associated with their religious history in the nation of Israel and nearby nations. The ancient city of Jerusalem, in particular, has sites that each of the three religions honor.

Technically, Christians don't have holy places—God and Christ are not tied to any land, city, or building. But for centuries Christians have enjoyed visiting—making pilgrimages—to sites associated with Jesus, Paul, King David, and other biblical figures. In fact, the Holy Land was probably the world's first tourist destination—as it still is.

By the way, the notorious Crusades of the Middle Ages weren't a matter of Christian warriors trying to convert Muslims to the faith. They were a matter of clearing a path for Christians wanting to visit the Holy Land sites. After the Muslims had conquered the land, they made life difficult for Christian inhabitants and tourists. So the Crusaders had the goal of reconquering the land on behalf of Christianity.

(*See also* Canaan, Israel, Palestine, Zion.)

IDOLATRY

What's so bad about statues?
Again and again in the Old Testament you'll find prophets condemning idolatry. Just what was idolatry? Essentially it was worshiping an image—a statue or something we might consider a "totem pole." The image represented a god or goddess. The people of Israel were strictly forbidden to worship such things. One of the Ten Commandments makes this clear: "You shall not

make for yourself an idol in the form of anything in heaven above or on the earth beneath or in the waters below" (Ex. 20:4). Why not? Because the religion of Israel was based on the worship of the one and only God, an invisible spirit, not an object and not a force of nature. Israel was surrounded by nations that worshiped nature gods—notably the weather-agriculture god Baal, who is mentioned dozens of times in the Old Testament. Like many ancient nature gods, Baal was a god of fertility (of crops, but of humans as well). The similar goddess Ashtaroth was also a fertility deity. People concocted elaborate myths about these human-like gods and their sexual shenanigans. Naturally the worship of such gods could—and did—lead to sexual immorality. Worship of these gods was often more like an orgy than a church service.

Modern readers puzzle over this constant harping about idols and images. Isn't this ancient history? Hardly. Most people don't literally bow down to an idol nowadays. But aren't most people still very materialistic, inclined to *worship* material things—cars, homes, bodies (our own or someone else's), the flashy images in advertising? It was this worship—this chasing after false gods—that the Israelite prophets condemned so strongly. We are supposed to worship the Creator (God), not anything created. So we aren't to worship Baal . . . or a Mercedes or the airbrushed images in pornography. It is possible to worship gods with names like Wealth and Power and Popularity and Worldly Satisfaction. According to Jesus, "No one can serve two masters. Either he will hate the one and love the other, or he will be devoted to the one and despise the other. You cannot serve both God and Money" (Matt. 6:24). The old idolatry problem won't go away.

(*See also* Israel, Sin.)

ISRAEL

Israelites, Hebrews, Jews, and Other Family Names

The name Israel refers to:

1. The patriarch Jacob, who was given this name after wrestling with a heavenly messenger. The name means "wrestles with God" (Gen. 32:28).

2. The nation descended from Jacob and his twelve sons (who were the ancestors of the "twelve tribes of Israel"). The nation could also be referred to as *Israelites, all Israel,* or *Children of Israel.*

3. The kingdom formed when the nation Israel divided in two after the death of King Solomon. Ten of the twelve tribes of Israel formed the Northern Kingdom of Israel. The two other tribes formed the Southern Kingdom, Judah.

In the Bible, Israel generally refers more often to the people than to the land itself. The land of Israel in the Bible did not necessarily cover the same area as the nation of Israel today.

The modern term *Israeli* refers to the people of the modern nation Israel. *Israeli* is not found in the Bible, which uses terms like *Israelites* or *Children of Israel.*

The word Hebrew refers to:

1. The language of the people of Israel. Most of the Old Testament was written in this language. A form of it is the national language of Israel today, and it is studied

by Jews and Christians who want to read the Old Testament in the original.

2. An Israelite. The first person called *Hebrew* is the patriarch Abraham. *Hebrew* means essentially the same as *Israelite*, although *Israelite* is much more commonly used in the Old Testament.

3. The group of Christians who received the Letter to the Hebrews, found in the New Testament. The author of this letter probably meant the word in a figurative sense—that is, in the Old Testament the Hebrews were "God's chosen people," so the Christians, now God's chosen people, are the "new Hebrews."

What are the Jews named for?

The word came to English from both Latin and Greek. It comes from the tribe of *Judah*, one of the twelve tribes of Israel (also the largest tribe). The kingdom of Israel split (after King Solomon's death) into two nations—the Northern Kingdom (called Israel) and the Southern Kingdom (called Judah). When the empire of Assyria conquered and devastated the Northern Kingdom, the name *Israel* ceased to have any real political meaning. The kingdom of Judah continued on longer, until conquered by the Babylonians. Years later, under the control of the Roman Empire, the region formerly called Israel and Judah had the name *Judea*, a province of Rome.

The word *Jew* in the Old Testament refers to inhabitants of Judah. The word occurs only in the very late books of the Old Testament—Ezra, Daniel, and others. By the time this word came into use, the words *Israel* and *Israelite* had ceased to have any real meaning, since the old kingdom

Israel no longer existed.

The New Testament uses the word *Jew* to refer to followers of the traditional religion of the land, the religion we call Judaism today. The Romans ruled over these people in the provinces of Judea (where Jerusalem was) and Galilee (Jesus' home territory). By this time there were also Jews living throughout the Roman Empire, including Rome itself. Devout Jews still longed to visit Judea, particularly the holy city of Jerusalem. And there were always some guerrilla movements aimed at creating a Jewish nation ruled by the Jews themselves. But by the time of the New Testament, it was clear that a Jew was a follower of a religion, not an inhabitant of a particular nation.

So, basically, in the Old Testament we have the people called *Israelites* and *Hebrews* (and, much later, *Jews*), and in the New Testament we have *Jews*. When the New Testament refers to *Israel, Israelites,* and *Hebrews*, it is referring to historical things—the same way an Alabama resident today would talk about the Confederacy. The Jews of Jesus' day thought of Israel only in a historical or spiritual sense—the way an Alabama resident today might say, "I live in the Confederacy," or "I'm a Rebel," while being fully aware that he technically lives in the U.S.A.

Because Israel no longer existed as a real nation, the early Christians could apply all the Old Testament words about Israel to themselves. That is, the old Israel, God's chosen people, gives up its place to the new Israel, God's chosen people, the Christians. The Old Testament prophecies about God "restoring Israel" were given a new spiritual meaning. Instead of God literally giving Israel its old land back and bringing peace, He will bring inner peace and a new heavenly land to His people.

(*See also* Chosen People, Covenant, Gentiles, Patriarchs.)

-ITES

Where are these -Ites from?

The *-ite* ending in the Old Testament refers to a group of people. So people of Israel are Israelites, people of Canaan are Canaanites, people of Moab are Moabites, and so on. The term *Israeli* is modern and not found in the Bible.

JEHOVAH

Who is Jehovah?

Did you ever wonder who Jehovah is (as in "Jehovah's Witnesses")? It is an older form of the name for God. In the original Hebrew Old Testament, God's name is *Yahweh*, a name meaning (probably) "I Cause to Be" or "I Am What I Am." Most English Bibles now translate *Yahweh* as "the LORD." But some older Bibles (the *King James Version*, for example) sometimes used the name Jehovah—which, believe it or not, is a form of the name *Yahweh*. (If you have a *King James* Bible, you'll find Jehovah in Ex. 6:3; Ps. 83:18; and Isa. 12:2.) Most newer translations do not use Jehovah at all. The name does occur in a lot of old hymns.

(*See also* Lord, Names.)

JEWS

(*See* Israel.)

LORD

One Lord—or Two?

If you look closely at your Old Testament, you'll notice the word "Lord" appears in two ways: *Lord* and *the LORD*. What's the difference?

Lord is a translation of the Hebrew word *Adonai* meaning "lord" or "master." The word could refer to God, or to a human master.

The LORD (note the caps and small caps) is a translation of the Hebrew *Yahweh*, the mysterious name of God. The actual name Yahweh means something like "I Am" or "I Cause Things to Be." (One loose translation might be "Supreme Being.") For hundreds of years, English Bibles have chosen to translate *Yahweh* as *the LORD* instead of fumbling for a way to really translate *Yahweh*. This choice goes back to the Jews, who had gotten into the habit of never actually saying the word *Yahweh*. Since it was the true name of God, they felt it was too holy to pronounce. So they got into the habit of saying *Adonai* instead of *Yahweh*. The translators followed this practice, but they use the small caps so you'll always know that *Lord* and *LORD* are translating two different words. (Curiously, in some isolated areas of the world, tribes still have a high God that is known by a name that the people believe is too holy to say out loud.)

Could we be sensible and just use *Yahweh* in our English Bibles? One version, the *New Jerusalem Bible*, does. In this version, Psalm 23 begins "*Yahweh* is my shepherd." Does that sort of jar your ears? Most people think so. After all these centuries of calling God "Lord," we could probably never adjust to calling Him *Yahweh*.

By the way, in the original Hebrew,

Adonai and *Yahweh* sometimes appear together when referring to God. How do we translate that? Wouldn't it seem clumsy to say *Lord LORD* in the same sentence? Most translators think so. So they came up with an alternate phrase. The *New International Version* and *Today's English Version* use "Sovereign LORD," for example. Some other versions use *Lord GOD*.

In the New Testament, the term *Lord* applies not only to God but to Jesus. This was natural, since the early Christians saw Jesus as the Son of God. You will find "the Lord Jesus" many times in the New Testament. In fact, the words "Jesus is Lord" express probably the earliest statement of faith in Jesus Christ. When people called Jesus "Lord," they meant that Jesus was the one they followed and worshiped.

(*See also* Christ, Jehovah, Names.)

MESSIAH

(*See* Christ.)

MIRACLES

One of the advantages of living at the beginning of the twenty-first century is that people seem very open to amazing things. Fifty years ago hardly anyone believed UFOs were real. Today, many people (including the well-educated and sophisticated) claim they believe. (Whether this particular belief is healthy or not is open to question.) Some people say we're living in a secular, materialistic, antisupernatural age. But it's obviously not true, with so many people fascinated by UFOs, astral projection, near-death experiences, etc.

So at least people may be open to the mir-

acles in the Bible. They are definitely there, in both Old and New Testaments. Jesus worked many miracles, most of them miracles of healing. Some of the Old Testament prophets, notably Elijah and Elisha, worked miracles. The curious thing is, even though there are miracle stories in the Bible, there aren't as many as you'd think. In fact, the lion's share of the Bible is down-to-earth, factual data that most historians would not argue with at all.

The Bible sees God as the Creator of all that is. He makes the universe and also the natural laws that (usually) apply. On occasion—in Bible times as today—things occur that even scientists cannot explain. In Bible times, when most people believed in God (or gods), the unexplainable was usually attributed to the supernatural. Interestingly, in the Bible these unusual occurrences are always for a purpose. Jesus never did miracles just for fun. He healed people and worked other miracles for them because He loved them. God is not a cosmic entertainer who likes to show off. He is a loving Father who does amazing things for a purpose. Like human beings, He is free. Being free, He can sometimes act in a way different from the normal, natural processes in the world. A miracle is a reminder that God is free to do this.

It is hard to read the Bible and overlook the miraculous parts. Some parts—the Book of Proverbs, for example, or the Book of Ruth—have nothing miraculous about them. But you can't avoid the miraculous, particularly in the New Testament, where every page carries the belief that the crucified Jesus was raised from the dead. Hard to believe? Yes, it is, and it was in the New Testament era too. But "hard to believe" and "impossible" are two different things. If intelligent, cultured people today can believe in reincarnation and UFO abductions, there is no reason they should rule out a man being raised from the dead. If you can believe in the Resurrection, the big miracle, you can probably accept the other miracles as well. Maybe not. But keep an open mind.

NAMES

Yah! El! What's in a name?

You can't help but notice that many biblical names—especially in the Old Testament—are peculiar. They seem less so when you realize that a name was picked because it had a meaning, not just because it sounded nice.

Notice how many Old Testament names contain a -iah or an -el at the end (or sometimes El- at the beginning of a name). The -iah (sometimes -jah also) was actually the Hebrew name Yah, referring to God. El was another name for God. So every name with -iah or -el has some meaning relating to God. Isaiah, for example, means "Yah [God] saves." Zechariah means "Yah [God] remembers." Daniel means "El [God] is judge." Elijah combines the two names and means "Yah is God."

When the Old Testament original uses Yah (or its longer form, Yahweh), English Bibles translate it as LORD.

(See also Jehovah, Lord.)

PALESTINE

Just where is "Palestine"?

Thanks to the political turmoil in the Middle East, we hear a lot about Palestine (as in Palestine Liberation Organization, the PLO). In the past, the name referred to the region that was also called many other names, depending on the time period—Canaan, Israel, Judea, the Holy Land, the Promised Land, etc.

Curiously, the name comes from Philistine, the name of a warlike people who were a constant thorn in Israel's side. The old name Palestina means "land of the Philistines." The Romans, who conquered the region, first made the name an official place on the map. The name has nothing to do with Arabs, by the way. The Philistines—and the Israelites—lived in the region long, long before the Arabs (or the religion of Islam) existed. The name was revived by the British, who governed the area beginning in World War I and gave it the name Palestine.

(See also Canaan, Holy Land, Israel, Zion.)

PATRIARCHS

To a lot of contemporary feminists, "patriarchy" is almost a dirty word. They use it to refer to any society dominated by men. (The word actually means "rule by fathers.") In the Bible, though, the patriarchs were the ancestors of the chosen people, the nation of Israel. The most important patriarchs were Abraham, the man to whom God promised the land of Canaan, Isaac (Abraham's son), and Jacob (Isaac's son, who also had the name Israel). These figures are especially important because of God's promises to them.

Abraham, whose story is told in Genesis 12 through 25, is the patriarch par excellence. Even though it was Abraham's grandson, Jacob, who lent his nickname Israel to the whole nation, Abraham is considered the true spiritual father of Israel. This is natural, since in most ways he was a more admirable and more moral character than Jacob. But, more importantly, Abraham was called by God to leave his idol-worshiping homeland of Chaldea and settle in Canaan, the Promised Land. Also very important is that Abraham endured a severe testing of his faith when God asked him to sacrifice his beloved son Isaac. This story, one of the most dramatic and most touching in the Bible, is found in Genesis 22.

Sometimes the patriarchs refers not only to Abraham, Isaac, and Jacob, but also to their distant ancestors in the Book of Genesis—Adam, Methuselah, Noah, etc. Also, Jacob's twelve sons—who were the ancestors of the twelve tribes of Israel—are referred to as patriarchs.

One easy way to remember who the patriarchs were is that they were all the important men who preceded the life of Moses, related in the Book of Exodus.

(*See also* Covenant, Israel.)

PROPHETS

Soothsayers, Preachers, or What?
We think of prophets as fortunetellers, those who predict the future, psychics like Jeane Dixon. When the Bible refers to a prophet, prediction may be part of his talents, but only a small part. In the tradition of Israel, a prophet was "God's proclaimer," a sort of "mouthpiece" for the words of God Himself. A true prophet (and there were *false* prophets around) had no message of his own and did not promote himself. He acted under the impulse of God, taking to the people—and sometimes to specific individuals—a clear message from God. Often this took the form of pointing out people's sins and urging them to repentance. The prophet's message was often a prediction of disaster if people did not repent.

Prophets are found throughout the Old Testament. The last section of the Old Testament is called the Prophets, and it includes books written by some of Israel's greatest prophets—Isaiah, Jeremiah, Ezekiel, Amos, and others. (In some cases it appears that the books may record the teachings of a prophet that were written down by his followers.) Some of the passages in the prophets' books are among the most inspiring in the Old Testament. Other passages concern ancient political wranglings that have no meaning for modern readers.

Some of the greatest prophets in the Bible wrote no books at all. In fact, the most famous prophet in Israel's history was the great Elijah, who wrote nothing at all. Elijah (whose story is told from 1 Kings 17 through 2 Kings 2) is a sort of wild man of the wilderness, a miracle-working man who dares to confront wicked King Ahab and his equally wicked wife, Jezebel. Elijah is "a man on fire for God," and he courageously opposes Ahab and the popular cult of worshiping the false god Baal. Elijah—and God—triumph over the false religion, but not until after Elijah's life has been threatened more than once.

Elijah doesn't die. In the sight of his successor prophet, Elisha, he is taken up to heaven in a "chariot of fire." Elisha continues Elijah's work as a prophet and miracle-worker and gains almost as much fame as Elijah did. But in Israel's tradition, Elijah became *the* symbol of the great prophets of God. The Old Testament's last book, the writing of the

Prophet Malachi, predicts that Elijah will one day return:

> *I will send you the prophet Elijah before that great and dreadful day of the LORD comes. He will turn the hearts of the fathers to their children, and the hearts of the children to their fathers; or else I will come and strike the land with a curse (Mal. 4:5-6).*

Interestingly, the Jews believed that there were no more prophets after the close of the Old Testament. In Jesus' time, many devout Jews wondered if a new prophet might be sent—perhaps the return of Elijah promised in the Book of Malachi. Apparently, Jesus Himself believed this had occurred: "All the Prophets and the Law prophesied until John. And if you are willing to accept it, he is the Elijah who was to come" (Matt. 11:13-14). The John He is referring to is His relative, John the Baptist, who had baptized Jesus. John, a sort of wilderness man as Elijah had been, was considered by many to be a prophet—the renewal of the prophetic tradition in the land. Jesus shared this belief, claiming that not only was John a prophet, but John was the Elijah people had been expecting to return.

PROSTITUTES

This may not be the "world's oldest profession," but it certainly is old, as the Bible proves. There were prostitutes in those days, some of them serving as "temple whores" in the service of some of the pagan gods. Whenever the people of Israel were tempted to abandon worshiping God and to worship false gods, the Bible authors refer to it as "prostitution." Sometimes it literally was, with a man of Israel having intercourse with one of the temple whores (some of whom were male, by the way). But to the Bible authors, worshiping a false god was also a kind of spiritual "infidelity." The Israelites' true master and "husband" was God Himself. To worship another god was like being unfaithful to one's spouse—only much more serious.

When you read the Old Testament, particularly the Prophets, you'll find frequent references to prostitution and adultery. Most often these are referring to this spiritual infidelity. The classic example is the Book of Hosea, where poor Hosea bears with his unfaithful wife (who had the unromantic name of Gomer). Gomer symbolizes Israel, the "unfaithful wife" who forsakes her true husband (God) and takes other lovers (the false gods of the surrounding nations). The other prophets, especially Ezekiel, often compare Israel's unfaithfulness to adultery and prostitution.

It is impossible to really understand the Old Testament unless you grasp this important concept: Prostitution and adultery were often code names for Israel's abandoning its faith in God.

SABBATH

The Bible sees the Sabbath as dating back to the creation of the world. "God blessed the seventh day and made it holy, because on it He rested from all the work of creating that He had done" (Gen. 2:3). Then, in the Ten Commandments, man is told that the seventh day is always to be a day of rest for man:

Remember the Sabbath day by keeping it holy. Six days you shall labor and do all your work, but the seventh day is a Sabbath to the LORD your God. On it you shall not do any work, neither you, nor your son or daughter, nor your manservant or maidservant, nor your animals, nor the alien within your gates. For in six days the LORD made the heavens and the earth, the sea, and all that is in them, but He rested on the seventh day. Therefore the LORD blessed the Sabbath day and made it holy (Ex. 20:8-11).

All business was prohibited on the Sabbath, and not even a person's animals could work. This rule wasn't considered restrictive. In fact, since the pagan world saw every day as a workday (a real burden for manual laborers), taking one day out of seven as a day off was progressive.

Strict Jews still observe the Sabbath; some live in buildings with elevators that are programmed (the day before the Sabbath) to stop on every floor; they will not push a button to have an elevator make a special stop.

The Christian Sunday—"the Lord's Day"—is not the same as the Sabbath. Jesus, a good Jew, did observe the Sabbath, though He claimed that one could do good deeds even on the Sabbath (Luke 13:15-16). He also claimed that "The Sabbath was made for man, not man for the Sabbath" (Mark 2:27)—His reaction to the burdensome rules that had grown up concerning Sabbath observance. The first Christians, being Jews, observed the Sabbath, but in time it began to lose its importance, particularly among Christians who had not been Jews. For Christians the first day of the week—the day Jesus rose from the dead—took

on a greater importance than the seventh day.

Some Christian groups choose to celebrate Saturday as the day of worship. Is this wrong? Not really. Neither is it wrong to celebrate the Sabbath on Sunday instead of Saturday. Why? Because the Bible's emphasis is on setting one day out of seven aside as a special day of rest and worship.

(*See also* Seven.)

SACRIFICE

(*See* Covenant.)

SATAN, DEVILS, DEMONS

The evil being known as Satan or the devil appears very rarely in the Old Testament, but several times in the New. In spite of his being pictured with horns and a pitchfork, the Bible says nothing whatever about his looks. (We can assume that, since Satan is evil, artists would portray him as very ugly and frightening.) Satan and the devils/demons who serve him are depicted as harmful to mankind, tempting us to do evil things and to reject God. The Bible's last book, the Book of Revelation, claims that Satan and his followers will be finally destroyed at the end of time. For the present, Satan and the devils can lead people astray—but not unless the people are willing. Comedian Flip Wilson's old line "The devil made me do it" doesn't square with the Bible. In the Bible, Satan doesn't *make* anyone do anything. Human beings are responsible for their own sins. The devil may tempt people, but people themselves choose to do wrong.

(*See also* Angels, Sin.)

SAVIOR

This is one of many titles that the New Testament applies to Jesus. Savior means, simply, "one who saves" or "deliverer." In the Old Testament, the name is often applied to God, the One who saves people from their worldly troubles—sickness, enemies, etc. The New Testament puts a different spin on it: Jesus is the One who saves people *from their sins*. He is also seen as the Savior from worldly troubles, but mostly He is the Savior who blots out people's sins so they can have fellowship with God. This fits with the New Testament's belief that our biggest problem in life is our own failings, our sins. Jesus is not a political deliverer, but a spiritual liberator.

(*See also* Christ, Lord, Sin.)

SCRIPTURE

Scripture means, simply, "written things." Many Bible study aids use "Scripture" or "the Scriptures" to mean exactly the same thing as "the Bible." Just as the Bible is often referred to as "the Holy Bible," it is also called "the Holy Scriptures." (The adjectival forms are biblical and scriptural. So you'll find books referring to biblical times and scriptural teachings, and so forth.)

You won't actually find "the Bible" in the Bible, except on the title page. But many times in the New Testament you will find the words Scripture or the Scriptures. Every time you see these words in the New Testament, they refer to the Old Testament, which the early Christians believed to be the holy and authoritative revelation of God to mankind. Later generations of Christians also regard the New Testament as Scripture, although Jews do not.

SEVEN

The Magic, Mystical Seven

Seven is considered a lucky number. Why? Lucky or not, it is a significant number in the Bible. God created the world in six days, then "rested" on the seventh, so seven symbolizes completion. The Israelites used the number seven in many ways. Mourning periods were seven days. Priests sprinkled sacrificial blood seven times. The unclean were isolated from the community for seven days. Seven Israelite priests marched around the city of Jericho seven times, then the city walls fell. Among the Israelites, every seventh year was a "sabbatical" year, and after seven times seven years (forty-nine, that is) came the "jubilee" year. Samson's wedding feast lasted seven days. Jesus told His followers to forgive people "seventy times seven" times. The symbol of the nation of Israel today is the menorah, the seven-branched candlestick.

(*See also* Sabbath, Twelve.)

SIN

This is an unpopular, old-fashioned-sounding word today, but it occurs so often in the Bible that you can hardly read a page without coming upon the concept of sin. We think of it as a killjoy word—that is, sin is something we enjoy that God doesn't want us to enjoy, like drinking, drugs, sex, maybe even dancing and card-playing. But in the Bible, sin is the broad concept of doing something that offends God and that harms others and ourselves. It is the idea that God wants what is best for us, makes His intentions clear, then we consciously disobey Him.

If the idea of sin seems old-fashioned, remember that most people in the modern world have the general feeling that we aren't all we're supposed to be. This explains why self-help books, psychologists, diets, exercise programs, personal growth workshops, and get-in-touch-with-yourself retreats are so popular. There is the feeling that something is wrong with each of us. We believe we ought to improve, change, grow, become better. All the world's religions carry the belief that whatever we are, we are not quite what we were meant to be. The Bible's idea of sin is much the same. The difference is that, according to the people who wrote the Bible, our failure is that we don't honor and love the God who made us. As a result of this, we do harm to others and to ourselves. Until we "get right with God" (as the old highway signs said), we can't be the people we were meant to be. I can't really be my true self until I'm relating to God in the right way.

In the first few chapters of the Bible, you'll read the story of Adam and Eve, the first human beings, who are given a beautiful place to live but who choose to disobey the one rule God imposes on them. According to the Bible, each human being repeats the mistake of Adam and Eve. (We call this beginning of sin "the Fall.") Each of us chooses to disobey God's orders. Each of us has "a Fall." Sin is universal—every human being sins, even good people. The New Testament says, "All have sinned and fall short of the glory of God" (Rom. 3:23). Sin is not confined to another nation or race or class or gender or political group. Sin is a part of all of us.

Sin is not just deeds but it is an attitude—worshiping ourselves, our own egos, instead of giving first honor to God. In fact, the idea of sin is connected with the idea of *idolatry*—worshiping something (or someone) other than God Himself. God wishes to be not only worshiped but also loved—freely, of our own will. We have the freedom not to love God—that is, we have the freedom to sin, to say no to God. Sin is bad, but it is a sign that God made us capable of choosing. We can choose to love God or snub Him. If we were not capable of sinning, we would be like robots, without free will of our own.

In the Old Testament, when people knew they had offended God by disobeying Him, they had a system of sacrifices—offering up an animal as a sign that they were sorry for what they'd done and wanted to make amends. A key idea in the New Testament is that Jesus was the ultimate sacrifice, who restores us to a right relationship with God. Jesus is often called *Savior* because He saves people from their sin.

Many people admire the Bible's good advice about human relationships. You'll find lots of advice in the Book of Proverbs, and in parts of the New Testament like Jesus' Sermon on the Mount (Matt. 5–7). But if you wish to understand the Bible fully, you'll have to come to grips with the very important idea of sin, and also the idea of sacrifice which restores us to a right relationship with God. That relationship with Him can't exist unless human beings confess their failures (sins, that is) and ask God's forgiveness.

It would be unfair just to view the Bible

as anti-sin. Looked at in a more positive way, it is pro-happiness. According to the Bible, we cannot find true happiness or joy in life unless we put God first. The purpose of avoiding sin is to have the most important relationship of all, peace with the Maker and Sustainer of everything.

In case you think the Bible is overly obsessed with sin, consider two important New Testament books, Paul's Letters to the Philippians and to the Colossians. Philippians mentions joy or rejoicing fourteen times, with no mention of sin. Colossians mentions joy twice, sin three times. Sin is important in the Bible, but so is joy.

(*See also* Christ, Covenant, Idolatry, Satan, Savior.)

SODOM

What is sodomy?
With our society's increasing frankness about everything sexual, people are more than ever aware of homosexuality—and the word sodomy.

The word comes from the loose-living city of Sodom (Gen. 19). One of its residents, Lot, entertains two heavenly visitors who are about to bring divine judgment on the immoral town. The men of Sodom surround Lot's house, demanding that he make his visitors available for sex. *The King James Version* reads, "Bring them out unto us, that we may know them" (v. 5). More directly, the *New International Version* reads, "Bring them out to us so that we can have sex with them." Lot offers an alternative the men of Sodom don't like: his two virgin daughters. The lecherous men become enraged and try to break down Lot's door.

Lot's two heavenly visitors strike the men with blindness. In the end of this sordid tale, Lot's family flees and God rains fire down on the wicked place.

THOU

You might think of "thou" and "ye" as "Bible language." It's true that older Bible versions like the *King James* use "thee" and "thou" and "ye" as well as "you." It wasn't just the language of the Bible, though—it was ordinary English for many centuries. It was also the English used by Shakespeare, whose plays are filled with "thees" and "thous." Modern English is amazingly simpler: we use "you" for both singular and plural, both subject and object. This seems like a great improvement, but not necessarily. Read on.

In the older versions, the different forms of "you" all had different shades of meaning. "Thou" and "thee" were singular, "ye" and "you" were plural. "Thou" and "ye" were subjects, "thee" and "you" were objects. So the four words weren't just all saying the same thing as "you." The words preserved some of the distinctions in the original Hebrew and Greek.

Does this matter today in terms of how we read the Bible? Actually, it does. In the *King James Version*, for example, the Ten Commandments in Exodus 20 begin with "Thou shalt"—and since "thou" is singular, the Commandments were addressed to each individual person, not just Israel as a whole. All modern versions have "you shall"—which could be plural or singular. In Luke 2:10, the angel tells the shepherds, "I bring you good tidings of great joy." The "you" here is plural—the angel is speaking to the shepherds as a group.

TRIBES

What were these "twelve tribes of Israel"?
We hear the word *tribe,* and we think of people in the pages of *National Geographic,* wearing loincloths and face paint. But *tribe* does not have this meaning in the Bible. The patriarch Jacob, also named Israel, had twelve sons—Reuben, Simeon, Levi, Judah, Issachar, Zebulun, Gad, Asher, Dan, Naphtali, Joseph, and Benjamin. The twelve "tribes" were clans, claiming descent from one of these twelve sons. When the land of Canaan was settled by the Israelites, the land was divided among the twelve tribes.

But, if you look at maps of Old Testament times, you won't find Joseph or Levi on the map. You'll find areas named for the other ten tribes. Why? Well, the tribe of Levi had no land of its own. It did have certain cities allotted to it. The people of Levi—the Levites—had the duty of serving as priests in the nation. (The great leader Moses was a Levite. So was his brother Aaron, Israel's first high priest.) The tribe of Joseph actually was divided into two "half-tribes" named for Joseph's two sons, Manasseh and Ephraim. So the maps show areas named for Manasseh and Ephraim, not for their father, Joseph. By eliminating Levi and dividing Joseph in two, we end up with twelve.

Judah, one of the largest tribes, was the tribe that the great King David came from. Israel's capital, Jerusalem, was in the territory of Judah. After the death of King Solomon (David's son), the ten northern tribes split off, calling themselves Israel. Judah, along with the smaller tribe of Benjamin, became the kingdom of Judah. When Israel was conquered by the brutal Assyrians, the ten northern tribes ceased to exist. (In literature you'll sometimes see a reference to the "lost tribes" of Israel. This refers to the ten tribes conquered by the Assyrians.) People living in the territory of Judah came to be called Jews. Jesus was descended from the tribe of Judah. Paul, the great missionary in the New Testament, was from the tribe of Benjamin, which was also part of the kingdom of Judah. Family trees were very important in the Bible, since people were eager to prove that they could trace their ancestry all the way back to Jacob/Israel himself.

Many people believe that when Jesus chose twelve men to be His disciples He was choosing to start a "new Israel"—one based not on family ties, but on being followers of Christ. He was establishing a "spiritual Israel" of people who chose to commit themselves to God. Even non-Jews could be part of this new Israel.

(*See also* Israel, Patriarchs.)

TWELVE

The Magic Twelve
Twelve, like seven, was a significant number for the Israelites. Why? It isn't a logical "body" number like ten. (Does anyone need to ask why ten is a significant number?) No, the significance of twelve lies in the stars—literally. The Israelites and other people of the Middle East divided the calendar into twelve months, based on the changes of the moon. The nations of the Middle East also were aware of the twelve

signs of the zodiac. Israel did not dabble in astrology as its neighbor nations did, but people were aware of the zodiac.

Because of its significance in the calendar, twelve became a key number. Jacob, also named Israel, had twelve sons, each one the founder of one of the tribes of Israel. Jesus chose twelve men to be disciples, and when one (the traitor, Judas) killed himself, the remaining eleven felt obligated to replace him. The disciples are sometimes referred to as the Twelve. The Letter of James, addressed to Christians throughout the world, goes out to "the twelve tribes scattered among the nations."

The Book of Revelation, with its visions and symbols, paints a picture of heaven that is filled with twelves—twelve pearl gates, twelve angels, twelve gems, twelve foundations, twelve kinds of fruit on the tree of life, and the names of the 12 Apostles and the twelve tribes of Israel.

Incidentally, what grade did you complete when you finished high school?

(*See also* Seven, Tribes.)

ZION

Where is Zion?

Jerusalem is considered a holy city by Jews, Christians, and Muslims. All three religions can point to sites in Jerusalem connected with their history and beliefs. In the Old Testament you'll find hundreds of references to Jerusalem—and other references to Zion. In fact, Zion is another name for Jerusalem (just as Chicago is the Windy City, New Orleans is the Big Easy, and Nashville is Music City). The actual Zion is a ridge within the city. The name came to refer to the city as a whole. The name also became part of the political movement known as Zionism. Many Christian hymns refer to Zion—usually applying the name not to the earthly city of Jerusalem, but to the New Jerusalem, heaven. This is based on Hebrews 12:22: "Mount Zion, the heavenly Jerusalem, the city of the living God."

(*See also* Canaan, Holy Land, Israel, Palestine.)

chapter 15

Help at Your Elbow: ◄···
Tools for the Bible Reader

You could read the Bible itself and never consult any study aids. You could, and many people do, and they profit from the Bible alone. The Bible presents a God for everybody—not just a God of the scholars and the self-appointed "experts."

But 2,000 years is a long time, and some parts of the Old Testament are much, much older than that. No matter how good and readable some of the modern translations are, you can still profit from various books to aid Bible study. You could spend a fortune on these, but it isn't necessary. A few basic ones (many of them in paperback) will do the job quite well.

A BIBLE

Yes, you do need one of these. In chapter 2 you'll find a discussion of contemporary translations and their merits. Picking a translation is only one factor when choosing a Bible. Consider these other factors.

A. Readability

Larger type is better than tiny type for most people. The tiny "pocket Testaments" and "pocket Bibles" used to be popular, but unless you have the eyesight of a rabbit, these won't be very useful. If your eyes are up to it, though, they do serve a nice purpose if you like to snatch a few minutes of reading when you're on the bus, waiting in the doctor's office, etc. You can decide for yourself which of the two editions, *The Smallest Bible* and *The World's Smallest Complete Bible*, is actually smaller. The very large "family Bibles" that are still sold in stores and door-to-door usually have very large and readable type (and pictures to boot). Unfortunately, family Bibles are almost always the *King James Version*— not the best translation for contemporary readers. And family Bibles aren't very portable, so you aren't likely to carry one with you when you travel. I have a suspicion that most family Bibles go unread. They are more often a decoration than anything else. (The next time you're in someone's home, sneak a moment to see if you pick up dust off the family Bible's cover. Better yet, check your own.)

B. Durability

A good solid binding makes for a longer-lasting Bible. "Deluxe" and "gift" Bibles often have elegant leather bindings and the very thin "Bible paper." These are attractive, and people like to give them as gifts, but my experience is that "classy" Bibles are seldom read. (The thin Bible paper is actually very durable. But if you think you'll be marking the pages with a pen or colored highlighter, you need to know that the ink can bleed through on Bible paper.) You can buy paperback Bibles, but they don't hold up too well. The worst problem with a paperback Bible is that it won't lie flat if you're studying at a desk or table. A cloth-bound Bible (with the binding you find on most hardback books) is a good choice—more durable than paperback, less expensive than leather. A good and inexpensive compromise is called *kivar*, a sort of heavy-duty paperback binding.

C. Writability

If you figure you'll be writing in the margins, choose a Bible that will give you room to do that. Many people (myself included) have this habit. Some Bibles have extrawide margins just for this purpose. But if you're going to do any serious study of the Bible, get into the habit of always keeping a notepad near the Bible.

D. Footnotes

You don't absolutely have to have a Bible with footnotes, but they are useful. (See the Footnote section in chap. 1.) Most Bibles do have them.

E. Study aids

Most Bibles have a few study aids, usually in the back. These include a few maps of Bible lands, a brief concordance (more on concordances later), maybe a brief Bible dictionary. Some Bibles also include brief introductions to each of the sixty-six books. Bibles with extensive study aids are sold as study Bibles. (I will discuss them in more detail later in this chapter.)

F. Red letters

Bibles called "red-letter editions" have the words of Jesus Christ in red. Some recent editions opt for green instead of red. I call this a nonessential option. Some people like it, others don't. I'm convinced that it's primarily a marketing tool that Bible publishers like to push.

G. Color coding

A recent variation on the "red-letter edition" Bible is the color-coded Bible. This kind of Bible features color highlighting on passages concerned with a certain topic—say, green highlighting for passages concerning salvation, orange highlighting for passages concerning heaven and hell, etc. Some readers like this, others find it gimmicky. If you like to underline or highlight, you'll probably find that these color-coded Bibles are more a hindrance than a help.

BIBLE DICTIONARIES

If you purchase just one study aid for the Bible, opt for a good Bible dictionary. These list names, places, and topics in the

Bible, explaining their meaning and pointing out where you'll find them in the Bible. A good Bible dictionary does something even more basic: it tells you how to pronounce words, which is particularly helpful with Old Testament names. There are dozens of Bible dictionaries on the market, some of them in multivolume sets. The larger ones are intended for scholars, and they tend to be expensive. One of my personal favorites is *Young's Compact Bible Dictionary* (Tyndale House, 1989). You won't find a better pocket-size Bible dictionary. It's in paperback, it's inexpensive, it gives the information you need and (Hallelujah!) leaves out all the scholarly gibberish you don't need. *The NIV Compact Dictionary of the Bible* (Zondervan, 1989) is also good. Another favorite is *A Theological Word Book of the Bible*, edited by Alan Richardson (Macmillan, 1950). Don't let the title scare you off. This book includes every word of importance, not just words we think of as "theological." It includes (just to name a few) *marriage, death, Christian, love, share, war,* and *boast.* Every word and topic of importance are found, along with what the Bible says about those words and topics. (One complaint: to save space, the editors have used a *lot* of abbreviations.)

If you want something more scholarly and in-depth, *The New International Dictionary of the Bible* (Zondervan, 1987) is a good choice. It's large, bulky, but very thorough.

CONCORDANCES

This is an alphabetical listing of all words (or just key words) in the Bible, listed in the order they occur. Besides listing each chapter and verse where the word is found, it will also show a few words from that passage, to give you an idea of the context in which the word occurs. So what purpose does it serve? Well, if you're looking for Bible verses on the subject of love, you could look up *love* in the concordance, and it would list all verses containing that word, from Genesis to Revelation. (It would also refer you to related words—*loved, loving,* etc.) This is, obviously, much easier than scanning the whole Bible, looking for places where the word *love* occurs.

Concordances serve another purpose. You may be thinking of a Bible verse but can only think of one or two key words in it. Try looking up one of those words in the concordance to find your verse.

A typical part of a page in a concordance would look something like this:

OPPOSES

Mk	3:26	And if Satan *o* himself
Luke	23:2	He *o* payment of taxes to Caesar
Jn	19:12	claims to be a king *o* Caesar
2Th	2:4	He *o* and exalts himself
Jas	4:6	"God *o* the proud
1Pe	5:5	because, "God *o* the proud

This is a list of verses in the *New International Version* that contain the word *opposes.* The verses are listed in the order that they occur in the Bible. Note that the books of the Bible are abbreviated to save space. Note that each listing shows the portion of the verse that contains the word *opposes.* Note also that instead of repeating *opposes* in each case, the list simply uses an *o* (again, to save space).

Bibles often have a small concordance

in the back. These cannot be very thorough, owing to space limitations. On the other hand, you may not want to buy a concordance that calls itself "exhaustive" because these can be expensive (and bulky to boot). Some of these even include Greek and Hebrew words—more than the average reader needs. You also wouldn't need the exhaustive concordance's list of all verses with the words *and* and *the*, would you?

Several good, handy-size concordances are available. *The NIV Handy Concordance* (Zondervan, 1982) is designed for the *New International Version*. *Nelson's Comfort Print Bible Concordance* (Nelson, 1995) is designed for the *New King James Version*. As its name implies, it is set in a readable type.

BIBLE COMMENTARIES

A commentary basically explains the text. It gives some background information on the particular book of the Bible (who wrote it, when, why) and then proceeds to explain the meaning verse by verse. Commentaries are usually written by Bible scholars and they bring their knowledge of the original languages and archaeology, helping to explain passages that may puzzle you. A good commentary is worth its weight in gold. Some of them are *too* weighty, though—filled with more information than you (or even other scholars) would ever need. (It's still a mystery to me how the brief Letter to the Ephesians in the New Testament could have warranted a two-volume commentary by scholar Markus Barth. In my Bible, Ephesians takes up a mere five pages.)

Commentaries can be one-volume (cov-

ering the entire Bible) or several volumes (you may find these giving more information than you'll ever need). There are also commentaries on individual books of the Bible. One of my favorite one-volume commentaries is *The International Bible Commentary*, edited by F.F. Bruce (Zondervan, 1986). Large, with a "library binding," it is based on the *New International Version* translation. It is scholarly and thorough. The introductory sections are probably too technical for most readers, but you can skip those.

Lawrence O. Richards' *Teacher's Commentary* (Victor, 1987) is another good one-volume commentary on the whole Bible.

There are dozens of excellent commentaries on individual books of the Bible, too many to mention here. One personal favorite is C.S. Lewis' *Reflections on the Psalms* (Macmillan, 1958). Lewis was an intellectual who wrote like a human being. This isn't a verse-by-verse commentary on Psalms, but a series of superb essays on one of the most important books in the Bible. Lewis does a great job of explaining the so-called vengeance psalms that many readers find distasteful. His essays are short, easy-to-read, and ought to be a role model for making the Bible interesting to people.

Several series also cover individual books of the Bible. You can avoid the larger ones, which are intended mainly for scholars and pastors. One series, with books of a manageable size and readability, is the Thru the Bible series published by Nelson.

Booklets that focus on one book of the Bible and are designed for group study are also commentaries. (I will discuss these in more depth later in this chapter.)

STUDY BIBLES

This is a sort of marriage of Bible and commentary. Study Bibles have extensive footnotes and other study aids to help explain the text. Their titles generally contain the words *study Bible* or *annotated*. ("Annotated" means "with notes," by the way.)

No one knows just how many study Bibles there are. Consider just a few currently available: *The Seniors' Devotional Bible, The Couple's Devotional Bible, The Men's Devotional Bible, The Women's Devotional Bible, YouthWalk Devotional Bible, The Parenting Bible, Spirit-filled Life Daily Devotional Bible, Word in Life Study Bible, Life Application Bible, NIV Study Bible, Teen's Study Bible* . . . well, you get the idea. The ones mentioned here are all fine.

Don't let the notes in a study Bible (or commentary) become a crutch for you. Footnotes and study helps are valuable, but try to interact with the Bible itself—just the words and your own mind (and the Holy Spirit, if you believe what the Bible says about the Spirit being active as we study the Bible). It is true of commentaries and study Bibles that many brilliant people offer us their wisdom and insights about the meaning of the Bible. But it is also true that the experts can sometimes be wrong. Learn from the scholars, but don't treat them as gods. They aren't.

TOPICAL BIBLES

Think of a topical Bible as a "mega-concordance." A topical Bible lists all relevant Bible passages on a particular topic—say, money, children, failure, etc. Instead of just listing where those topics are covered, it actually gives the whole passage. So if you looked up *money* in a topical Bible, you would find all the Bible passages on that subject. (Note that the topical Bible lists topics, not words. The section on *money* would have passages dealing with money, even if the actual word *money* did not occur in that passage.)

Topical Bibles are wonderful. You can find at a glance every significant passage on every major topic. Topical Bibles are sort of addictive, like popcorn. You'll find yourself browsing, turning from one interesting topic to another.

Topical Bibles are usually hefty volumes, but they are a good investment. Buy one on the basis of the translation it uses. You can buy topical Bibles that use the *New International Version,* the *New King James Version*, etc. I don't recommend buying one of the older versions that use the *King James Version.*

Similar to topical Bibles are Bible promise books. These are designed to give aid and comfort by presenting Bible passages on key problem areas in life—marriage, children, career, ambition, money, etc. *The Complete Book of Bible Promises* (Tyndale House, 1997) is the most thorough.

BIBLE HISTORIES

You may never feel terribly interested in the minute details about how Bible translators do their work. But you might enjoy *A Concise History of the English Bible* (American Bible Society, 1983). This booklet, updated from time to time, is just what it says: a brief history of English Bible versions. It makes some interesting comparisons of the various versions available.

You probably want to put off reading the multi-volume *Cambridge History of the Bible in English*, even though it is very interesting.

BIBLE BACKGROUND STUDIES

A lot of people ask, "Just what was the world like in Bible days?" If you know the answer to that, you're well on your way to understanding how the Bible authors thought. You might enjoy *Harper's World of the New Testament* (Harper & Row, 1981). Lavishly illustrated, this is a good introduction to the world Jesus and the first Christians lived in. It looks at the Jewish religion of those times, Roman life and thought, and the many religions that competed with Christianity. Ronald Brownrigg's *Who's Who in the New Testament* (Oxford, 1993) is just what it says, and quite good. A book by David Watson and Simon Jenkins, *Jesus Then and Now* (Lion Books, 1983), is full of color pictures and very easy to read. It is a perfect introduction to the Bible's key figure. It also provides a good summary of basic teachings of the Bible.

Some of the most attractive Bible background books ("suitable for coffee tables") are published by *Reader's Digest*. As with all the *Reader's Digest* products, they are easy to read and lavishly illustrated.

TOPICAL STUDIES

These are books that look at a particular subject—sin, death, marriage, family, money, whatever—from the Bible's standpoint. There are hundreds of these. Highly recommended is David Ewert's *And Then Comes the End* (Herald Press, 1980). It deals with a sticky subject: the end of the world. The author gives a fine overview of the Bible's teaching about heaven, hell, the last judgment. Another good book on this topic: Peter J. Kreeft's *Everything You Ever Wanted to Know about Heaven, but Never Dreamed of Asking* (Harper & Row, 1982).

BIBLE ATLASES

Does an atlas sound boring? Why would you even need maps of a place you don't expect to drive through? Ah, but a good Bible atlas is more than maps. It shows the flow of biblical history, gives information on the movements of key Bible characters, and gives you the feel of place and time (reminding you that the Bible events were real, not just religious fiction). You could live without a Bible atlas, but some are inexpensive. A favorite is *Eerdmans' Atlas of the Bible* (Eerdmans Publishing, 1983). Full of color photos as well as maps, it shows the flow of biblical history. It also contains a dictionary of all important places mentioned in the Bible, and it is smaller, less expensive, and more readable than any other Bible atlas. If you'd like a good reference book *and* something that looks nice on a coffee table, the *Reader's Digest Bible Atlas* is worth looking for. *The NIV Atlas of the Bible* (Zondervan, 1989) and the *Oxford Bible Atlas* (Oxford, 1974) are good but may be too technical and scholarly for most readers.

PARALLEL BIBLES

If one Bible translation isn't enough for you, you'll love a parallel Bible. It is designed so that each page spread shows several translations (usually four) of the same text. The key idea is that you can compare the different translations. Parallel Bibles are, by necessity, bulky. You might find them helpful, but there are better things to spend your money on. One problem with parallel Bibles is that some readers fall into the habit of using them to find the translation they particularly *like*—because it sounds good, or because it interprets a particular passage in a way they like. But our likes and personal tastes should have nothing whatever to do with our main goal—finding an accurate translation that clearly communicates what the original translators meant.

COMIC BOOKS

Do you think I'm kidding? Not at all. Highly recommended is *The Man Who Moved the World: The New Testament Story* (Tyndale House, 1986). This is a comic-book version of the New Testament. Kids would like it, but adults can enjoy it just as much. Fast-moving and with good artwork, it covers the life of Jesus and the apostles. In its own way it might be the best way to get introduced or reintroduced to the New Testament (if you can get over the initial obstacle of admitting you're reading a comic book).

BIBLE STUDY BOOKLETS

These cover a lot of ground. If you enter a religious bookstore, you'll find booklets (they're usually too small to be considered full-fledged books) that will lead you through a particular book of the Bible (such as Matthew or Proverbs) or focus on a particular topic as presented in the Bible (such as love, work, friendship). There are many excellent ones available. Most are suited for group study, and some even have guides for the group leader. Most of them have fill-in-the-blank sections and space for taking notes. Churches often use these for adult Sunday School material or midweek studies. But most can also be suitable for an individual reader.

The Great Books of the Bible series (Zondervan) looks at the most important books—John, Psalms, Proverbs, Philippians, and others.

The TruthSeed series (Victor) covers both books and topics.

The Christian Basics Bible Studies series (InterVarsity) has guides on Christ, Character, Prayer, and other subjects.

The Life Application Bible Studies (Tyndale) covers individual books of the Bible. A distinctive of this series is that it includes the text of the book being studied. It uses the *New International Version.*

The Knowing God Bible Studies (Zondervan) is topical.

Fruit of the Spirit Bible Studies (Zondervan) has guides on the "fruits of the Spirit" mentioned in Galatians 5:22: Love, Peace, Patience, and others.

Fisherman Bible Study Guides (Harold Shaw) cover The Parables of Jesus, The Sermon on the Mount, James, Romans, Guidance, Prayer, and other books and topics.

The LifeGuide Family Bible Studies (Standard Publishing) is a topical series with a difference: it's designed for parents and kids to use together.

If you belong to a church, your denomination may publish its own series similar to these. These have a plus that is also a minus: they may have a particular denominational slant. Check with your pastor or Sunday School superintendent about these. Many churches choose not to use studies from their own denomination.

ETHICS, MORALS, VALUES

You can't do any better than Robertson McQuilkin's *Introduction to Biblical Ethics* (Tyndale House, 1995). It's called an "introduction," but this is a very large book covering every conceivable moral issue—marriage and family, racism, abortion, euthanasia, war, government, the media, work and leisure, etc. The author is a college president who knows how to think and write like an ordinary human being.

Lewis Smedes' *Mere Morality: What God Expects from Ordinary People* (Eerdmans, 1983) is also excellent. As its title suggests, it is for "ordinary people," not theologians or "religious pros."

C.S. Lewis' *Mere Christianity* (Macmillan, 1952) is still readable. Chapter 3, titled "Christian Behavior," is probably the best introduction to the Bible's view of morality and values. (This book is also one of the best investments you could ever make—and one of the least expensive as well.)

A WORD ABOUT BUYING REFERENCE BOOKS

Good reference books can be expensive. Some of the books recommended above fit that category. Others (like the excellent *Young's Bible Dictionary*) are both useful and inexpensive. You should not spend a fortune on Bible study tools. Two or three basic reference books should serve you quite well. But if you are thinking of purchasing some of the larger books, check them out—literally, through a local library. If you find that a particular book is helpful to you, you might want to purchase one for yourself. But it's better to make that decision after using one for a few days—not just after flipping through one in a bookstore.

Most of the books mentioned above can be purchased in regular bookstores or in religious bookstores. If a book isn't in stock, someone can usually order it for you. But don't order any book over ten dollars without first finding a copy you can browse through.

COMPUTERS: THE BIBLE IN BITS AND BYTES

Neil Diamond had a hit song containing the line "We're headed for the future and the future is now." This is certainly true in the field of Bible publishing. Companies have been swift to make various kinds of Bible software available to the public. Before you invest in some of it, ask yourself, "Is this better than just sitting in a chair with my own Bible?"

In a sense, no. The words of the Bible are words—the same words whether they're on a printed page or on a computer screen. Most people agree that the printed page is easier to read than a screen (especially a screen on a laptop computer). You can carry your Bible anywhere—the beach, the woods, work, train, wherever. Computers with readable screens aren't so portable—not yet, anyway. And laptops are still frightfully expensive.

But, technology marches on. There is now much more available in software than just the Bible text itself.

Parsons Technology has produced *QuickVerse*, available in several translations. *QuickVerse* is one of several Bible softwares that enables you to do more than just read text. You can also search for key words and names—the same as you can do with a concordance, but much faster. You could have your computer search for, say, all the verses that contain the word *husband*. You can also search for more than one key word—something you can't do with a concordance. Let's say you were thinking of a Bible verse that says something like "Love your neighbor as yourself." Where is that? You could look for this by telling the computer to search for all verses with the word *love*. But you'd end up reading through a lot of verses with that word. With the computer software you could look only for verses that contain both *love* and *neighbor*. This is something a concordance can't do.

Some of the Bible softwares are a regular Bible library. Some, like BibleSoft, contain not only the Bible text (sometimes more than one translation), but also aids like a topical Bible, a Bible dictionary, maps, a concordance, etc. If you're computer-oriented to the point that you'd prefer working the computer to leafing through books, you might enjoy a product like this.

The book *Computer Bible Study* by Jeffrey Hsu (Word, 1993) is an excellent guide to the many software packages available. I'm guessing that Hsu's book will probably be updated from time to time, considering how quickly this whole field changes.

But a word to the wise: Don't get caught up in electronic toys if your real goal is to get to know the Bible better. People have managed to get by for hundreds of years with just the printed Bible, and chances are you can do the same.

NOW HEAR THIS: AUDIO BIBLES

The Bible on cassette has been around for years. It's amazing in our busy age, with so many people with cassette players in their cars or offices, that the Bible-on-tape does not sell better.

True, it has limitations. You can't underline a favorite passage or write notes in the margins. And you can't pause over a passage as you could with a printed book.

Remember that the Bible was part of an oral culture. The original readers of the Old and New Testaments weren't lucky enough to have one Bible per person. They generally learned the Bible by hearing it read aloud. This happened in church and within families. We don't necessarily want to return to that era. But there is some value in bringing our ears as well as our eyes into absorbing the Bible. Teachers know that the two can reinforce each other. We learn best when we use both eye and ear.

Most religious bookstores have several versions of the Bible-on-tape. Some are in the *King James Version,* usually read by someone with a resonant, majestic voice. Unfortunately, they are dignified but not understandable. I recommend a more contemporary translation.

I highly recommend *The One-Year Bible on Tape* (Tyndale House). This is available in more than one translation. For the busy person, this tape set is ideal. The Bible is

A Word about "Bible Criticism"

When we talk about "criticism," we don't mean "put-downs." We mean evaluating, explaining, critiquing. A movie critic is someone who reviews movies. In a similar way, Bible critics "review" the Bible. They serve a useful purpose, since they study the Bible closely, often in the original Greek and Hebrew. Some of them make a career of knowing the Bible deeply, studying how it fit in with the ancient world, what the words meant in the original languages, etc. All this knowledge is a good thing.

The problem is, some of these critics really do become criticizers—people who knock the Bible and cast doubts on its divine origin. Studying the Bible closely builds up some people's faith. Unfortunately, in a few cases it has torn down people's faith. The old phrase "familiarity breeds contempt" sometimes applies. A Bible scholar can spend so much time with the Bible that it becomes "old hat." Instead of the inspired Word of God, the Bible is "just my job." It is sad, but true, that some of the Bible pros have come to view the Bible in the same way other scholars regard the ancient writings of Greece and Rome—interesting writings, but not truly divine, and not really relevant to life today.

The books and other materials listed in this chapter are ones I can recommend heartily because they approach the Bible as it presents itself: something authoritative, with a divine origin. Hundreds of other commentaries and other reference tools take the same approach. But many don't. Even some religious publishing houses print books that treat the Bible as simply human, nothing more. They present the Bible as an interesting book—something worth studying, but not particularly relevant to today (unless they have some particular social agenda they wish to push, in which case they may use the Bible as a tool to promote it).

You can learn about the Bible from books like these. Even an atheist could write (and probably has written) a useful commentary on the Bible. From such a book you could learn facts, dates, useful bits of information. But you wouldn't get a deep appreciation of the Bible as the authoritative book it claims to be. So be careful in choosing reference books to aid you.

The Bible critics, whether they are true believers or not, share the joy of debating academic issues. Whether any of these issues is of any concern to anyone (except other Bible critics) is immaterial to them. For example, they've been arguing for decades about whether the Book of Isaiah had one author, or two, or three. They've observed (as have some readers) that the style of the Book of Isaiah changes abruptly after chapter 39. But most readers put this into the So What? file. Not the scholars! Arguments like these are their bread and butter.

Consider an incident in the life of American evangelist D.L. Moody. Moody probably preached to more people than any other man of his generation. He knew the Bible extremely well, even though he had no formal training in it. Once he invited a scholar friend to speak at a conference. The friend replied, "Do you want me to speak, knowing I believe there were *three* Isaiahs?" Moody replied, "It's all right. You'll be addressing people who don't even know there is *one* Isaiah." In other words, "Get people familiar with Bible basics before getting them involved in academic issues." (And if they *never* get involved in the academic issues, they won't be missing anything.)

divided into 365 readings. January 1 begins with the Old Testament (Gen. 1) and the New (Matt. 1); a reading from Psalms and Proverbs is included for each day. Each daily reading runs about twelve minutes. It is a painless way to go through the entire Bible in one year. You can listen while jogging, doing housework, shaving, commuting, whatever. Ideally, you can also read along with the tapes. (If you feel like fast-forwarding through some of the dry passages in Lev. or 1 Chron., don't feel too guilty.)

Incidentally, in case you were wondering, yes, the Bible is on video—sort of. Back in the 1980s a group decided to produce *The New Media Bible,* which would be the whole Bible on video. Bible on video means that the Bible text was read by a narrator while actors portrayed the story on camera. It was a good idea—but how could anyone film the laws in Leviticus and Deuteronomy and the long sermons of the prophets? Anyway, the project didn't materialize fully, but parts of it did. Genesis and Luke are available on videotape, and they are quite good, actually. Luke is especially good, having a "real" feel to it, very different from some of the overproduced Hollywood movies like *King of Kings* and *The Greatest Story Ever Told.* You get the feeling you are watching an actual videotape of the life of Jesus.

PLAYING WITH THE BIBLE

If the Bible is meant to be taken seriously, can it also become a source of amusement? Play? I raised that question in 1988,

the year my *Complete Book of Bible Trivia* was published. The book was on the religious best-seller list for almost a year, went into numerous printings, and has been translated into five languages so far. I've concluded that we do like to "play" with the Bible. We see the Bible as something approachable, something we need not keep our distance from. It is still holy, of course, but through quiz books and games we can

> *If a man is not familiar with the Bible, he has suffered a loss which he had better make all possible haste to correct.*
> —THEODORE ROOSEVELT

approach it as user-friendly.

Most religious bookstores, and some secular stores as well, stock Bible games. The many board games—like Bibleopoly and The Book Game—are variations on the popular game Trivial Pursuit. But game producers have gone well beyond board games. If your household is wired for computer games (and it probably is), fear not: Bible games for computer play are available.

None of these games will actually get you into the deeper truths of the Bible. What they will do—aside from passing the time in good clean fun—is reinforce some of the material you are (we hope) absorbing through your regular study of the Bible. And there's no better way to make the Bible approachable to kids than with Bible video games.

chapter 16

From Adam ◄⋯
to the Apostles:
A Concise Chronology of Bible Times

Y ou can read and enjoy the Bible without knowing when events in the Bible took place. Learning valuable life lessons by reading about King David is more important than knowing that David reigned in Israel around 1000 B.C. Still, it helps to see the sequence of Bible events. It also helps us to remember that events in the Bible actually took place—they weren't just visions or legends.

This chapter presents the actual historical dates when key events in the Bible took place. More importantly, this is a "quickie" tour of the Bible from beginning to end, giving you a concise overview of major people and movements.

CHRONOLOGY OF THE OLD TESTAMENT PERIOD

The Beginnings
We do not know, obviously, the precise dates for the events in the early chapters of

Genesis. However, long, long ago, God created the universe, including man and woman, out of nothing and called all His creation "good." Man and woman (Adam and Eve, that is) chose to disobey God (this is called "the fall of man" or "man's fall into sin") and were punished by being expelled from the beautiful garden God had given them and forced to work hard for a living.

Their firstborn son, Cain, became the first murderer by killing his younger brother, Abel. Human wickedness escalates, and God resolves to punish mankind with a universal Flood. God spares one righteous man, Noah, along with Noah's family, who also survive (along with specimens from the animal kingdom) in an enormous boat, the ark. After the Flood subsides, Noah's sons populate the world again. Human evil continues, however, and arrogant people try to "reach heaven" by building the Tower of Babel. God punishes their arrogance by changing one universal language into hundreds of incomprehensible tongues. Creation (*Gen. 1–2*)

Adam and Eve in the Garden of Eden (*Gen. 3*)

Cain and Abel (*Gen. 4*)

Noah and the great Flood (*Gen. 6–9*)

The Tower of Babel (*Gen. 11*)

THE PATRIARCHS

The nation of Israel has its beginnings with Abraham, whom God calls to be the "father of a great nation." Abraham moves from Ur, a pagan country, to the land of Canaan. Abraham and his nephew Lot witness the destruction of the immoral cities of Sodom and Gomorrah. In old age Abraham fathers his longed-for son, Isaac. Strangely, God then asks him to sacrifice (kill) Isaac.

Abraham, a man of faith, obeys, but an angel intervenes at the last minute, commending Abraham for his faithfulness. Isaac fathers the crafty trickster Jacob, later nicknamed Israel. (Collectively, Abraham, Isaac, and Jacob are known as the *patriarchs*.) By his wives and concubines, Jacob/Israel fathers twelve sons, ancestors of the "twelve tribes of Israel." His favorite son, Joseph, provokes his brothers' jealousy and ends up sold into slavery in Egypt.

With wisdom and God's oversight, Joseph becomes the Pharaoh's right-hand man. Later this works out to save Jacob's family, who are suffering a famine in their homeland. The brothers are reunited, Jacob finds the long-lost Joseph, and the families settle happily in Egypt.

Abraham comes to Canaan ca. 1900 B.C. (*Gen. 12–20*)

Isaac, son of Abraham, is born (*Gen. 21–22*)

Jacob, son of Isaac, is born (*Gen. 25*)

Jacob (also named Israel) has twelve sons, the ancestors of the twelve tribes of Israel

One son, Joseph, becomes chief adviser to Egypt's Pharaoh (*Gen. 27–50*)

ISRAEL IN EGYPT

A new ruling family in Egypt decides the numerous Israelites there are a threat. They are enslaved by the Egyptians. Through a curious turn of events, an Israelite child, Moses, is raised in the Egyptian court. Later, identified as an Israelite, he is forced into exile in the wilderness, where God calls him to lead the Israelite slaves to freedom in their homeland of Canaan. Aided by his brother Aaron (ancestor of Israel's high priests), Moses confronts the Egyptian Pharaoh, demanding that he release the slaves. Pharaoh finally does—after God sends several horrible plagues on the Egyptians. The Israelites depart, and when Pharaoh, after a quick change of mind, sends his armies after the Israelites, the soldiers are drowned miraculously at the Red Sea.

Following God's deliverance of the Israelites, He delivers His divine Law (including the Ten Commandments) to Moses. The liberated Israelites prove ungrateful to both God and Moses. As they make their way slowly from Egypt to Canaan, Moses and God must put up with rebellions and attacks from the nations Israel passes through. After forty years in the wilderness, poor Moses dies before the nation finally enters the land God had promised them.

Moses is the great hero of the Old Testament, Israel's Law-giver and Liberator. He has his faults (the Old Testament shows him "warts and all"), but he is highly moral, and one of the great leaders in world history. He is considered the author of the first five books of the Old Testament, and is mentioned in the Old Testament more than any other person.

The exit—Exodus—from Egypt is the key event in the Old Testament. For the Israelites/Jews, it was the Great Thing that God had done to show that Israel was His chosen people. The feast known as Passover, still celebrated by Jews today, commemorates the liberation from Egypt.

The Israelites (Jacob's sons' descendants) are enslaved in Egypt
ca. 1700—ca.1250 B.C. *(Ex. 1)*
Moses, an Israelite reared in the Egyptian court, leads the Israelites out of Egypt, preceded by miraculous plagues on the Egyptians
ca. 1250   *(Ex. 2–15)*
The Israelites wander in the desert for forty years before entering the land of Canaan. In this period Moses receives the Law at Mount Sinai and passes on divinely given laws to the Israelites.
ca. 1250–ca. 1210   *(Ex. 16–Deut. 34)*

CONQUERING AND SETTLING THE LAND OF CANAAN

Moses' successor, Joshua, leads the Israelites as they settle in Canaan, their homeland promised by God. The conquest/settlement is extremely violent, since the native inhabitants resist the invasion (naturally). God often intervenes miraculously to aid the Israelites in defeating the idol-worshiping Canaanites. (The famous story of the walls of Jericho falling down is from this period.) This is a violent age, and tribes constantly fight each other. (The world hasn't changed much—think of Bosnia and Serbia.)

In the Book of Judges, the Israelites are more or less settled in Canaan, but they still face attacks from neighboring tribes. Worse yet, the idol-worshiping tribes threaten to lead the Israelites away from worshiping the true God, the one who delivered them from Egypt. Charismatic leaders, the "judges," arise to lead the Israelites from time to time. With no unified government, though, the Israelites suffer numerous political and spiritual setbacks.

Joshua leads the first wave of the invasion of Canaan
ca. 1210   *(The Book of Joshua)*
Israel in Canaan is a loose confederation of tribes, still often at war with the resident idol-worshiping Canaanite tribes. Occasional leadership is exercised by the "judges" (Gideon, Samson, and others) *(The Book of Judges, the Book of Ruth)*
While under the leadership of Samuel, the Israelites demand to have a king
                     (1 Sam. 1–8)

THE UNITED KINGDOM OF ISRAEL

Israel's last judge is the beloved Samuel. The people pressure him to give them a king to unite the country. He reluctantly agrees, and he anoints Saul as the first king. Saul is handsome and a good leader, but he also proves temperamental and unstable. God rejects him as king and chooses David as Saul's successor. Saul and David are sometimes friends, sometimes enemies, though David is always forgiving and respectful. Saul is killed in battle with the Philistines, and David officially becomes king and makes Jerusalem his capital. Despite his numerous character flaws and sins, David is essentially a good king, one who loves God dearly. With many wives and children he endures revolts and all sorts of domestic squabbles. With the exception of Moses, he is probably the best-loved figure in the Old Testament.

David's peace-loving son Solomon succeeds him as king. As often happens in peacetime, Solomon pursues a tax-and-spend policy, building lavishly, including a beautiful temple for God in Jerusalem. Solomon gains a reputation for both wealth and wisdom. His many pagan wives, however, lead him away from God.

Reign of Israel's first king, Saul
ca. 1030–ca.1010   (1 Sam. 9–31)
Reign of David, noted not only as a military leader but as a poet. He makes Jerusalem the nation's capital. His numerous wives and children lead to major crises in his own home and in the nation.
ca. 1010–ca. 970   (1 Sam. 16–
                          1 Kings 2)
Reign of Solomon, David's son, who builds lavishly, including the first temple of God in Jerusalem. Solomon's wealth and wisdom become legendary, as do his marriages to numerous idol-worshiping women.
ca. 970–931   (1 Kings 2–11)

THE TWO KINGDOMS, ISRAEL AND JUDAH

Restless under Solomon's government, part of the kingdom of Israel revolts after his death. The breakaway kingdom in the north keeps the name Israel, while Solomon's son Rehoboam rules the Southern Kingdom, now called Judah (which contains Jerusalem). For years the two kingdoms exist side by side, sometimes friendly, sometimes hostile. Israel's kings are, for the most part, immoral and corrupt rulers who have no interest in the true God. Judah's rulers are a mixed bag. Some (Asa, Hezekiah, Josiah) are godly men who try to bring the people back to God. Others (Ahaz, Manasseh) allow and encourage worship of other gods, including rituals of child sacrifice.

Prophets arise to confront the kings and preach a message of repentance. The most famous are Elijah and Elisha, working in Israel. Elijah confronts wicked King Ahab and his wife Jezebel. In a contest with the prophets of the pagan god Baal, Elijah, God's man, triumphs. Later, Elisha anoints a (somewhat) good king, Jehu, who wipes out the entire family of the wicked Ahab. Still, the Northern Kingdom's unstable government and immorality lead to decline, and in 722 B.C. the nation falls to the brutal Assyrian Empire.

Judah, the Southern Kingdom, hangs on longer. Prophets like Isaiah and Micah preach messages of spiritual purity and social justice, and a few good kings like Josiah lead spiritual renewals. (Immorality, by the way,

The Two Kingdoms

Judah (Southern Kingdom)		*Israel (Northern Kingdom)*
Kings	*Prophets*	*Kings*
Rehoboam 931–913		Jeroboam 931–910
(*1 Kings 12:1-24; 14:21-31*)		(*1 Kings 12:25–14:20*)
Abijah 913–911		Nadab 910–909
(*1 Kings 15:1-8*)		(*1 Kings 15:25-32*)
Asa 911–870		Baasha 909–886
(*1 Kings 15:9-24*)		(*1 Kings 15:33–16:7*)
Jehoshaphat 870–848		Elah 886–885
(*1 Kings 22:41-50*)		(*1 Kings 16:8-14*)
Jehoram 848–841		Zimri 7 days in 885
(*1 Kings 8:16-24*)		(*1 Kings 16:15-20*)
Ahaziah 841		Omri 885–874
(*2 Kings 8:25-29*)		(*1 Kings 16:21-28*)
Queen Athaliah 841–835	Elijah	Ahab 874–853
(*2 Kings 11*)		(*1 Kings 16:29–22:40*)
Joash 835–796		Ahaziah 853–852
(*2 Kings 12*)		(*1 Kings 22:51–2 Kings 1:18*)
Amaziah 796–781		Joram 852–841
(*2 Kings 14:1-22*)		(*2 Kings 9:14-26*)
Uzziah 781–740	Elisha	Jehu 841–814
(*2 Kings 15:1-7*)		(*2 Kings 9–10*)
Jotham 740–736		Jehoahaz 814–798
(*2 Kings 15:32-38*)		(*2 Kings 13:1-9*)
Ahaz 736–716		Jehoash 798–783
(*2 Kings 16*)		(*2 Kings 13:10-13*)
Hezekiah 716–687	Amos	Jeroboam II 783–743
(*2 Kings 18–20*)		(*2 Kings 14:23-29*)
		Zechariah 6 months in 743
		(*2 Kings 15:8:13*)
		Shallum 1 month in 743
		(*2 Kings 15:13-16*)
	Hosea	Menahem 743–738
		(*2 Kings 15:17-22*)

Timeline markers (left margin): **900 B.C.**, **800 B.C.**, **700 B.C.**

	Micah	Pekahiah 738–737
		(*2 Kings 15:23-26*)
	Isaiah	Pekah 737–732
		(*2 Kings 15:27-31*)
		Hoshea 732–723
		(*2 Kings 17:1-4*)
		Fall of Northern Kingdom to Assyria 722
		(*2 Kings 17:5-41*)

The Last Years of the Kingdom of Judah

Kings	*Prophets*
Manasseh 687–642	
(*2 Kings 21:1-8*)	
Amon 642–640	
(*2 Kings 21:19-25*)	
Josiah 640–609	Zephaniah
(*2 Kings 22; 23:1-30*)	
Joahaz 3 months in 609	Nahum
(*2 Kings 23:31-34*)	
Jehoakim 609–598	Jeremiah
(*2 Kings 23:35–24:7*)	
Jehoiachin 3 months in 598	Habakkuk
(*2 Kings 24:8-17*)	
Zedekiah 598–587	Ezekiel
(*2 Kings 24:18–25:7*)	
Fall of Jerusalem to Babylonians, 587 or 586	
(*2 Kings 25:1-17*)	

was never just a matter of sexual shenanigans. The prophets condemned greed, dishonest dealing, oppressing the poor, materialism, etc. All of this followed when people neglected Israel's true God.) But in 586 Judah falls to the Babylonian Empire under the famous King Nebuchadnezzar. Much of the population of Judah is deported to Babylon, leaving only the lower-class people. The Prophet Jeremiah, who had predicted the nation's political and spiritual ruin, painfully watches it take place. The people of Judah (now called Jews) live in Babylon many years. One of them, the Prophet Ezekiel, writes most of his prophecies in Babylon.

Keep in mind that this period of the Old Testament involves many interactions with foreign empires. The history here is real history, not fiction, and 1 and 2 Kings frequently refer to the invasions and conquests of real figures like the Babylonian King Nebuchadnezzar, the Assyrian King Tiglath-Pileser, and the Egyptian Pharaohs Shishak and Necho.

BABYLONIAN EXILE AND RETURN

Empires come and go, and the Babylonians lose ground to the Persians. (Persia is modern-day Iran, by the way.) The Persians are more tolerant than the Babylonians, and the Persian Emperor Cyrus decrees that the Jews may return to their homeland to resettle and rebuild. Under leaders like Nehemiah and Ezra, the city of Jerusalem is rebuilt (sort of), and an attempt is made to practice a pure faith, with faithful attention to the Old Testament laws. Prophets like

Haggai, Zechariah, and Malachi arise to encourage the people in rebuilding their faith and their homeland.

Jews taken into exile in Babylon after the fall of Jerusalem.
 (2 Kings 25:18-21)
Persian rule begins 539
Decree of Persian King Cyrus allows Jews to return 538
 (Ezra 1)
Foundations for a new Jerusalem temple laid 520
 (Ezra 3–6)
Restoration of Jerusalem's walls 445–443
 (Neh. 2–6)

THE PERIOD BETWEEN THE TWO TESTAMENTS

The Bible doesn't say much about this period, but through other writings we've learned a lot about it. The Greek conqueror Alexander the Great expands his empire all the way to India, conquering the area of Israel in the process. Alexander then dies at an early age, with his vast empire divided up among his generals. Several of them, and their descendants, rule over the Jews, sometimes peacefully, sometimes not. Briefly, under a Jewish family called the Maccabees, the Jews achieve political freedom.

During this period, Greek (the language of Alexander and his empire) becomes widely spoken among the Jews. In fact, a Greek translation of the Old Testament (known as the Septuagint) has to be done to serve the many Greek-speaking Jews across the vast empire Alexander leaves behind.

Along comes an even more powerful empire, the Romans. The Jews' territory is divided into three Roman provinces—Judea, Samaria, and Galilee. In the New Testament period, Judea (with Jerusalem as its chief city) is the site of most of Jesus' activity (He is born in the Judean town of Bethlehem). He is also active in Galilee, site of His hometown of Nazareth.

More important than this period's politics is its spirituality. Between the two Testaments, the Jews come gradually to believe in an afterlife (barely hinted at in the Old Testament). Most Jews come to believe that faithful people will live in heaven, while a sad fate awaits bad people. Also, living without a real king, many Jews come to believe in a Messiah, a political deliverer who will oust the Roman rulers and establish a saintly Jewish nation that will endure forever. As time passes and the Romans still rule, some Jews began to wonder if the real Messiah might be a spiritual liberator, not a political or military leader.

During this period, two noted Jewish religious parties arise. One group, the Pharisees, emphasizes being faithful in every detail to the Old Testament laws given to Moses. Since Israel had failed in a political sense, the Pharisees believe it could succeed in a spiritual sense. At their best, the Pharisees are good, idealistic, moral people who tried to honor God by obeying His laws. At their worst, they are self-righteous and legalistic, more concerned with petty rules than with really loving God and other people. In the New Testament, Jesus sometimes praises the Pharisees, but often He speaks harshly against their legalism.

The other important religious group is the Sadducees. This is the religious upper crust of the Jews, mostly high-class Jerusalem families that control the very important priesthood. They hobnob with their Roman overlords and look down their noses at the common folk and, sometimes, at the Pharisees. Unlike the Pharisees and the common people, they do not believe in an afterlife. Comfortable in this world, their religion is mainly a ritual matter centered on animal sacrifices at the temple in Jerusalem. Theirs is a religion with little emotional appeal and no hope for eternity. They have a lot of clout, but aren't very important spiritually.

Note: From now on in the time line, the name *Israel* refers to a geographical area, since Israel as a political unit no longer exists.

Alexander the Great establishes Greek rule over Israel   333 B.C.
Israel ruled by the Ptolemies, descendants of one of Alexander's generals 323–198
Israel ruled by the Seleucids, descendants of another of Alexander's generals 198–166
Jewish revolt led by Judas Maccabeus reestablishes Jewish independence.
Israel ruled by his family and descendants 165–63
Israel conquered by Roman General Pompey and made part of the Roman Empire 63

CHRONOLOGY OF THE NEW TESTAMENT PERIOD

When Jesus was born, the Jews were still under Roman rule. Most people accepted it, but there were always agitators around wanting to overthrow (and throw out) the Romans. (One of Jesus' disciples was a Zealot, one of these anti-Roman activists.)

Before Jesus began His public life, His kinsman, John the Baptist, was already preaching and gathering followers. John was a sort of "nature boy" prophet, living a simple life and urging people to repent of their sins and turn to God. He baptized Jesus (though he believed Jesus had no sins to repent of), and this marked the beginning of Jesus' public career. Jesus gathered around Him numerous followers, in particular twelve known as the apostles. They followed Him around the towns of Judea and Galilee, while Jesus cured people of illnesses (including exorcising demons) and preached His message of repentance and turning to God, a loving and forgiving Father. Unlike many Jews, Jesus showed deep compassion to the poor, to outcasts, and to foreigners.

Jesus criticized the religious establishment (the Pharisees in particular) for caring more for the rules than for genuine kindness and mercy. Like most rebels, His words got Him into trouble. The Jewish authorities looked for some excuse to arrest Him, and with the aid of a turncoat disciple (the notorious Judas) they succeeded in arresting Jesus and bringing Him to trial before Pilate, the Roman governor. On flimsy charges of being a political subversive, Jesus was executed by the cruel method known as crucifixion. His disheartened disciples fled in dismay. But shortly afterward Jesus' tomb was found empty. Numerous followers claimed He had appeared to them in the flesh. He ordered them to preach His method of salvation to the ends of the earth.

The Book of Acts tells how they did that. Gathered in Jerusalem, the apostles receive an amazing surge of spiritual power when the Holy Spirit comes to them, as Jesus had promised. They boldly preach that Jesus is the Messiah—Christ—the Jews had been expecting. Like Jesus, they also perform numerous miracles of healing. Also like Jesus, they are persecuted by the Jewish authorities (one, the Apostle James, is executed). Still, their message spreads, not only to the Jews but to the Gentiles (non-Jews) as well. One eloquent preacher, Stephen, is stoned to death by an angry Jewish mob, thus becoming the first Christian martyr. Aiding in the persecution of Christians is a devout Pharisee, Paul. Miraculously, Paul later becomes the best-known Christian preacher, the "apostle to the Gentiles" who travels over the Roman Empire to spread the new faith. The tireless Paul suffers imprisonment, shipwrecks, and other adventures. When the Book of Acts ends, Paul is in prison, awaiting his trial before the Roman emperor.

Paul not only helped start Christian communities wherever he traveled, but he also maintained contact with them via his many letters that are now in the New Testament. Like Acts, these letters tell us much about the new faith and how the first Christians believed the faithful person should live.

Jesus' other disciples were also busy as missionaries and authors. Two of the Gospels were written by disciples (Matthew and John), and two letters were written by Peter. John may also be the author of Revelation, the New Testament's last book, which describes the persecutions Christians must endure and how God will finally

	New Testament Events	Roman Emperors	Rulers of Judea
40 B.C.			*King Herod the Great 37–4* B.C.
30 B.C.		*Augustus* 27 B.C.–A.D. 14	
20 B.C.			
10 B.C.	Birth of Jesus 5 or 4 B.C. *(Matt. 2; Luke 2)*		Archelaus 4 B.C.–A.D. 6
0	Ministry of John the Baptist; baptism of Jesus and beginning of His ministry *(Matt. 3; Mark*		
A.D. 10	*1; Luke 3; John 1:6-35)*		Coponius A.D. 6–9 Marcus Ambivius 9–12 Annius Rufus 12–15
A.D. 20		*Tiberius* A.D. 14–37	Valerius Gratus 15–26
A.D. 30	Death and resurrection of Jesus 30 *(Matt. 27–28; Mark 15–16, Luke 23–24; John 18–21)*		*Pontius Pilate 26–36*
A.D. 40	Conversion of Saul, later called Paul 37 *(Acts 9:1-31)*	Caligula 37–41	Marcellus 37 Marullus 37–41 *King Herod Agrippa 41–44*
A.D. 50	Paul's ministry ca. 41–65 *(Acts 13–28)*	Claudius 41–54	Cuspius Fadus 44–46 Tiberius Julius Alexander 46–48
A.D. 60		*Nero* 54–68	*Antonius Felix 59–62* *Porcius Festus 62–65*
70	Final imprisonment of Paul ca. 65		

bring about an end to all sorrow with a new heaven and new earth.

Politically, the Roman Empire was in control during the entire New Testament period. The international language of the Roman Empire, though, was Greek. Because this one language was so widely spoken, the Gospels and Letters in our New Testament were all written in Greek and could be widely circulated throughout the Empire. This, along with the Romans' excellent roads and communication systems, made it easy for any new faith to spread. Many of the Jews scattered across the Empire believed that God would send a Messiah, and many (but definitely not all) of these Jews listened readily to the message of the early Christians.

Roman rulers in *italics* on the chart on page 246 are those who are mentioned in the New Testament. The New Testament sometimes refers to the Roman emperor as "Caesar" without mentioning his actual name. (They used "Caesar" generically, just as we might use "the President" instead of "President Smith.") Luke does mention that when Jesus was born, the Caesar named Augustus was ruling (Luke 2:1). In Jesus' adult life, when He referred to Caesar (as in Matt. 22:21), He was referring to Tiberius. When the Apostle Paul requests a trial before Caesar (Acts 25:11), the Caesar (emperor) at that time was Nero, who later became notorious for persecuting Christians. According to tradition, Nero had the Apostles Paul and Peter executed.